Right With God

Right With God

A DEVOTIONAL STUDY OF THE EPISTLE TO THE ROMANS

JOHN G. MITCHELL

with Dick Bohrer

MULTNOMAH

Portland, Oregon

Cover design by Durand Demlow
Edited by Rodney L. Morris

RIGHT WITH GOD: A DEVOTIONAL STUDY
OF THE EPISTLE TO THE ROMANS
© 1990 by Richard W. Bohrer
Published by Multnomah Press
10209 SE Division Street
Portland, Oregon 97266

Multnomah Press is a ministry of Multnomah School of the Bible, 8435
NE Glisan Street, Portland, Oregon 97220.

Printed in the United States of America.

Library of Congress Cataloging-in-Publication Data

Mitchell, John G., 1892-1990
    Right with God : a devotional study of the Epistle to the Romans /
John G. Mitchell with Dick Bohrer.
        p.   cm.
    ISBN 0-88070-411-X
    1. Bible. N.T. Romans—Commentaries. I. Bohrer, Dick. II. Title.
BS2665.3.M56   1990
227'.107—dc20   90-49328
                                                              CIP

91 92 93 94 95 96 97 98 99 - 10 9 8 7 6 5 4 3 2 1

Contents

John Greenwood Mitchell
(1892-1990)

A Tribute

His office at Multnomah School of the Bible where he was a much-loved Bible teacher, the founder, and for many, many years chairman of the Board of Trustees lay in the east wing of Sutcliffe Hall, the administration building.

As you entered, possibly you greeted Marian O'Connor, for many years his faithful secretary, or one of the other dedicated women who took her place after she retired.

Told that Dr. Mitchell is waiting for you, you turn to your right and enter his room. On his walls you see the pictures of his dear friends, men whose preaching ministries touched his own, decades ago—marvelous men like Arno C. Gaebelein, B. B. Sutcliffe, Lewis Sperry Chafer, W. H. Griffith Thomas, and Harry A. Ironside.

John G. Mitchell sits facing away from you in a large swivel chair behind a strong wooden desk. He's finishing a telephone conversation, and he motions you in with a sweep of his husky arm.

You've come to talk to this veteran preacher-teacher about something that seems to be missing from your life, something that he knows so very much about.

He hangs up the receiver and says in his baritone brogue (he was born in England near the Scottish border), "Come in, my friend. Sit down. Sit down."

You look at the piles of letters around him and say, "Let me come back another day. You look terribly busy."

"Oh, I'm busy," he admits, "but there's always time for us to have a wee little talk together. In fact, I don't know why you don't come more often. I love to have you come."

You enjoy the sound of his rich voice. He's attached to his R's and not only rolls them as they occur to his tongue but supplies them when they don't.

He has just returned from having preached a week each at a midwest college, a theological seminary and a west coast church. And he's just finished an assignment of cutting thirty-eight broadcast tapes in the book of Genesis for his half-hour daily radio program, aired across a good number of states. So you know he's been busy.

He sees you looking at his piles of letters and he picks one up and reads it to you. It's from a lady in California who thanks him for his program and asks him three questions.

"You see?" he says at the end. "I have to answer these good letters myself. There's no other way. All these are from people who are listening and writing in questions. They want to grow; they want to know the Lord."

"But don't they go to church? Can't their pastors answer these questions?" you ask.

He shakes his head. He's reluctant to indict his brethren in the ministry. But soon he leans back and reminisces through his seventy-some years as a Bible teacher and pastor.

"The Lord's sheep are hungry for food," he says. "If they don't find it in one place, they'll turn to find it in another. They cannot grow without the Word of God."

"But aren't all pastors shepherds?" you ask.

"A real shepherd will take care of his sheep. And certainly a shepherd cannot lead his sheep to the pasture unless he knows from experience that there is food there," he says. "In some churches the pastor becomes so occupied with his pastoral duties that he doesn't give the time to study and prayer. On the other hand, some men give all their time to study and have no heart for the people of God. Some teach the Word of God with intellectual clarity but do not reach the hearts and lives of God's people. Others are warm in their ministry, but they don't have an intellectual grasp of the truth.

"I would say that the neglected gift in the gospel ministry today is the gift of expository preaching and teaching."

He turns to the letters in a small pile directly in front of him and riffles through them.

"They tell me, 'If it were not for your program, I do not know where I would be fed the Word of God.' Now, that's tragic. I certainly don't have outstanding gifts, except that I love the Savior and I want people to love Him. I may not be reaching their heads, but I think I'm reaching some hearts for the Savior."

"But not all pastors have an expository gift," you say.

He leans forward. "You know, if a pastor loves his flock, he'll feed it. But he cannot feed a flock if he's not feeding himself. He must be a man of the Book. Whatever our gift may be, we need to saturate our minds with the Word of God so that we'll be both available and usable in the hands of the Holy Spirit. Why, the truth must live in us.

"Now, when I was a young preacher just starting out in the ministry, I asked Dr. G. Campbell Morgan what was his method of Bible study. And he informed me that he would read a book through forty or fifty times before he even started to study that book. In other words, he saturated his mind with the text. Now, it's true that some pastors have another gift, not expository preaching. They may be evangelists or they may be teachers. But whatever the gift God has given to a man, He has not changed His method of reaching people. The Spirit of God uses the Word of God through the man of God. It says that in 1 Thessalonians 1:5."

"Then what's your definition of expository preaching and teaching?" you ask.

"We preach for a verdict. We teach for edification. A pastor should be able to expound the Word of God, not some theory, not

Right with God

some topic. The Bible is not a textbook. It's God's personal revelation of Himself to my heart, and it brings me His purpose and His counsel. It's God's word to me—personally; but, until I get to the place of recognizing that, I'm not going to heed it. It will be just another book. Now, I'm not speaking of its inspiration here but only of its practical use in my life.

"Expository teaching is expounding the Word of God—exposing it to the mind and heart and life of God's people. It is preaching the truth in the light of the context. It's giving the content of what's in the passage."

"How do you yourself go about preparing an expository message?" you ask.

"When I prepare a message, I read the passage through a great number of times and I pray about it. I write down what I see, and then I do some more praying. I look at what I've written and I may cross it out and start over again, searching for something more out of the passage. Then, when I've gotten all I can, I go to my library and read what someone else has received from the same passage. Often, when I read what someone else has written, I find he's received the same thing I have—only it's mine. I didn't get it from him.

"Now, oftentimes, these men will give you a little nudge. They give you a thought that you will follow through. In other words, you are digging all the time. And, after all these years, I'm still digging.

"Why, a student said to me the other day, 'It must be nice to have preached and taught all these years, Dr. Mitchell, because now you don't have to study any more.'

"I told him, 'Man, I never stop studying.' You never get to the end of it. You never get through!"

His blue eyes flash.

"But what if you have other things to do?" you ask. "You can't study *all* the time." You're getting close to what you came to talk to him about.

"Listen, my friend, a person has to budget his time and guard his time with the Lord and with His Word. A great many of God's servants are too busy with programs and with running around in the pastorate on a lot of details that someone else could do. Their main object (as Peter could say in Acts 6) should be to give themselves to the ministry of the Word of God. That's what these men did."

He points to the pictures on his wall.

"A man has to discipline himself to stay in the Word of God and to get the mind of God. Only then can he teach the Word in the power of the Spirit, and only then will he have a tenderness and compassion for the people of God who need feeding, guidance and direction in their spiritual lives."

"But can't he ever go out?" you ask.

"Now, don't get me wrong. A man must be out among his people. Why, when I was a pastor, I'd be in the hospitals three or four afternoons a week. A man must know the problems and the heartaches of his people if he's going to minister to them where they are. But the danger today is that it is so easy to become lazy mentally. We don't give ourselves. It's going to cost us something to get to know the Word of God. We receive according to our capacity, and our capacity grows as we lay hold of the truth. The truth must live. We can't feed God's people if we His servants are not feeding on His Word. The truth must live."

He moves his hand across the desk and puts it for a moment on yours.

"And, remember, this is true for you, too, you know. You don't have to be in the pulpit to minister God's Word to other people."

You know this man cares about you. You can hear it in his voice.

"God has given you a gift, you know," he says gently. "He's given you a gift so you can minister to your own generation."

"But how do I—?"

"Paul told Timothy to take heed to himself and to the ministry. He was to give himself to reading and to exhortation. Then Paul ends up the passage by saying, 'Take care of your own soul.' If you don't take care of your own soul, how are you going to take care of others? In other words, I relate to people what's in me. I cannot relate what I don't have.

"Some of the most wonderful truths I ever learned as a young Christian, I learned in old sod shacks way up in northern Canada from old homesteaders who knew the things of God. There was a sweetness, an aroma about them that stirred in me a tremendous yearning. I saw the reality of life in Christ and my heart responded.

"If the truth is not living in my life, I can talk about it intellectually, but I'm not reaching the heart and the needs of God's people."

He pauses. "Neither can you, you know. We can't imitate the life of the Lord Jesus; but it can be reproduced in our lives by the Spirit of God. But He doesn't reveal more truth to our life or to our heart until we walk in the light of the truth we already have.

"All of us believers, not just pastors, need the reality of the presence of Christ by His Spirit in our lives if we're to know the needs of God's people and be of service to them. We need to understand their tests, their heartaches, their disappointments, their sorrows, yes; but we need to know something of the compassion and tenderness of our Savior. That's the important thing. Only then can we really communicate the Word of God. And, of course, we need to pray."

"Pray?" you ask.

"It's no use my reveling in the fact that I am a child of One who is God if I do not seek to please Him and if I do not seek to come into His presence to spend time with Him.

"Oh, we must be men and women of prayer," he says fervently. "I believe that waiting on the Lord in prayer and having fellowship with Him is just as important as the study of the Word. The more I go into the Word of God, the more I feel the need of seeking His face to direct me by the Spirit of God in that Word. You can't divide Bible study from prayer. For example, I would not say I was going to study for four hours in my Bible from eight in the morning to twelve o'clock and after lunch spend two hours in prayer. It doesn't work out that way.

"Oftentimes, when you're studying, you'll spend an hour in the Word of God; and, for some reason, you're not getting anything. What do you do? You get down and talk to the Lord about it. You come back to the Word and all of a sudden the whole thing opens up like a rose. But your mind's got to be full of the text.

"That's why I come back to emphasize continual reading of the Word. And, as a person does this, he or she becomes God's channel of truth to human hearts and minds.

"But we need time. The pastor needs time. His people need to insist that he take time to study and to pray. And they need to insist that he make time for them, too, as well as for his own family.

"I'm sure that when a pastor is in love with the Savior, he'll also be in love with his people and will feed them and shepherd them. And that goes for you, too, in your ministry to your neighborhood, you know. Just as you fall in love with the Savior—oh, what it would mean to Him and what it would mean to you. God grant that our vision of Christ may be enlarged so that we will truly fall in love with Him."

"Yes," you whisper. You realize this is the word you came for.

"Every once in a while," he says, "someone tells me I should have this experience or that experience or some other experience. As wonderful as those experiences may be, I have the Lord Jesus and you can't add anything to Him. I have everything in Him. And, thank God, the day is coming when through eternity I'll continually be experiencing what I have in Him."

He pats my hand. "It's a wonderful thing to come into the presence of God in eternal glory and be known." His face lights up in a wistful smile. "He will know me and I will know Him. I shall see God and, oh! He'll be no stranger."

He clears his throat. "I don't know when God wants to call me Home. But I know He numbers my steps and He bottles my tears and my times are in His hands."

It's late. You need to leave. You look up at the pictures of those old saints—those great men of God—and you know it's fitting that he should have those pictures on his wall. A man is known by the company he keeps.

You sense that you may not see him again for a long, long time.

"Do you have a word just for me?" you ask. So much of what you know of Christ and of His Word you've learned from this dear, loving, faithful man.

He puts his hand on yours again.

"Some years ago, a friend of mine was on his way to a mission field in southeast Asia. He had all his belongings on the ship and, just before departure, he called me and asked if I had a word to give him for China.

"Let me give you that same word today—for you and your 'mission field' wherever you go.

"I said to him, 'Sit at the feet of Jesus—and tell the people what you see.' "

You leave his office, your heart warmed and full. You've just sat at the feet of Jesus with one who is himself so very much at home there.

And, now, our Lord has him with Himself. He's finally Home after ninety-seven years. Finally Home, joyously sitting at the feet of his Lord Jesus, whom he loved with all his heart.

And he, who in modesty would so often brush aside our praise, has surely reveled in the supreme tribute he has received from our Lord: "Well done, My good and faithful servant!"

And we echo it—oh, we shout aloud, "Well done, Dr. Mitchell. "Well done!"

Dick Bohrer

Introduction

Martin Luther, the great reformer, called the book of Romans the chief book in the New Testament. Samuel Coleridge, the English writer, said, "It is the most profound work in existence." Melanchthon, a contemporary of Luther, wrote it twice in longhand just for the joy, the blessing, and the thrill of getting into it.

W. R. Newell, one of the outstanding teachers of the book of Romans in the past century, told me one day, "I have taught the book eighty times and the pastures are still green." Someone has well said, "To know the book of Romans makes one heresy-proof."

It may be that I'm conscious of this for the simple reason that, when I first went out preaching, I was asked, "Don't you know there are other books in the Bible besides the book of Romans?" (I had preached Romans all across the Canadian prairies.) People have told me, even though I haven't been back in more than forty years, that they have found people all over the prairies who are established in the gospel of God's grace . . . and they got it from a man named Mitchell, who doted on the book of Romans. So I hope you won't mind if I dote with you a while on the book of Romans.

The Place of Romans in the New Testament

It's folly to build a building without a foundation. This wonderful, amazing book of Romans is the foundational book; the epistles that follow are all based on this book. What Isaiah, the great prophetical book, is to the prophets of the Old Testament, the book of Romans is to the New Testament. Romans is the only book in the New Testament (in fact, I would say the only book in the Bible) that gives us the gospel of God in a systematic way. In the Gospel of John the gospel is declared, but in Romans it is systematically set forth.

Why Romans Was Written

When Paul wrote Romans, he had in mind the Jew with his laws and ceremonies and also the Gentile, who needs to be told that the gospel is for him as well. In this book you see both Jewish unbelief and Gentile faith. Chapters 9 and 10 show that what the Jews missed by their works and ceremonies, the Gentiles received by faith.

Paul wanted to assure the Jewish people that this message was God's message for them as well as for the Gentiles. When he wrote this book, many Jewish people were opposed to him because his message was being believed by the Gentile world. Paul wrote to prove to them that the message he was giving the Gentiles was also God's message for Jews, and that they must receive it on the ground of faith, just like anyone else. Likewise, he had the Gentiles in mind when he declared that this message which had so transformed their lives was also for the Jews; he wanted the Gentiles to take heed that, if God set the Jews to one side because of their unbelief, He could also set the Gentiles to one side because of their unbelief.

That is the line of argument Paul follows in the book. You have the Jewish people with all their laws, ceremonies, traditions, and ordinances on one side and the Gentiles with their need of enlightenment regarding God's gospel on the other.

Time and Place for the Writing of Romans

Paul wrote from the city of Corinth about the year A.D. 50. You remember, he was in Corinth for eighteen months and while he was there, he wrote to these Roman Christians whom he had never seen. He wrote to establish and to encourage them in the gospel.

The Great Theme of Romans

Romans presents the righteousness of God displayed in the gospel of His Son. God has made provision whereby every man, Jew or Gentile, can be brought into a place of relationship and acceptance before God. It is a wonderful thing that, irrespective of background or tradition or experience, God has made provision whereby men and women can be fitted to come into His presence.

I was greatly amazed when I visited the Orient to see transformed lives. On one hand I saw people in darkness, in despair, in fear, in bondage to paganism. But I also found wonderful men and women who have been transformed into the sons of God, proving that God has a message and has made provision whereby men of any age and under any circumstance can be transformed and fitted for His presence.

When men and women can be transformed and become the children of God, when they can stand righteous in the presence of their holy God and can have a sanctified life through the Lord Jesus Christ, when they can manifest the character and beauty of the living God and become bearers of the good news to their generation, I wonder why we're not more diligent to spend our time and our money to support the spreading of that gospel.

An Overview of Romans

Romans is an amazing book! I want to take the time as we study it together to bring to you the jewels and the pearls that are along the way—that we might be refreshed and strengthened and established in the Word of God. I want you to be especially helped, so that, as the apostle Paul would say, by our "mutual faith" we might be edified by the precious Word of God.

Let me take a moment to whet your appetite. In the first seventeen verses of the first chapter, Paul introduces the truth of the righteousness of God. He is introducing the gospel of God, which was prophesied by the prophets and is now made manifest. He takes up the whole degenerate human race in chapters 1 through 3. In chapter 1 he specifically has the Gentiles in mind—how God gave them up to their sins. That's the history of the Gentile nations from Genesis 10 right through to the coming of our Lord.

In chapter 2 Paul has a little more difficult job. He has to prove that the moralist and the religionist—both Jew and Gentile—are just as unrighteous before God as those in the first chapter. He specifically takes up the fact that God is going to judge them according to truth.

Then, from chapter 2:17 to 3:9, Paul talks about the Jew in his rebellion against God. Paul ends up with a verdict in 3:18-20 where every man's mouth is shut and the whole world is guilty before God.

Having shut man's mouth from glorying in his own goodness and self-righteousness, God turns around and opens His heart. Starting at 3:21 and running through chapter 5:11, we have the unfolding of God's heart toward men. Here are the great doctrines of justification, redemption, and propitiation. We find in chapter 4, for example, that the Christian life is by faith; it is without works, without ceremonies, without law. It is faith in the God of resurrection.

The question is raised at the beginning of chapter 5: Can we lose our faith? Paul answers that the love of God will guarantee the faith of every believer. The provision for man's redemption is received on only one ground—the ground of faith. Not only does the gospel give us forgiveness and redemption and fit us for the presence of God, it also gives us a new life. It brings us into a new relationship with God. It delivers us from death, from sin, and from the law. It sanctifies us and will eventually glorify us.

In chapter 5 we are delivered from death. In chapter 6 we are delivered from sin as a master, as a principle of operation. In chapter 7 we are delivered from the law and its curse. The law can't make us righteous, no matter how we strive to keep it. We must turn from the law, which condemns, to a Savior who redeems and sets us free. Then we come to that amazing eighth chapter, telling all the marvelous things we have in Christ. This is the crowning chapter of the book. Here we are glorified together with Christ.

I'm not surprised that the apostle Paul says, "I reckon that the sufferings of this present time are not worthy to be compared with the glory which shall be revealed in us" (8:18). And then, at the end of chapter 8, the chapter that starts with "no condemnation" and ends with "no separation," we have the glorious verse, if God "spared not his own Son . . . how shall he not with him freely give us all things?" (v. 32).

Chapters 9, 10, and 11 give us what is commonly known as dispensational truth. Here a question is raised: Is God righteous in His dealings with the people of Israel? In chapter 9 we find that God chose Israel for a distinct purpose—not because these people were better than anybody else, but because they could be the avenue through which Messiah would come. Their language would be the depository of the Word of God. They would relate to the nations of the earth the wonders of our sovereign God. But they failed in that. So in chapter 10 we are shown that the Jews rejected both a personal salvation and a universal salvation for Jews and Gentiles.

When we come to chapter 11, another question is raised: Is God through with Israel? No, He will still fulfill His promise to the nation. He still has a remnant He is going to bring right through to where His purpose and His counsel will be fulfilled according to the word of the prophets.

Then in chapters 12 through 16, we have the practical side of the book, dealing with practical righteousness as well as the question of responsibility. The moment you and I receive the Savior, we have a responsibility. In chapter 12 we are responsible to God, we are responsible to our position in the body of Christ, and we are responsible to act righteously toward our enemies.

In chapter 13, we find our position as Christians with respect to the government under which we live. We are to be in subjection to the powers that be. The same chapter, starting with verse 11, describes our relationship to society. In chapter 14, up to the first two or three verses of chapter 15, the issue is our relationship to weaker brethren. Some Christians are still babes and some are in trouble. In chapter 15 we have an exhortation to God's people about their own relationship to the God of hope, the God of all grace, the God of peace.

Finally, chapter 16 gives us that great list of dear men and women Paul salutes at Rome, and he ends up with a few parting words.

A broad general outline of the book would be:

I. Doctrinal, 1:1-8:39
   A. Introduction, 1:1-17
   B. The need for righteousness, 1:18-3:20
   C. God's way of justifying sinners, 3:21-5:11
   D. God's way of sanctifying saints, 5:12-8:39

II. Dispensational, 9:1-11:36

   A. God is righteous in electing grace, 9:1-33
   B. God's present dealings with Israel in governmental discipline, 10:1-21
   C. God's future dealings with Israel in the fulfillment of prophecy, 11:1-36

III. Practical, 12:1-16:27

   A. Relationship to God, 12:1-2
   B. Relationship to the body, 12:3-18
   C. Relationship to our enemies, 12:19-21
   D. Relationship to civil authorities, 13:1-7
   E. Relationship to society, 13:8-14
   F. Relationship to weaker brethren, 14:1-15:7
   G. Exhortations, 15:8-33
   H. Salutations, 16:1-27

Introduction

I have given you this brief rundown of the whole book of Romans because I want to whet your appetite to read it. You can't read it too much nor can you study it or meditate on it too much. Sometimes I think about Ezekiel, who, when he received the Word of God, was told to eat it; when he swallowed it, it became life to him.

Some of you have studied Romans before, but it will not hurt you one little bit to go over it again. After all, the book of Romans will make you heresy-proof. It is because of their lack of study and knowledge of Romans that so many Christians have been led astray. They have become shipwrecked in their hearts and lives before God. They have also become "double-minded" and "unstable" in all their ways, to quote the book of James.

Many of God's people, even in evangelical circles, are in confusion regarding all the "isms" and the doctrines that are being tossed around today. They have not been established in the book of Romans. They need the book of Romans. We all need the book of Romans.

You may say, "I read the Bible, but I get nothing out of it." The one thing Satan desires above all else is that we not spend time in the Bible. It is God's revelation to us and to men everywhere. So let us come to know our Bibles. Let us not be ignorant of the marvelous things God has done for us through His Son, Jesus Christ. As we begin this study, ask the Father to open your mind and heart to show you His beloved Son and to prompt you to truly fall in love with Him.

Romans 1

Paul begins the book of Romans with the only comment he has to make about himself. The moment he mentions the gospel of God, Paul is forgotten. It would be a wonderful thing if we who minister the Word of God could forget ourselves and exalt the Person of Christ and what He has done for us.

INTRODUCTION (1:1-17)

Paul Separated unto the Gospel of God (1:1)

1:1. *Paul, a servant of Jesus Christ, called to be an apostle, separated unto the gospel of God,*

Here we have a three-fold statement about the relationship, the character, and the dignity of Paul's work. "Paul, a bondslave of Jesus Christ"—this is his relationship to the Savior. He recognized he was bought from the markets of sin and set free. Paul, once purchased, is also surrendered to Jesus Christ as his Master. He has no will of his own, no mind of his own, no possessions of his own, no time of his own. Everything he has belongs to Christ. Nothing is kept back.

That doesn't mean Paul is not going to use his will, his mind, his possessions, or his time for himself. It means that Christ is the Master and Paul His bondslave. How well we measure up as bondslaves before God is the measure of our usefulness to Him.

It is possible for a Christian to take that place voluntarily, to surrender himself to the Son of God as a bondslave. Then he grows in knowledge as he continually yields various areas of his life over to the Lord. Paul writes in chapter 12, "I beseech you therefore, brethren, by the mercies of God, that ye present your bodies a living sacrifice." That's an act, once for all, a giving of yourself to Him. And, after that, we progress in understanding and progress in experience and progress in knowledge. Some people question your salvation unless you are wholly abandoned to the will of God. I disagree with that. My relationship with God is a matter of my acceptance of Christ as Savior. The matter of growth, the matter of giving areas of our life over to Him, comes according to our knowledge.

I have been a Christian for more than seventy years. Years ago, as far as I knew, I gave myself to the Lord. I would love to have called myself a bondslave of Jesus Christ; but as we go along in the things of God, we learn more and more from the Scriptures of the desire God has for our lives.

If we acknowledge that He is absolute in authority, then we must give Him absolute obedience. But there's a danger sometimes that we become so occupied with the things of Christ—our experience with Christ and our service for Christ—that we miss being in blessed fellowship with Christ, where He is the center of our life. In so far as you give the Lord Jesus His rightful place in your heart, in your life, and in your love, just so far can you be a bondslave of His.

Paul was also called an apostle. In 1 Corinthians 9 he tells us, "Am I not an apostle? am I not free? have I not seen Jesus Christ our Lord?" He defends his apostleship as given by a risen Christ. This is his office. Being a bondslave is his relationship. He is called to a ministry. He is God's messenger.

Likewise God has called you, whoever you may be, to a ministry. Not necessarily to be a preacher or a missionary or an evangelist, but every Christian has been called by God to communicate the good news of the gospel to our generation by our lives, by our words. If we don't, how are people going to hear?

And by the way, if you are witnessing for the Savior, be sure your life matches up to what you say. People watch a Christian to see how he is living. They'll even go out of their way to try to make you fail God. The world sets traps for your feet so it can say, "You're no better than the rest of us." But that doesn't change the situation. If you have accepted the Lord Jesus Christ as your Savior, you have a job right where you live to communicate the Word of God to somebody else.

There's one more thing in the verse. Paul is not only a bond slave and an apostle, but he also was separated unto the gospel of God. This was his duty, this was his position before God. He was separated to no other message—man had no part in it. All the religions in the world want you to do something, to merit something. The gospel of God is telling people not what you can do for God, but what God has done for you.

God has separated you and me unto the gospel. It's God's gospel, it's His good news, a message that can't be improved upon, a message that must not be distorted, a message that manifests to men the divine provision for their acceptance by the living God. It's high time we believers got this message across to this age.

This Gospel Is in Accord with Old Testament Scripture (1:2)

1:2. *(Which he had promised afore by his prophets in the holy scriptures,)*

I am well aware that many of you can say, "Why, Mr. Mitchell, I have known these truths all my life." Yes, but in many cases you are dried up to the truth for lack of usage. When you don't dwell in it, it dries up in your soul. That's a principle all through the Bible. If we do not use the truth God gives us, we lose it.

This gospel of God is in accord with Old Testament Scripture, which is the documentary defense of the gospel. In Romans alone there are some sixty references to the Old Testament. The prophets wrote as they were moved upon by the Holy Spirit. If

God is going to give us a revelation of Himself, He will make that revelation clear and real and worth our accepting it. He will also protect His revelation down through the centuries, so that today you and I may have the revelation of God, His purpose, His counsel, His Person, and His gospel.

The Gospel Concerns a Person Who Is Both Man and God (1:3-4)

1:3-4. *Concerning his Son Jesus Christ our Lord, which was made of the seed of David according to the flesh; and declared to be the Son of God with power, according to the spirit of holiness, by the resurrection from the dead:*

Mankind was so thrilled, so full of awe when we put men on the moon, a dead satellite. They returned to the earth to tell us what was on the moon, and they brought back rock because they found nothing alive there.

In contrast, almost two thousand years ago, heaven sent a Man to the earth, a heavenly Man. He was made of the seed of David according to the flesh. He was a real Man in the midst of men. What did that heavenly Man find here? He found the human race dead in trespasses and sin, a race under the bondage of sin, death, and hell. He took His place in the human family, and that human family killed Him. Heaven took Him back but, when He went back to heaven, He became a Prince and a Savior.

A real Man is there in heaven, a Man who is touched with the feelings of our infirmities, a Man who was "declared to be the Son of God with power, according to the spirit of holiness, by the resurrection from the dead." In other words, He was marked out from everyone else as God's Son by the resurrection. The resurrection is the proof that this Jesus is God's Son.

People often say that the resurrection is contrary to human experience, and that's true. I have conducted funeral services for hundreds of people, but not one has been raised from the dead.

How do we know Jesus is real? How do we know He put away

our sins? How do we know He is the Savior? How do we know He was the Son of God? We know because God raised Him from the dead. That's a personal proof to you that this Jesus, born in David's line, is God's Son.

I am anxious to get this amazing fact across because it is the key to the whole book. The gospel of God concerns His Son who belonged to man and who belonged to God. He was in two realms. He was made of the seed of David according to the flesh. He is a real man who came among men, and He is a real man now in heaven at the right hand of God. But He also is from heaven; He is the Son of God. He always was the Son of God and He became a man.

When the Lord healed the man by the pool of Bethesda on the Sabbath day, the Jews were angry and they accused Him of breaking the Sabbath. Our Lord's answer was, "My Father worketh hitherto, and I work" (John 5:17). Then the Jews sought all the more to kill Him, not just because He had broken the Sabbath but because He had made Himself equal with God.

But instead of telling them, "You have made a mistake jumping to that conclusion," Jesus said, "Yes, you are perfectly right. I am making Myself equal with God. For as the Father has power to raise the dead and make them alive, that's just what I do." What was He claiming? To be God!

God the Son came into the world for a purpose—to make it clear to you that He is the Savior of men. Your sins, my sins put Him on the cross and in the tomb. But God raised Him from the dead and gave Him glory so that your faith and your hope might be in God.

Do you see, my friend? This gospel of God is not only authenticated by the Old Testament, but it declares that the Lord Jesus Christ is the Son of God with power. He is God manifested in the flesh, manifested further by resurrection.

This is fundamental to our Christian faith. "If Christ be not raised," says Paul in 1 Corinthians 15, "[we] are yet in [our] sins." In fact, I would say boldly, justification and sanctification are guaranteed by the resurrection. This gospel of God, this good news of how to receive eternal life, is from a risen Christ.

I am thrilled with this. I would to God that I might be as separated unto the gospel of God, the gospel of our Lord, as the apostle Paul or anyone else down through the centuries. Oh, to so fall in love with Him that we have our minds saturated with the truth of it!

You and I not only have our sins forgiven, but we have been joined to a risen, glorified Savior. This is the guarantee of life, the guarantee of redemption. This is the guarantee of our hope, the guarantee of eternity. Our very position, our standing before God, is guaranteed by the resurrection of Jesus Christ.

The Gospel Is Universal (1:5-7)

1:5-6. *By whom we have received grace and apostleship, for obedience to the faith among all nations, for his name: Among whom are ye also the called of Jesus Christ.*

This gospel is for everybody. It is "for obedience to the faith among all nations." It's universal in its appeal. It doesn't matter what color you are, what language you speak, what your background is, where you were born, or anything about you. This gospel of God is good news received on only one ground—the ground of faith. Man has no part in it. All the religions of the world want you to do something to merit faith. But God did the whole business and offers us a salvation free from works. It is received by faith. When we put our trust in the One the gospel declares, my friend, we pass from death to life. The salvation He purchased is ours the moment we put our trust in Him.

And then Paul says that they, the Roman believers, were called of God even as he was called. Paul belonged to Christ and so did they. He had been called by a risen Lord and so had they. And so have you. Since we have received Jesus Christ as our Savior, it is our job to communicate to the world the work He has accomplished for us. You see, the gospel is different from any other message. It brings life, satisfaction, peace, forgiveness, and hope. Think about that. It brings a person into relationship with the eternal God.

Paul's heart longs for everyone in the whole world to have the privilege of hearing this good news from God, that anyone in any nation—under any circumstance—will have the right to hear and to receive this message and become a member of the family of God.

The church has failed in this matter down through the centuries. We have never acquired this passion, this great yearning of the apostle's heart, that our message be truly universal. We send a few out here and a few out there. We pay a few dimes and a few dollars to send messengers out to the different parts of the world. But, oh, how miserably the church has failed in reaching the world with the Word of God.

Do you realize, my friends, that paganism is increasing at a far greater rate than the gospel of Christ? We have been authorized by the living God to bring the message of His Son as the only Savior to every man and woman, every boy and girl under the shining sun. Yet more than two billion people in the world today have never heard God's message. How this ought to convict your heart and mine. How we need, if we believe the coming of the Lord is near, to rise up with the dignity and character and honor that God has bestowed upon us and give His message concerning His Son to the nations.

PAUL'S GREAT DESIRE (1:7-17)

Paul's Salutation (1:7)

> **1:7.** *To all that be in Rome, beloved of God, called to be saints: Grace to you and peace from God our Father, and the Lord Jesus Christ.*

We do not know who took the gospel to Rome. Perhaps saints scattered abroad after the stoning of Stephen went to Rome, and the moment they came they began to witness. Paul had heard of a number of believers there who loved the Savior, and he longed to see them. So he writes "to all that be in Rome, beloved of God, called to be saints."

I love this little statement. God loves to call His people His "beloved." Everyone who professes the name of the Lord Jesus becomes the beloved of God. You become the object of the love and devotion of the living God Himself.

Isn't it wonderful that God can pick up the children of wrath—men and women who have been rebels against His law and order, people who have sinned against Him—and can redeem them, put His arms around them, and call them His beloved. This is grace, absolutely grace.

Christian friend, revel in that today. As you go to work, as you work around the house, as you take care of the children or drive the car or whatever you do, remember that you are the beloved of God.

It's marvelous that God loves to call us His beloved ones. Do you men look upon your wives as your beloved ones? Isn't there something special there? You don't call just anyone your beloved. Only the special ones in our lives are marked out as our beloved and we manifest that love by living for them. God says, "You are My beloved ones. You are the object of My affection, the special ones in My heart."

But He not only calls you His beloved, we are also saints. Having been redeemed from sin, pronounced righteous by God and set apart for His fellowship, we are called saints, holy ones.

Some churches make people saints after they are dead; the Bible doesn't do that. Paul is writing to living people in Rome and calling them saints. He has never seen them, he doesn't know much about them, but he knows they love the Savior. So he writes this book to establish them in the gospel, to let them know what God has done for them—and he calls them saints. He spends more time on this theme in chapters 12 through 16 where he says we are to walk "as becometh saints."

There is a difference between being a saint and being saintly. I was raised in an Irish settlement where there was a lot of fighting going on, and I was one with the rest of the kids. We fought quite a bit. We kind of liked to fight. But sometimes my mother would send us out and say, "Now, remember what you are. I expect you to act like a Mitchell." We are saints by calling. Every member of the family of God is a saint, but He also wants us to act saintly.

When I first became a believer I was working in the machine shops. One day I began witnessing to one of the die makers in our little shop, telling him the best I knew, how God can come into our lives and transform us. When I got through, He said, "Now, listen to me, Jack Mitchell. There's no use giving that to me. I couldn't do that in this shop. Why, a saint couldn't work in this shop."

"Oh?" I said. "There are some saints in this shop."

"I'd like to see just one."

"Well, there's one talking to you now."

You ought to have seen his face and heard the explosion that followed: "You, a saint?"

It's true that just a few weeks before I had been swearing along with the rest of them, and now I could claim to be a saint? Yes, I could. And then he added, "And are you going to be like that fellow outside, that Barney? Are you going to be like him?"

Barney was a toolsman who tempered the dies. He went to church in the morning with a Bible under his arm, but he had one of the filthiest tongues I have ever heard. He had absolutely no testimony among the men.

"Are you going to be like him?"

I said, "I trust not. I do know one thing—I have received some good news from God and I know that Jesus Christ is my Savior and I know He calls me a saint."

We are not saints because of what we do. We are saints because God has called us into His family. We are the beloved of God; we are His holy ones. Now, He says, "Walk like saints." Every believer is called a saint, but not all believers are saintly. One is a position before God, the other is a walk before men. We are to be holy because God is holy.

Then Paul uses a common salutation, "Grace to you and peace from God our Father and the Lord Jesus Christ." This is a precious message Paul includes in all his epistles. Peace is the result of grace. Because God has made the provision, we can enjoy peace.

Paul's Prayer (1:8-10)

1:8. *First, I thank my God through Jesus Christ for you all, that your faith is spoken of throughout the whole world.*

Is your faith known in your neighborhood, in your suburb, throughout your city? Is it known throughout the world? Is your church known for its faith toward God, for its love for the Lord Jesus and for the saints? Paul thanks God through Jesus Christ because their faith "is spoken of throughout the whole world." This was also true in the Thessalonian church.

Paul said, "I don't need to speak for you. Everybody knows how you walk before God." What a wonderful thing to have your faith known far and wide.

1:9. *For God is my witness, whom I serve with my spirit in the gospel of his Son, that without ceasing I make mention of you always in my prayers;*

Paul talks about both his thanksgiving for them and his unceasing prayer for them. How diligent this man was in his prayer life. He even calls God to be his witness that what he is saying is the truth. In fact, he does this often—in Galatians 1:20; 2 Corinthians 1:23; Philippians 1:8; 1 Thessalonians 2:5; and again in Romans 9:1-2. He calls God to be his witness that what he is saying is the truth;

they can believe him when he says he is praying for them.

I wonder, my Christian friend, could you call God to be a witness that without ceasing you make mention of others in your prayers? What a heart for God's people this man had. He speaks in Ephesians 6:18 of "praying always with all prayer and supplication in the Spirit, and watching thereunto with all perseverance and supplication for all saints." He prayed continually. He had upon his heart every Christian he knew and even Christians he had only heard of but had never seen.

Oh, this man! How he loved the people of God. He loved them because they were the beloved of God. We too are the beloved of God, and if God loves us in spite of our failures, then we ought to love each other in spite of our failures. Instead of being hypercritical, may we love. Even though we may disagree on doctrine, we ought to love each other. If you are going to stand for the faith, do it in love. And God grant that you and I might be much in prayer for other believers.

1:10. *Making request, if by any means now at length I might have a prosperous journey by the will of God to come unto you.*

Paul yearned that God's people might be built up in the faith, which was the reason for his great desire to go to Rome. But first he prays for "a prosperous journey *by the will of God* " to come to them. He did not act until he knew God's will, which at this point he did not know. We may yearn for something and God may put it upon our hearts, but circumstances hold us back from the fulfillment of that desire. But if you wait before God and go on day by day, He will open the door in His own time as He did for Paul.

The apostle waited, praying for God's will, and when God did finally allow him to go, it was a prosperous journey. God used him even through the peril of a storm and shipwreck, which gave him the opportunity to reveal the wonderful grace of God not only to the sailors but also to the islanders who gave them refuge (Acts 27-28).

Paul's Longing (1:11-12)

> **1:11-12.** *For I long to see you, that I may impart unto you some spiritual gift, to the end ye may be established; that is, that I may be comforted together with you by the mutual faith both of you and me.*

Paul is yearning to establish them in the gospel. He wants them to know all about the good news from God. But one is only established through the Word of God, not through experiences. Paul says it again in chapter 16, "Now to Him that is of power to establish you according to my gospel." Here in chapter 1, he says, "When I come to you, I want to impart to you some spiritual gift. I want you to be established, and I want to be comforted by our mutual faith." It is the revelation of God, given to us in His Word, that causes us to be established in the faith. As we share together what we know about Christ and what we know about the Word of God and as we impart to one another what Paul calls "some spiritual gift," we not only edify one another, but we comfort each other.

This is one of the greatest needs today among God's people—to share with each other the blessed Savior whom we love, irrespective of organization, irrespective of what label we may have. If you love the Savior, you share together the things of Christ for fellowship, for comfort, and for edification. We comfort one another through our mutual faith—in the home, around the dinner table, in the car, on the street.

Paul's Obligation (1:13-14)

> **1:13.** *Now I would not have you ignorant, brethren, that oftentimes I purposed to come unto you, (but was let hitherto,) [prevented thus far], that I might have some fruit among you also, even as among other Gentiles.*

Not only did he want to comfort the believers and edify them, but he also wanted to reach some of the unsaved in Rome. How this man's heart yearned to make Christ known to believers and unbelievers, to comfort and edify the one and to bring the other to the knowledge of Christ. Now we come to Paul's responsibility, Paul's obligation:

> **1:14.** *I am debtor both to the Greeks, and to the Barbarians; both to the wise, and to the unwise.*

Paul is saying, "I owe the gospel to everyone, everywhere."

I'm sad to say, the church of Jesus Christ has failed to reach each generation with the Word of God. We can't reach the past generation, we can't reach the future generation, but we are responsible to reach our generation—everyone we can find—with God's message. We owe the gospel to the campuses of our universities. We owe the gospel to the men on the streets. We owe the gospel to our neighborhood. God has put us where we live to reach people with the Word of God by our life as well as by our testimony.

It's a wonderful thing to sit down beside someone and tell him the Word of God the first time he's ever heard. And it's more wonderful if he receives the Savior. I love that. But when you meet people who oppose you over and over again, the danger is that you want to go after somebody else. No, you live before them. Remember, Christ died for them, too. Remember, everyone to whom you witness is a prospective child of God, a prospective saint. God still yearns that men and women receive His Son.

Paul says, "I am obligated. I'm a debtor." He says in 1 Corinthians 9:16, "Woe is unto me, if I preach not the gospel!" Preach to whom? Anybody and everybody where they are. I say again, sadly, we have failed in this matter.

If we did what we expect our missionaries to do, we would evangelize America in a short time. We expect missionaries to represent the Savior, winning people to Christ, building up the saints of God, keeping everlastingly at it. How much could you do at home, in your neighborhood, in your family? Oh, how we have failed. How the church has failed. Instead of America being drawn closer and closer to God, it has gone in the opposite direction. Instead of our lives being spiritual, they have become secular. Instead of having a passion for God and for men, we have a passion for material things. God has committed to us—to you and to me—a responsibility. We are debtors.

You say, "But Mr. Mitchell, I can't preach." I'm not asking you to preach. I'm asking you to live for Christ. I'm asking you to live like one who belongs to the Savior, to act toward your neighbors as to people you love. God can put in your heart and my heart His divine love. Paul says in Romans 5:5, "The love of God is shed abroad in our hearts." Try to love them. The first thing you know, you will be loving them and barriers will be broken down. Believe me, I'm preaching to myself. I'm not talking only to you. We are debtors.

Paul's Yieldedness (1:15)

> **1:15.** *So, as much as in me is, I am ready to preach the gospel to you that are at Rome also.*

There is an inference here that Paul is answering his critics who don't think he is qualified to go to Rome. It's all right for him to preach the gospel in out-of-the-way places or in colonies such as Philippi or Ephesus or Corinth. But to come to the great metropolis of Rome where the sinners are, where Caesar is—to the heart and pulse of the empire—why, that's better left to those better equipped.

Paul says, "That's where I want to be, in the very center of the empire. I'm not ashamed of the gospel. I want to bring it to you. I want fruit among you even as among other Gentiles." You can just see the passion of this man's heart.

May God give you and me some of that same passion, that yearning to come to God's people, to love them and to pray for them, to build them up in the faith and comfort them, to encourage them and edify them so they can go out to teach and witness to others.

Notice the three "I am's" in these verses. In verse 14 he says, "I am a debtor", that is my stewardship, my obligation. In verse 15 he says, "I am ready" to discharge my obligation. And then in verse 16, he says, "I am not ashamed of the gospel"—that's my message.

When I think of this, I think of that little story in John 6 where five thousand people were hungry in the wilderness. A lad was there with five loaves and two fish, and that was all the Lord needed. The Lord took that lad's lunch (and that in itself was a miracle—that a boy would give up his lunch!) and fed the whole five thousand.

God said to Moses, "What do you have in your hand?" He had a dried-up old stick, a rod. That was enough for God. He could say to the disciples, "What do you have to feed these people?"

I'm full of amazement at the kind of people God uses. I know many hundreds who are ministering the Word of God in every part of the world. He takes the most unlikely ones and uses them. His servants don't have to be brilliant orators, He takes us as we are. God's good news is received by faith, not illumined to minds through brilliance.

The Spirit of God indwells you. You have the Son of God in whom the Father has hidden all His treasures of wisdom and knowledge. All He wants is you. He'll do the rest. He can take a Gideon and thrash Midian. He can take a boy with five loaves and feed a crowd. He can take the rod of Moses and bring water from a rock and split the Red Sea.

What do you have in your hand? Are you going to say with Paul, "As much as in me is, I am ready to preach the gospel to you that are at Rome also"?

Paul's Message (1:16)

> **1:16.** *For I am not ashamed of the gospel of Christ: for it is the power of God unto salvation to everyone that believeth; to the Jew first, and also to the Greek.*

There is more power manifested by God in the gospel than there was in the creation of the universe. Where is God displaying His power today? In creation? No, though we do see His power there. The greatest place where God reveals His power is in the simple presentation of the gospel of Jesus Christ. Christ died, He was buried, He was raised again. It is the only message that transforms the human heart.

I cannot for the life of me understand how church leaders can bring to unsaved people anything but the message of the gospel of Christ. I am opposed to any insidious ways of trying to reach hearts through psychology, through sad stories, through eloquent language that leaves out the blood of Christ. There is only one message. It is the power of God to deliver!

Paul said, "I am not ashamed of the gospel." He could have said, "I am proud of the gospel." I am proud of it because it takes sinners and rebels and transforms them into saints. It reveals the grace of God. It exposes the guilt of man. It can deliver and transform if men will but put their trust in the Savior.

The gospel of God is the only message that guarantees deliverance, that rescues (and that's what the word *salvation* means) us from sin, that rescues us from death and its authority and power and causes us to live forever.

Paul was not ashamed of it because he had experienced its saving and transforming power. He was so in love with the Savior that he was ready to go even to Rome with this wonderful message of the Lord Jesus, the message that reveals God's grace and man's guilt.

It is in the gospel that God portrays His power to rescue you and me—anyone—from the bondage and penalty and guilt of sin, from the fear of death, from the powers of hell, and to fit us for His presence.

Paul was not ashamed of this message, but I find some Christians who are. They are afraid of letting people know they are Christians. Maybe, sometimes, it's a good thing they don't speak up. Maybe their lives don't measure up to what they claim.

Christ came to put away your sin and my sin. He died your death and my death that He might set us free. He who knew no sin became the Sin-bearer that you and I might stand before God without sin. The gospel alone guarantees eternal forgiveness and eternal life. It's the only eternal gift with no strings attached. It's received on only one ground, the ground of faith. And it has only one requirement, our trust. We are saved by faith alone.

This is what the early reformers died for. Many were martyred for this one thing. Ecclesiastical leaders said, "You have to do more than just believe on Jesus Christ and be saved, more than just have the blood of Christ cleanse you from all sin." But this is what Martin Luther stood for. This is what Zwingli stood for. It is salvation by faith alone.

Faith is not assenting to the facts with your mind and leaving out your will. That's not New Testament believing. Three things are involved with believing in the Lord Jesus Christ—your mind, your will, and your emotions. It takes all three. Some people have what we might call "a soulish experience." At some point, somebody preached, maybe told some moving stories and worked on their emotions. That doesn't make a person a Christian. Salvation involves your mind and will, not just your emotions. Some people have their minds open and may say, "I believe that!" With their mind they see the truth, but that doesn't make them a Christian.

God tells us that whoever sins must die. He tells us that Christ died in the sinner's place. Then He asks me what I will do with the One of whom the facts speak. I respond, "Heavenly Father, I repent of my sins. I hereby stand in the good of the death of Christ. He suffered the judgment I should have borne. I accept Him as my own Savior. I put my trust in Him." Now my will is involved. With my mind I see the truth, but with my will I accept the truth, and I am brought into a relationship.

Then, often, one's emotions become involved. Some people cry. Some are very happy. No two of us have the same experience. We don't have the same personality. Some people cry easily. Some hardly ever cry. Some people keep their emotions under control. Others don't. So if you are saved and you have had a certain experience, don't demand that every other person have the same experience.

What I want to know about people who say they have received

the Lord is, have they repented of their sins, believed in the Lord Jesus, and come into a right relationship with the Savior? Everyone who believes on the Lord Jesus experiences the power that saves. A rest and peace come into his heart.

It is an amazing thing to me how many people spurn the good news. They don't want it. So then there is nothing left except judgment and death. If I spurn the divine provision for my eternal welfare, what is left but judgment?

This gospel is for everybody. It is "to the Jew first, and also to the Gentile." In the first twelve chapters of the Book of Acts the message is preached mostly to the Jews. And then, starting in chapter 13, the Christians go out to the Gentiles. I believe at the present time that God is pleading with everyone, Jew and Gentile. There is no difference. All have sinned and come short of the glory of God.

The Key Verse (1:17)

1:17. *For therein is the righteousness of God revealed from faith to faith: as it is written, The just shall live by faith.*

This is the great theme of Romans; seven times in this epistle he talks about the righteousness of God—a righteousness that is bestowed on sinners who believe, giving them a righteousness that avails with God.

Remember, there is just one righteousness in God's universe and that is His own. Man doesn't have any. Isaiah 64:6 informs us that our righteousness is as filthy rags in God's sight.

You see, friend, for you and me to stand accepted in the presence of God, we must not only have our sin question settled and have eternal life, but we must have His righteousness—a righteousness that equals the righteousness of God. John Bunyan said, "Our righteousness is at the right hand of God where our good works can't help and our failures can't hurt." That righteousness is put to the account of every believer. Christ is our righteousness, and the gospel reveals the righteousness of God.

Today, men have so minimized the character of God that sin is no more sin. We're living in a permissive society. Things we would have frowned on twenty-five years ago are taken for granted today. You say, "Well, twenty-five years ago the same sins were in society, but we kept them under cover." That may be true, but the reason we kept them under cover was because we had some estimate of the righteousness of God.

But today we have lost that concept. The very essence of God's character is His holiness, His absolute righteousness. Having turned our backs on that, having ignored the character of God, we have become permissive and sin is no longer sin. The more we see the character of God, the more we see how awful sin is and the more we appreciate His grace.

I am continually amazed at the boldness and the arrogance of even so-called religious leaders who want our government to legalize the filthy sins that brought the flood upon the world (Genesis 7-8) and the fire of God upon Sodom and Gomorrah (Genesis 19). These are the very sins that caused Israel to go into the Babylonian captivity and that caused God to judge Israel in A.D. 70.

The less you and I understand the righteousness of God, the more we will look upon sin as being nothing. I tell you, anyone who preaches moral permissiveness today doesn't know much about the Savior or anything at all about the righteousness of God.

I've had men say to me, when I've presented the good news concerning Jesus Christ to them, "Well, Mitchell, I'll take my chance with God." Will you? I'll tell you frankly, if that is your attitude, you are going to end in eternal night, eternal death, absolute separation from God and, as Jude 1:13 says, "in the blackness of darkness for ever."

Listen, Isaiah saw the Lord and he cried out, "Woe is me! for I am undone; because I am a man of unclean lips, and I dwell in the midst of a people of unclean lips: for mine eyes have seen the King, the LORD of hosts" (Isaiah 6:5).

Take this dear man Job. He cried out, "I have heard of thee by the hearing of the ear: but now mine eye seeth thee. Wherefore I abhor *myself*" (Job 42:5-6). He didn't say, "I abhor some of the things I am doing." He said, "I abhor *myself*." How did he get that way? He saw the Lord, and the Lord is righteous.

Take dear old Peter in Luke 5. When the Lord said to him, "Launch out into the deep and let down your nets for a draught," Peter said, "We fished all night and we caught nothing. And the nets are still dirty. It's the wrong time to fish. Nevertheless, at your word I will let down the nets." And they had a tremendous catch of fish. (I would like to have been there. When I go fishing, I generally catch what Peter caught that night—nothing.) And when he saw the miraculous catch, you know what Peter did? He fell at the feet of Jesus and said, "Depart from me; for I am a sinful man, O Lord" (v.8). Was he wicked because he got a draught of fish? Of course not. He saw the Lord in His majesty, in His power. He saw that the One he was following controlled nature, and he worshiped Him.

If you want to get a real picture of yourself, just look at the Lord Jesus. Do you want to know the kind of man God will accept? Just look at Him. He always did the things that please the Father. He was the only one of whom God could say, "This is my beloved Son, in whom I am well pleased" (Matthew 3:17).

There is only one righteousness—divine righteousness—and that same righteousness is put to our account when we trust the Savior. That's why a Christian can come at any time into the presence of God and be accepted. He stands in all the righteousness of Jesus Christ. It is "revealed from faith to faith; as it is written, The just shall live by faith."

Faith is the starting point, and faith is the course we follow. Faith is confidence in Another as opposed to confidence in ourselves. It's a life of continual trust. If you want a picture of that, look at Hebrews 11 where the believer is justified by faith and maintained by faith. Or to put it another way: The righteous by faith shall live, and only those who are righteous shall live.

This statement is used four times in the Bible. It is first used in the little book by the prophet Habakkuk, chapter 2:4. Then it is used here in Romans 1:17 with the emphasis on the righteousness of God. In Galatians 3:11, the emphasis is on the just shall live by *faith*, and in Hebrews 10:38, the just shall *live* by faith. Romans emphasizes the righteousness of God, Galatians emphasizes faith, and Hebrews emphasizes the question of life.

I'm saved by faith; I continue in faith.

THE NEED FOR RIGHTEOUSNESS
(1:18-3:20)

The Gentile World Guilty (1:18-20)

Paul now begins to give us the absolute unrighteousness of men—of all men, whether Jew, Gentile, moralist, religionist, you name it. He's going to reveal in chapters 1, 2, and part of 3 that there isn't a man on the face of the earth who is righteous and is able to stand on his own before God and say, "This is what I am." It would be folly for Paul to speak of the righteousness of God when men are occupied with their own righteousness. Therefore he asks, "Is the gospel necessary? Can man do anything to please God?" And then he proves that man cannot.

In Romans 1:18-32, Paul argues that the Gentile world is guilty before God and without excuse. And when Paul gets through with the first chapter, all the Jews will say, "Amen! That's a real picture of the Gentile world." It was, and it still is.

Man Is without Excuse (1:18)

1:18. *For the wrath of God is revealed from heaven against all ungodliness and unrighteousness of men, who hold the truth in unrighteousness.*

The gospel is not only a revelation of the righteousness of God, but it is also a revelation of the wrath of God. And His wrath is just as real as His love. If a generation rejects His love, His grace,

His mercy, then there is nothing else for a righteous God to do but to judge and manifest His wrath.

First, I read here that the wrath of God is revealed against man's ungodliness. Now an ungodly man is one who leaves God out. He has no regard at all for God. There are men and women who have absolutely no regard for God. They are ungodly. They might be moral, they might be wonderful people, but they leave God out of their lives. They go to bed at night, get up in the morning, go to work, come back home, do a few things they want to do, and go back to bed with no thought, no room, no time for God. They live in a world all their own, and God is outside of it. That's the ungodly.

"Then they're atheists," you say. No, I'm not saying they're atheists. They just have no regard for God. They go their own way, they live their own lives. The great majority of people live just that way. Sadly, many Christians do, too.

Second, the wrath of God is revealed against the unrighteousness of men. This deals with their wicked conduct. Ungodliness means God is out of their lives. Unrighteousness describes their conduct.

Third, they hold down the truth in unrighteousness. They suppress the truth. They stifle the truth because they want to sin in willful opposition to revealed truth. In his wickedness man would suppress the truth. And do you think for one moment he is going to escape the wrath of God or the judgment of God? My friend, God is going to judge men in righteousness.

God Has Revealed Himself (1:19-20)

1:19-20. *Because that which may be known of God is manifest in them; for God hath showed it unto them. For the invisible things of him from the creation of the world are clearly seen, being understood by the things that are made, even his eternal power and Godhead; so that they are without excuse.*

Man doesn't have a lick of excuse. And if you ask about the heathen, well, that's who Paul is talking about. What man out of Christ can stand before a holy, righteous God and have any excuse?

God has revealed himself to man and in man. Man has in himself the capacity to worship and trust the living God, and when he does, God gives him more truth. But man has refused it and cast it out. Every man, everywhere, knows what he ought to do. God has given him a conscience. I don't care what part of the world you go to, men know this. God revealed himself to them even before Christ came.

Creation was man's first Bible. Even if he knew nothing of the writing of books, he could find God through creation. Psalm 19:1-3 proclaims: "The heavens declare the glory of God; and the firmament showeth His handiwork. Day unto day uttereth speech, and night unto night showeth knowledge. There is no speech nor language [no place], where their voice is not heard."

Men—heathen men, all men—down through the centuries, whether they had a Bible or not, whether they ever heard of Christ or not, are responsible to worship their Creator, the One who made them and made the universe.

Man did not sin through lack of knowledge, but in spite of that knowledge. Man had the light, but he rejected it; and by spurning God, man lost sin-consciousness. Sin was not sin to him any more.

That's the history of man, by the way, not only in the first century but also in the twentieth.

THE SINFULNESS OF THE GENTILE WORLD (1:21-32)

Their Degeneration (1:21-23)

"Because that, when they knew God, they glorified him not as God. . . ." Man is not evolving to the place where he is going to know God. No, man knew God, then he didn't glorify Him as God. In fact, we had men who were polytheistic, who worshiped all the gods that men have created.

Man first of all knew God. He knew he was responsible to God. But when Cain went out from the presence of God (Genesis 4), he tried to make this world a fit place to live without God, and that has been going on ever since.

Whether you like it or not, we were born in sin. We were children of wrath like the rest, unrighteous and unholy. And either we were filled with our own self-righteousness or filled with outbroken sin.

Now let's look at the degeneration. It's a sad picture.

> **1:21-23.** *Because that, when they knew God, they glorified him not as God, neither were thankful; but became vain in their imaginations, and their foolish heart was darkened. Professing themselves to be wise, they became fools, and changed the glory of the uncorruptible God into an image made like to corruptible man, and to birds, and fourfooted beasts, and creeping things.*

Even in their sinfulness men go down instead of up. They did not glorify Him as God. They became unthankful, they became puffed up, they were godless and thankless. Having stopped the worship of God, they lost the knowledge of God. We have these all around us today. Men still misuse the knowledge they have and become puffed up. Man becomes independent of God and vain in his reasoning.

Professing himself to be wise, man became a fool. The proof? He changed the glory of the incorruptible God into an image; and even in his worship, there is degeneration. First, he worshiped God as a man, then as a bird and as a quadruped, then as a creeping thing.

Is God like these? No. The only true image of the invisible God is Jesus Christ (Colossians 1:15). If you want to know God, you must find Him in Jesus Christ, the sinless One, the righteous One. But man became a fool, turned his back on the revelation of God, refused to have God in his knowledge, and entered decline and degeneration not only in his thinking but also in his actions.

"Knowing God," they became fools in preferring themselves

and the work of their hands to a God who loved them and wants to manifest His mercy to them. They made gods who can neither hear nor see nor act nor do anything—chunks of stone and wood. And, my friend, when men make idols, they condemn themselves when they worship them. When I take a piece of wood and make it into something, I am greater than the thing I made. The creator is greater than the thing made. The fact that someone made me, makes me responsible to worship Him. And if I worship anything else, I condemn myself. I have made what I worship greater than I.

Their Judgment (1:24-32)

1:24. *Wherefore God also gave them up to uncleanness through the lusts of their own hearts, to dishonour their own bodies between themselves.*

When "God gave them up," He deliberately turned them over to be dominated, to be controlled by their own lusts. Here we have a positive act of God. He gave them over as slaves to the very thing they wanted. Sad, isn't it? Having refused the person of God, having spurned His righteousness, His love and grace and mercy, they became slaves to what they craved. They made what they served greater than they.

God gave them over to uncleanness because they changed the glory of God into an image. The fruit of their idolatry was immorality. Their bodies were defiled and their minds were diseased. They were given up to it.

God gave them up to vile affections (1:25-27).

1:25-27. *Who changed the truth of God into a lie, and worshiped and served the creature more than the Creator, who is blessed for ever. Amen. For this cause God gave them up unto vile affections: for even their women did change the natural use into that which is against nature: And likewise also the men, leaving the* *natural use of the woman, burned in their lust one toward another; men with men working that which is unseemly, and receiving in themselves that recompence of their error which was meet.*

They changed the truth of God into a lie. They refused His revelation. They persisted in their sin. The fruit of their unbelief in the Word of God was vile passions, passions of disgrace, moral perversion. Men are morally perverse because they worship and serve themselves, the creature, more than the Creator. God gives them up to vile passions. You just can't play fast and loose with God.

How bad is the human heart? When you and I think of sin, we think of the outbroken sins of society—drunkenness, drug abuse, sexual perversion, immorality, moral corruption. Name it, you have it.

But some things are even more vile than that in the presence of God. When men take the Word of God and pull it to pieces and change it, they traffic in souls. They delight to take people who love the Savior and try to destroy their faith. In God's sight, that is far worse. They break down the simplicity of faith in the Savior; they dethrone the Savior. They throw the Word of God out as untenable and the fruit is right here. Having changed the truth of God into a lie, having worshiped and served the creature—or man—more than the Creator, "God gave them up unto vile affections." Men are given up to the very things they want to do because of their refusal to have God in their lives.

God gave them up to a reprobate mind (1:28-32).

1:28-32. *And even as they did not like to retain God in their knowledge, God gave them over to a reprobate mind, to do those things which are not convenient [ought not to be done]; being filled with all unrighteousness, fornication, wickedness, covetousness, maliciousness; full of envy, murder, debate [strife], deceit,* *malignity; whisperers, backbiters, haters of God, despiteful, proud, boasters, inventors of evil things, disobedient to parents, without understanding, covenantbreakers, without natural affection, implacable, unmerciful: who knowing the judgment of God, that they which commit such things are worthy of death, not only do the same, but have pleasure in them that do them.*

Here is an amazing thing. Paul says they refused to have God in their knowledge. They preferred to be ignorant of God and the things of God and the Son of God and the salvation in Christ. As a result, God gave them over to a reprobate mind to do despicable things.

In this first chapter of Romans, we have the history of man right down to this century. And don't tell me that man today lives any better life than he did three, four, five thousand years ago. The human heart hasn't changed. Once a man rules God out of his life, there is nothing left but lawlessness.

I am well aware that my generation reaped the fruit of the character of our forefathers who loved God. Our lives were changed, our characters were changed, through the gospel of Christ. We had the Word of God, we loved the Savior. And even though a great many of our people did not accept the gospel of Jesus Christ, their lives were affected by the character and testimony of Christians.

The wrath of God is not revealed on America and Canada because God's people are still here. The blessing of God keeps this nation, this continent, from some of the vileness we see in other lands. We ought to thank God, my friend, that we are living in a land where the Word of God is still believed, where we can still buy a Bible and read about our precious, wonderful Savior.

The picture Paul paints in Romans 1:18-32 is a picture of God removing His restraints from men and letting them have their uncleanness, their vile affection, their reprobate mind. And why did God do this? Because they changed the glory of God into an image, because they changed the truth of God into a lie, because they refused to have God in their knowledge. In spite of it, God still loves men and women.

God doesn't love their sin, He doesn't love their corruption, He doesn't love their self-righteousness, He doesn't love their folly. Why do you think He is holding back the forces of wrath and of judgment from the world? He loves them and "is longsuffering to us-ward, not willing that any should perish, but that all should come to repentance" (2 Peter 3:9).

But the day is coming when the wrath of God is going to be revealed from heaven against all ungodliness and unrighteousness of men.

Romans 2

As we went through Romans 1, we saw the universality of sin. Paul had wanted to talk about the righteousness of God, but he realized the folly of spending time talking about that when men think they have a righteousness of their own.

So when you read Romans 1, you find the universality of sin, especially in the Gentile world. God gave the Gentiles up—they had spurned the God of creation, they had changed the glory of the incorruptible God into an image. He had given them over to uncleanness, and because they changed the truth of God into a lie, He gave them up to vile affections. Then, because they refused to have God in their knowledge, He gave them over to a reprobate mind to do despicable things. This is Romans 1.

THE MORALIST AND THE RELIGIONIST GUILTY
(2:1-16)

But in Paul's day, there were those who could say, "We don't belong to Romans 1. We haven't sinned like that." And there are a great many people in our age who are quite ready to condemn others and justify themselves.

So when we come to the first sixteen verses of Romans 2, we have Paul addressing this group who think they are not as bad as the people in Romans 1. We have him proving that the moral person and the religious person are just as guilty as the immoral and the irreligious.

Paul does not deal in this second chapter with salvation, but with how God will judge men. This is important to keep in mind. Some verses will look as if they affirm that salvation is by works. That's not true. The fact that men have sinned means they have to be judged. God is righteous. Never forget that.

"But," you say, "God is love." Yes, but He cannot manifest His love at the expense of His righteousness. We are dealing with a righteous God. If you and I have sinned, then sin pays wages and death is the wages. So Paul gives to us four grounds on which God is going to judge men.

God Will Judge in Truth (2:1-5)

God is going to be dealing not with empty profession but with reality. Remember that. Second Thessalonians 2:10,12 gives us two reasons why God is going to judge them: because they did not love the truth and because they did not believe the truth.

> **2:1-3.** *Therefore thou art inexcusable, O man, whosoever thou art that judgest: for wherein thou judgest another, thou condemnest thyself; for thou that judgest doest the same things. But we are sure that the judgment of God is according to truth against them which commit such things.*
>
> *And thinkest thou this, O man, that judgest them which do such things, and doest the same, that thou shalt escape the judgment of God?*

Why is the one who judges not excused? Because he does the same things, and he thinks God is going to let him get by. Although Paul primarily has the Gentile moralists and religionists in mind, he also has the Jew in mind. Like the moralist, the Jew judges others; yet in his heart he wants to do the same thing.

The Pharisees in John 8 came to the Lord, dragging a woman

with them. They threw her down before Him and said, "Rabbi, according to Moses' law this woman ought to be stoned. We caught her in the act of adultery and, according to Moses, she should die. What do you think?"

Jesus did a wonderful thing. He ignored them. But, when they persisted, He said, "All right, I appoint you men as the executioners of this woman if you are without sin." And from the oldest to the youngest, they sneaked out of the crowd one by one until the woman stood alone. The Lord lifted up His head and asked, "Where are your accusers?"

"There are none, Lord."

And He said, "Neither do I condemn you. Go and sin no more. If there is no one to accuse you, then no one can judge you." The Lord was not condoning her sin because He said to her, "Go and sin no more." She was a transformed woman, standing in the presence of God.

Why did her persecutors vanish? Because of what Romans 2:1 says: "You are without excuse, O man, for when you judge somebody else, you judge yourself because you do the same things." And even if you don't do them, it's not because you wouldn't like to do them.

How quick we are to judge and accuse people when we ourselves are doing the very same thing. God is going to judge men according to truth. No man can escape the judgment of God unless he comes God's way. And in the next two verses, we find that man despises God's grace.

> **2:4-5.** *Or despisest thou the riches of his goodness and forbearance and longsuffering; not knowing that the goodness of God leadeth thee to repentance? But after thy hardness and impenitent heart treasurest up unto thyself wrath against the day of wrath and revelation of the righteous judgment of God.*

Let me stop here a minute. Acts 17:30 says God commands all men everywhere to repent. From Abraham to Christ, God allowed the Gentile world to go on. How patient He was and how patient He is yet with those who despise Him even though there is nothing left for them but judgment.

It just seems that sinners get away with their sin. They sin with impunity, with arrogance. They despise the righteous God. And because God is good and loving and merciful, "not willing that any should perish, but that all should come to repentance" (2 Peter 3:9), they think they can do anything they want.

But, my friend, they still have to meet God. Those who despise His goodness are storing for themselves judgment and wrath against the day of wrath and the revelation of the righteous judgment of God. Remember, God is bound to judge righteously, and the very goodness of God should lead them to repentance. Regrettably, man has exchanged the goodness of God for His wrath.

God Will Judge Men's Deeds (2:6-10)

We come to the second ground whereby God is going to judge men. He will do it according to their deeds, and it is a solemn thing.

> **2:6-7.** *Who will render to every man according to his deeds: To them who by patient continuance in well doing seek for glory and honour and immortality, eternal life.*

Verses 8 through 10 give us the other side of the coin:

> **2:8-10.** *But unto them that are contentious, and do not obey the truth, but obey unrighteousness, indignation and wrath, tribulation and anguish, upon every soul of man that doeth evil, of the Jew first, and also of the Gentile; but glory, honour, and peace, to every man that worketh good, to the Jew first, and also to the Gentile.*

God is not going to judge men according to what they profess, He is going to deal in righteousness and in reality. Believe me, it is a solemn reality because God knows everyone's thoughts and motives.

But in verses 7 and 10, Paul speaks of every man "who by patient continuance in well doing" seeks for "glory and honour and immortality." He will receive eternal life. "Glory, honor, and peace, to every man that worketh good, to the Jew first and also to the Gentile." God in His righteousness is judging men according to reality. Those who trust the law seek for glory and incorruptibility.

But how can they find them unless they are in touch with God? In other words, what they are in themselves is revealed by their actions. God doesn't cultivate people who live a life of empty profession. If their actions do not measure up to what they say, God is going to judge them according to their deeds. He is going to judge in truth. He is going to judge in reality.

Verses 8 and 9 speak of those who are opposed to God, who are contentious and do not obey truth but obey unrighteousness. I read "indignation and wrath, tribulation and anguish upon every soul of man that doeth evil, whether Jew or Gentile." This man has no trust in God. As a result, his life is a life of evil; he yields himself to sin. The end is going to be anguish and tribulation and wrath. The attitude of men's hearts to God is revealed by their works. Paul is not dealing with being saved by works, but rather with divine judgment as a result of works.

God is going to judge righteously. Those who are arrogant, self-righteous, and self-willed are going to do what they want to do, whatever it may be. But they are going to stand before God who is righteous. He is going to judge them on the reality of their life before Him. He is going to shut the mouths of men from glorying in their own self-righteousness and goodness. He is going to judge the very thoughts and idle words they have spoken. They may fool you and me, my friend, and that wouldn't be hard to do; but they are not going to fool God.

"But we haven't sinned much," these people say. It's not a question of the amount of sin but the fact that they *have* sinned;

there is unrighteousness in them. Would they be willing for God to blaze abroad the thoughts of their heart—the thoughts that never find expression in words or actions?

They say, "You mean to tell me that God knows my thoughts?" Psalm 139:1-2 says He knows my thoughts "afar off." God knows the innermost secrets of your life, things that only you think you know. Not another living soul knows what goes on in your heart—not even your wife or your children. But God knows. Would you be willing to stand before a righteous God and let Him tear the veil off and let everybody see?

No, you want to keep it covered. Although you may not have said or done bad things, you know in your heart the things you would like to have done. You didn't do them because you didn't want to injure yourself or somebody else or your reputation.

You are not fooling God, my friend. You can fool people, but you can't fool God. God must judge according to truth, according to your character, according to the very depth of your being. Everything that is unrighteous is going to be judged, and the wages of sin is death. God judges according to what a man is in his heart.

God Will Judge without Partiality (2:11-15)

2:11-13. *For there is no respect of persons with God. For as many as have sinned without law shall also perish without law: and as many as have sinned in the law shall be judged by the law; (for not the hearers of the law are just before God, but the doers of the law shall be justified.*

We come now to a tremendous passage of Scripture, and it's a passage that has been greatly misunderstood. God is going to judge men in absolute impartiality. There are going to be no favorites. Paul especially singles out the Jew. Watch what he says: The doers of the law, not the hearers of the law, are justified before God.

You say, "Well, there you are, Mr. Mitchell. Salvation is by works." Not so. No man (except the Lord Jesus) has ever kept the law. For the fifteen hundred years between Moses and Christ the Jews had the law, and no Jew ever fully kept the law. Even the best men in the Old Testament, somewhere along the line, failed God. The law was not given to save mankind. It was given to prove man is sinful. It is impossible for you or for me to keep the law of God from the moment we are born until the moment we die. It is impossible because we are born in sin.

The Jews were sticklers for keeping the law, but their hearts were far from God. As the Lord himself said through the prophet, "With their mouth they praise me, but their hearts are far from me."

To say the doers of the law shall be justified is true if you can find a man who keeps the law. But the Book also says that if you break the law in one point, you are guilty of all. "Cursed is everyone that continueth not in all things which are written in the book of the law to do them" (Galatians 3:10). You see, we are all sinners, we have all "sinned and come short of the glory of God." What the law demanded, we could never do.

What about the Gentiles?

> **2:14-15.** *For when the Gentiles, which have not the law, do by nature the things contained in the law, these, having not the law, are a law unto themselves: which show the work of the law written in their hearts, their conscience also bearing witness, and their thoughts the mean while accusing or else excusing one another;)*

The question is raised then, "If the Jew could not be saved by keeping the law because he was just a hearer not a doer, what about the Gentiles?" Well, my friend, the Gentiles have no excuse either. We discovered that in Romans 1: "For the invisible things of him from the creation of the world are clearly seen, being understood by the things that are made, even his eternal power and Godhead; so that they are without excuse" (1:20).

The moral law has been revealed to the Gentiles, and they are responsible to do the right and not the wrong. Notice what it says: "He that sins without law shall perish without law." Even though they had no revealed law, they had sinned because they knew what was right and they knew what was wrong. And if the Jew claims that the law will save him, then the Gentile can claim that his law of conscience will save him. But both Jew and Gentile are absolutely guilty, and both must stand before God who is righteous.

The conscience God put in man has become so distorted today that what used to be called sin is called sin no longer. Unsaved young people have no conscience concerning sin. "As long as you want it, do it," they say. "As long as it's love . . ." It's not love, it's lust. And do you think they're going to dodge the judgment of God? Not a bit of it.

God Will Judge according to the Gospel (2:16)

2:16. *In the day when God shall judge the secrets of men by Jesus Christ according to my gospel.*

The Jew had the law of Moses. The Gentile had the law written on his conscience and his heart. Both must stand before God who "will judge the secrets of men by Jesus Christ according to my gospel." The very secrets of men, the very motives of the human heart are going to be judged by Jesus Christ.

"Why, Mr. Mitchell, no one will be able to stand." That's right. No man will be able to stand before God because He is going to judge according to truth, without respect of persons, according to each one's works.

THE JEW IS AS GUILTY AS THE GENTILE (2:17-29)

The Jew's Knowledge Accuses Him (2:17-20)

Paul comes right out and goes after the Jew. He is going to prove that the Jew is equally guilty with the Gentile sinner of chapter 1. The first thing he takes up is what the Jew knows—his knowledge.

2:17-20. *Behold, thou art called a Jew, and restest in the law, and makest thy boast of God, and knowest his will, and approvest the things that are more excellent (or the things that differ), being instructed out of the law; and art confident that thou thyself art a guide of the blind, a light of them which are in darkness, an instructor of the foolish, a teacher of babes, which hast the form of knowledge and of the truth in the law.*

This is what the Jew knew, and if Paul can prove the Jew to be as guilty as the Gentile, then the Jew is in a worse condition than the Gentile because of his added knowledge and responsibility.

Notice that the Jew rests in the law and makes his boast of God. Here you see his blindness. He never did see the reason for the law. The law is an executioner—"The soul that sinneth it shall die." It's like a man with his neck on the block, and as the executioner raises his ax, the man about to lose his head glories in his executioner.

Though a foolish thing, that was what the Jew was doing. He made his boast in the law, and he rested in the law. Because he had the law from God, he thought that covered a multitude of sins. Instead, the law was the revealer of sin; and he was blind, blinded by his own self-righteousness, blinded by his own egotism, blinded by the thought that he was a favorite of God.

He made his boast that Jehovah was his God. He claimed to know the will of God, to know right from wrong according to the law. He claimed to be a leader of the blind, of those who were in darkness. He claimed to have the knowledge of God's law.

He made all these claims—his God was the only God, he had the law of God, he had the Word of God, the Jews were God's people and Abraham's children. They were the people of the covenant. Oh, how they boasted about their God and about their relationship to Him.

But notice the condemnation of the Jew in verses 21 to 29. The Jew failed in the exact thing he knew best. His deeds denied his doctrine. I want you to mark it—he refused to walk in the light of what he taught.

The Jew's Practice Accuses Him (2:21-29)

2:21-22. *Thou therefore which teachest another, teachest thou not thyself? thou that preachest a man should not steal, dost thou steal? thou that sayest a man should not commit adultery, dost thou commit adultery? thou that abhorrest idols, dost thou commit sacrilege?*

The Jew refused to walk in what he himself taught. "Thou that teachest a man that he should not steal, do you steal?" The Jew thought nothing, for example, of going down to the heathen temple and stealing the gold and the silver and the precious stones, whatever was of any value in the heathen temple. "This is for the glory of God," he would say. "We are putting down idolatry."

"You that preach a man should not commit adultery, do you commit adultery?" The answer, of course, is obvious.

"You that abhorrest idols, do you commit sacrilege?" If a Gentile came into the temple courtyard in Jerusalem, the Jews would cry out, "Sacrilege!" and get ready to kill that Gentile. But they thought nothing of going to the Gentile temple and defaming it and smashing things up. As I mentioned, they would plunder the heathen temples and steal everything they could lay their hands on.

2:23-24. *Thou that makest thy boast of the law, through breaking the law dishonourest thou God? For the name of God is blasphemed among the Gentiles through you, as it is written.*

The Jews tarnished the very name of God. Their lives made the Gentiles curse Him. For example, in Ezekiel 36:19-20, the prophet says, in effect, "When you were in Israel, you were in idolatry and moral corruption. You are in captivity among the nations of the earth, and even now, the very name of Jehovah is blasphemed because of you."

I can't help thinking that the name of our Savior is often blasphemed because Christians are not walking uprightly before God. I've had people say, "Mr. Mitchell, if that is Christianity, I don't want it." My friend, what you are looking at is not Christianity. Someone once pointed out to Dwight L. Moody a man who was drunk, lying in the gutter, and said, "Mr. Moody, there goes one of your converts." "Yes," said Moody, "he might have been my convert. He certainly wasn't the Lord's."

Oh, I say sadly, how often the lives of the saints have been used by Satan to hinder people from coming to Christ. May you and I so walk before God that our Savior will not be dishonored because of what we say and do. I know we are all frail and have certain weaknesses, but let's look to the Lord for them. If you know you have a weakness, look to the Lord that He may give you victory over it and that you may become a testimony for God.

I pray that we may so walk before God that we will shed abroad something of the sweetness of the aroma of Christ. Our lives will be a benediction to people, so they might say, "You have something we don't have. I'd like to have what you have. I'd like to have that peace, that loveliness of character, that sweetness of disposition that you have and I lack."

In verses 25 to 29, Paul talks about the inconsistency of empty profession, especially for the Jew:

> **2:25-29.** *For circumcision verily profiteth, if thou keep the law: but if thou be a breaker of the law, thy circumcision is made uncircumcision. Therefore if the uncircumcision keep the righteousness of the law, shall not his uncircumcision be counted for circumcision? And shall not uncircumcision which is by nature, if it fulfill the law, judge thee, who by the letter and circumcision dost transgress the law? For he is not a Jew, which is one outwardly; neither is that circumcision, which is outward in the flesh: but he is a Jew, which is one inwardly; and circumcision is that of the heart, in the*

spirit, and not in the letter; whose praise is not of men,
but of God.

What in the world is Paul talking about? The Jews boasted
about being the circumcised. The Gentiles, of course, were the
uncircumcised. Circumcision was a sign of the covenant God
made with Abraham and his seed, and it became a national sign.

Another example of a national sign is the Sabbath day (Exodus 31).
The Sabbath day is not an individual sign, it is a national sign—
the sign of a covenant between God and the people of Israel. It
was a sign of the Mosaic covenant.

Circumcision was a sign of the faith covenant made to
Abraham and to his seed. Circumcision didn't make a person a
real Jew; circumcision was of the heart. Ishmael was circumcised
just as Isaac was—they were both sons of Abraham—but God
said, "In Isaac shall your seed be called." His descendants were
called the "children of faith," the "children of Abraham." Our
Lord said in John 8:37,39: "I know that ye are Abraham's seed
[his natural descendants]"; but "if ye were Abraham's children
[children of faith], ye would do the works of Abraham." In other
words, they would believe Messiah.

Outward ordinances benefit you if your heart is right with God.
For Jews, circumcision was an outward manifestation that they
belonged to God. But that would do no good if they didn't live for
Him.

Some people today say, "I have joined the church. I've been
baptized." That may be true, and I'm not opposed to that. But baptism is a sign to the world that you belong to God. So your life
should be godly. Paul is saying, "You Jews who have the rite of
circumcision, if you are not walking before God, you are in a
worse plight than the Gentile who seeks to please God but who
has never been circumcised. It's no use glorying in the label if you
don't have the content." The Gentiles had no label, but they had
reality, whereas the Jews who had the label had no reality.

When a man boasts of his knowledge of God but lives like a

man that is unsaved with no desire to change, then I question whether he really is trusting the Savior. You say, "Well, Mr. Mitchell, you can't judge a man's heart." That's right, only God can see a man's heart. But men see a man's works, and Paul is saying it's no use boasting about being a Jew, being circumcised, being superior to the Gentiles if your life is not real before God. God would rather accept the Gentile without the rite of circumcision, without any ordinances at all, if his heart is right.

Is your heart right with God? I'm not opposed to ordinances or ceremonies. What I'm after is the reality of your heart-life before God. You and I can discuss and argue about ceremonies, but that is not important if your heart is not right with God. Does your life show forth the transformation that comes to one in whom Christ dwells?

Romans 3

God has revealed to us the gospel concerning His Son, who was a real Man, God manifest in the flesh. He was the Son of God, raised with power and now sitting at God's right hand. When I think of what we have in the Book of Romans, my heart goes out that every Christian might be established in the wonderful truths of the grace of God as it is given to us in this amazing book, this most foundational book of all of the epistles. I say very frankly, my friend, if you are not established in the Book of Romans, then you are not established in the gospel God has for us.

Paul has just said (Romans 2:25-29) that empty profession isn't worth a thing. Outward ordinances are empty if your heart is not right with God. So he raises the question, "What's the advantage of being a Jew?"

THE JEW'S ADVANTAGE ACCUSES HIM (3:1-8)

3:1-2. *What advantage then has the Jew? or what profit is there of circumcision? Much in every way: chiefly, because that unto them [the Jews] were committed the oracles of God.*

If a Gentile can be acceptable to God without being circumcised, what's the use of circumcision? If this rite that marks him as a Jew is of no value, what's the use of being a Jew?

Paul says, "Much every way." Privilege always increases one's responsibility; it never frees you from it. And this very advantage is what accuses the Jew.

Why didn't Paul say here that God was through with the Jew? Now that Christian churches have been established, what's the use of being a Jew? He answers his own question by saying that God has given three things to the Jews and we have to acknowledge them.

First, to the Jews were committed the oracles, the revelation, of God. Where did we get our Bible? From the Jews, who were the depository for the Word of God. God spoke through their prophets, through their leaders, through their sages, through their apostles.

Second, through them the Messiah came. When He was talking to the Samaritan woman, our Lord said, "Salvation is of the Jews," referring to Himself.

Third, God chose the Israelites not because they were many or because they were good. He chose them in sovereign grace to be His witnesses to the nations even though they failed in their job and have been scattered among the nations for nineteen hundred years. That choosing has never been abrogated. Israel is to be restored to fellowship and relationship with God. She is again going to be His testimony to the Gentiles of the wonderful grace of God (Isaiah 43).

So circumcision only profits when one is exercised in heart. What profit is there in circumcision? Everything, if you are right before God.

In verses 3 through 8, some other questions are raised:

3:3-4. *For what if some did not believe? shall their unbelief make the faith of God without effect? God forbid: yea, let God be true, but every man a liar; as it is written, That thou mightest be justified in thy sayings, and mightest overcome when thou art judged.*

What if some did not believe? Will God not keep His Word and bless Israel so that all will share in the blessing? Isn't God faithful to His Word? Yes, even if some did not believe. Mark the subtlety of this thing. Is it not true that whatever God has promised, He will do? If God is going to keep His Word and bless Israel, then we are all going to share in His blessing. God will keep His Word in spite of the unbelief of those who profess His Name.

But God's faithfulness does not free man from God's judgment. When Jesus returns, He is going to purge out of Israel all the unbelieving Jews. They are not going to come in under the promises of God. There must be faith, personal and individual faith, before they can have the blessing. That's true among the Jews; it's also true among the Gentiles today.

Now the second question is raised:

3:5-6. *But if our unrighteousness commend the righteousness of God, what shall we say? Is God unrighteous who taketh vengeance? (I speak as a man) God forbid: for then how shall God judge the world?*

Well, Paul, if Jewish unfaithfulness, if Jewish unrighteousness makes the righteousness of God stand out with more glory—if it exalts and exhibits His righteousness—what are you finding fault for? You ought to be thankful that the Jew's unrighteousness is going to bring more glory to God. Why judge the Jew if his unrighteousness is going to glorify God?

Again, mark the subtlety of this situation. Paul has a tough time trying to get the Jew to realize he needs a Savior. The Jew runs from one hole to the next. Paul pulls him out of one and he dives into another. Let me repeat the question. What if some did not believe? Well, what of it? Will God keep His Word and bless sinful Israel? Is God unrighteous because He won't?

The answer is, "God forbid." If God did bless an unrepentant Israel, He would have no basis for future judgment. If He lets the Jew with his privileges go because he glorified God by his unfaithfulness, God must let the Gentile who has no privileges go, too. In fact, if anyone is going to be set free, it will have to be the Gentile because the Jew has had more responsibility and is just as big a failure.

If you take two fellows out into the sea and tie a block of cement to one and throw them both overboard, which one will go to the bottom quicker? Of course, the one with the cement block. That's the Jew with his privileges. He was just as bad as the Gentile so he was under greater judgment than the Gentile. If God lets the Jew go, He has to let the Gentile go.

But Paul's not through yet:

> **3:7-8.** *For if the truth of God hath more abounded through my lie unto his glory; why yet am I also judged as a sinner? And not rather, (as we be slanderously reported, and as some affirm that we say,) Let us do evil, that good may come? whose damnation is just.*

If through my lie God is glorified, that doesn't free me from being a liar. I'm still a liar and under judgment. It's true that everything ultimately is going to redound to the glory of God. But that does not free you or me from the fact that we have sinned and fallen short of the glory of God, and that we are to come under the judgment of God unless we accept Jesus Christ as our Savior.

Remember what Paul is doing. He is not talking about the gospel. He's not giving us good news. Indeed, it's far from good news. He is telling us that the law with all its ceremonies has only one point and that is to prove that man cannot fit himself for the presence of God.

The Scriptures have included all under sin. God has included all in unbelief that He might have mercy upon all. God has so much in store for man in the future and He is going to keep His Word. He is faithful. Every jot and every tittle is going to be fulfilled whether you like it or not. Whatever man does, God is going to do His job.

If God is glorified through our failures, that doesn't give me ground to glory in my sin. As Paul says, "If I lie and God is glorified through my lying, I am still a liar and I must stand before God for lying. If the truth of God has more abounded through my lie to His glory, I am still a sinner, and I am going to come under the judgment of God. I must never say, 'Let us do evil that good may come.' "

GOD'S GREAT INDICTMENT OF THE HUMAN RACE
(3:9-20)

Paul is not about to talk of the wonderful righteousness and grace of God when man is occupied with himself, with his own so-called goodness, with his boasted religious experiences instead of Christ. So he must shut the mouth of man from glorying in his own self-righteousness before Paul can reveal to us the righteous character of God, which he does starting in verse 21. But between verses 9 and 20, Paul takes up the great indictment of the human race. He takes the Jew's own Scripture and shuts his mouth.

> **3:9.** *What then? are we better than they? No, in no wise: for we have before proved both Jews and Gentiles, that they are all under sin.*

Paul begins by making the flat statement that no one is better than anybody else. People are always saying that today. "I'm not as bad as he is," or "I'm not so bad after all." God has declared everybody "under sin."

Man's Character (3:10-12)

Having said that, Paul takes the Old Testament Scriptures and proves that all men in their character and conduct are absolutely unrighteous. In verses 10 to 12, he takes up the question of the character of man. He is not talking about any individual, he is talking about everyone in the human race. As God sees men, this is their character.

> **3:10-12.** *As it is written, There is none righteous, no, not one: There is none that understandeth, there is none that seeketh after God. They are all gone out of the way, they are together become unprofitable; there is none that doeth good, no, not one.*

That's not a nice picture, is it? But Paul is simply reminding the Jews of what David wrote in Psalm 53:1-3. This is how God looks at man. It may not be the way you look at man. You might say to me, "I'm just as good as anybody on earth." I'll take your word for it, but what are you going to tell God? It's how God sees us that's important.

I remember one time preaching on this portion of Scripture when a great big fellow stood and waved his fist at me right in the meeting. He said, "I want you to know, sir, that I sought God. That's why I was saved—because I sought God." (It happened that the year before I had led this great big brother to Christ, but in the meantime he had been told that he had been saved because he sought God.) So I said to him, "I didn't know that God was lost and that he had to be sought. We were the lost ones and God came seeking us." Luke 19:10 says, "The Son of Man is come to seek and to save that which was lost."

Man is incurably bad, my friend. Just look in your own heart. Don't line yourself up with somebody else and say, "I'm not as bad as he or she is." That isn't the question. The question is—how do you stand before God? How does God see you?

It's true that you and I may do good things. We may do good works as far as man counts them good. If we go by the standards of men, we could argue with Paul. But this is not the standard.

It is God who is declaring man unrighteous. This is the way God sees people who are out of Christ.

Man's Conduct (3:13-17)

If that is our character as God sees us, let's read what our conduct is as God sees us:

> **3:13-17.** *Their throat is an open sepulchre; with their tongues they have used deceit; the poison of asps is under their lips: whose mouth is full of cursing and bitterness: their feet are swift to shed blood: Destruction and misery are in their ways: and the way of peace have they not known.*

This is the history of man from the beginning. Even in my brief space on earth, we have had a number of wars. In fact, there is always some war going on.

Look at the actions. Our conduct corresponds to our character. If my character is unrighteous, then my actions will be unrighteous. Listen to Paul: "Their throat is an open sepulchre"—like a grave with a body in corruption. "With their tongues they have used deceit." Did you ever deceive anyone? "The poison of asps is under their lips." We do more damage with our tongues than we can do with anything else. No wonder James says, "The tongue is set on fire of hell." My, the nasty things we can say with our tongues. Aren't we all guilty? Sometimes things come out of our mouths we never intended to say. But when we hear ourselves say it, our pride forbids us taking it back or apologizing. If someone were to accuse us of murdering someone's character, we would look so self-righteous. Why, we wouldn't do a thing like that. No, but it comes out just the same.

You can't read your newspaper without seeing it. You can't walk among people without realizing it. Deceit, the poison of asps, villainy—where does it all come from? "From within," as the Lord said in Mark 7. From within proceed all these things.

Before I came to know the Savior, I wasn't taught to curse. I just cursed. That was part of the language. You work in shops or shipyards or railroad yards, wherever your employment may be, wherever men and women are, mouths are there full of cursing and bitterness.

Even among Christians I have seen that bitterness as they speak with a bitter tongue. Oh, the damage that is done, the friendships that are broken, the fellowships that are smashed, all because of a bitter heart. No wonder Paul wrote to the church and said, "Let there be no root of bitterness springing up in defilement."

Before we were saved, our mouths were full of bitterness and cursing. Isn't it wonderful that when one accepts the Savior, the cursing goes out. He puts a new song in our mouths, even praises to the Lord. Instead of cursing people, we bless them.

What made the transformation? We've come into a relationship with the Savior.

And then we come to verse 15. I needn't spend time there. "Their feet are swift to shed blood." That's the history of the human race. Wars and bloodshedding abound.

I remember when I was a youngster having fistfights with the kids in the neighborhood. We used to fight about every other day. If we didn't find somebody to fight or if we had no reason to fight, we would pick a fight by hitting someone on the shoulder. And believe me, brother, if you landed one on someone's nose and the blood came out, there was an exultation there. Where did it come from? From a rotten heart, a heart that was sinful, unrighteous, unredeemed. That's the history of man. "His feet are swift to shed blood. Destruction and misery are in their ways."

Even today, with all our knowledge and technology, we see destruction and misery. Much of the world's population doesn't know where the next meal is coming from. And yet we in our land take our produce and dump it in the ocean to keep prices up. "Destruction and misery are in their ways: And the way of peace have they not known." It's a terrible picture!

The Cause (3:18)

What's the cause of it all? What's the reason for man's unrighteous character and conduct?

3:18. *There is no fear of God before their eyes.*

They rip God out of the picture. They leave God out of their life and let sin and corruption come in. There is no way out of it. Rule God out of a nation and what do you find? Corruption. Sinfulness. Brutality. Bloodshedding. I want to say to you, the more we leave God out of our nation, out of our cities and schools and out of our own individual lives, the more there will be of moral corruption, lawlessness, bloodshedding, bitterness, and cursing. Why? "There is no fear of God before their eyes."

The Verdict (3:19)

> **3:19.** *Now we know that what things soever the law saith, it saith to them who are under the law: that every mouth may be stopped, and all the world may become guilty before God.*

It has taken Paul nearly three chapters to shut all mouths—"that every mouth may be stopped." Jew, Gentile, moralist, religionist must all stand before God with their mouth shut. Their only plea is "guilty."

Then, to keep these moralists and religionists and especially the Jews from running to some cover, Paul immediately closes everything up by saying:

> **3:20.** *Therefore by the deeds of the law there shall no flesh be justified in his sight: for by the law is the knowledge of sin.*

The law was never given to save anyone. The law was given to reveal what sin is. The law was a schoolmaster to bring us to Christ; and, after we come to Christ, we're no longer under the schoolmaster. The law gives a distinctive character to sin. The law works wrath. As James says, the law is a looking glass. And, as Mr. Moody used to say, you don't take the looking glass to wash your face. The looking glass reveals how dirty your face is.

The law is given to reveal sin and there was a misunderstanding in the minds of the Jews—just as there are misunderstandings today in the minds of a great many religious folk who call themselves Christians—that by keeping the law they're going to be justified in the sight of God. We found that in chapter 2—the Jew cannot be saved by his law; neither can the Gentile be saved by walking according to his conscience. Neither law nor conscience was given to save anyone. If God saves the Jew by the law, He must save the Gentile by his conscience. Then God would have no ground for the judgment found in chapter 3.

By the works of the law "there shall no flesh be justified in God's sight." That closes the door, doesn't it? There is not a thing anyone can do to fit himself for the presence of God. God must be righteous. How is anyone going to stand before Him? There's not an excuse any of us can make. We are all incurably bad and totally helpless. When God gets us to recognize our position, then He will step into the picture and do something for us. After shutting man's mouth from glorying in himself, now God must open his heart and make provision whereby men and women can be saved. This is the message of Romans.

Someone may protest, "I know that God is righteous, but God is also love. The God I worship is love." Yes, my friend, but God cannot manifest His love at the expense of His righteousness. Let me get this clear in your mind. I grant you that in 1 John 4:8 and 16 we have the statement that "God is love." But where did God manifest His love? How do you know that God is love? "Herein is love, not that we loved God, but that He loved us, and sent His Son to be the propitiation [the sacrifice] for our sins" (1 John 4:10).

God, of necessity, must be righteous. He must be holy or He wouldn't be God. When you tell me you are putting your trust in a God who is love, then you must accept what that love has done for you in the Person of His Son. Those who say, "My God is a God of love," have never realized that God is essentially righteous and holy.

Friend, we are not dealing with a namby-pamby, jellyfish sort of a god. We are dealing with God who is absolute in holiness, absolute in righteousness. He is the Sovereign God; I'm a creature born in sin. All of us are not only natural sinners, but we are also cultivated sinners. This is the history of man—your history, my history, the history of everyone.

Having proved that man is unrighteous, that he is guilty before God and his mouth is shut, God begins to open up His own heart. God brings the man who is afar off, dead in trespasses and sin, near to himself through the work of His Son. Through the blood of Jesus, we may receive by faith the righteousness of God.

Remember, God doesn't open up His heart and reveal who He is and what He has done for man until man has stopped his deadly doing. When man realizes his need of a Savior, you will find God

74

ready on a moment's notice to save anybody—no matter how bad
he is—who will come to Him. God has good news: God Himself,
in the person of His Son, has come into this world to take away our sin.

GOD'S WAY OF JUSTIFYING SINNERS (3:21-5:11)

If there is any doctrine in the Bible I love to talk about and
revel in, it is this one. Divine righteousness is put to the account
of a sinner who accepts the Savior so that sinner stands before
God in all the merits of Christ. He stands and has the joy of stay-
ing in the presence of God.

As Paul could say in Ephesians 3:12, "In whom we have boldness and access with confidence by the faith of him." Isn't it wonderful that you and I can come with confidence, with boldness,
having our access into the presence of God because we stand there
just as Jesus Christ, His Son, stands?

As we look at these verses in Romans 3:21-31, stop for a
moment and read the passage through. It's the basic passage, the
foundation upon which the rest of Romans is built. Many
Christians love to read Romans 8, but you will appreciate chapter 8
so much more if you have Romans 3.

That's why I want to stress this amazing passage about God
opening His heart and revealing to man His righteousness. I can't
overemphasize that there is only one righteousness in the universe
and it is God's. If you and I are going to stand before God, we must
stand in a righteousness that is comparable to God's righteousness.
Otherwise we can't stand. The marvel of it is that God is offering
His own righteousness to everyone who will trust His Son.

GOD'S RIGHTEOUSNESS IS RECEIVED BY FAITH
(3:21-31)

This Righteousness Is Apart from the Law (3:21-22)

3:21-22. *But now the righteousness of God without the
law [without works] is manifested, being witnessed by*

> *the law and the prophets; even the righteousness of*
> *God which is by faith of Jesus Christ unto all and upon*
> *all them that believe: for there is no difference.*

Look at all we get out of the first word in Romans 3:21—*But.*
If you follow that through your New Testament—especially in
Pauline revelation—it's a common thing for Paul to reveal the
utter helplessness and sinfulness of man. When he brings you to
that point, then he begins to reveal to us the righteousness of God.

For example, in Ephesians 2:1 he says we were dead in trespasses and sin. He says we were controlled by the prince of the
power of the air, that we lived in the lust of the flesh, the lust of
the mind. We were by nature children of wrath like the rest. He
pushes us way down, with our mouths shut, incapable of produc-
ing anything that will please God.

Then he reveals this amazing fact: "But God, who is rich in
mercy, for His great love wherewith he loved us, even when we
were dead in sins" (2:4-5). Before he reveals the greatness of
God's love and the richness of His mercy, Paul brings man down
to where he actually is—in God's sight.

We have this same structure here in Romans: "But now the
righteousness of God without the law is manifested, being witnessed by the law and the prophets." Paul begins to display the
righteousness of God, and from 3:21 to 5:11, he explains God's
way of justifying sinners.

Having declared that man is void of righteousness, Paul shows
us where the righteousness of God *is* manifested. There is only
one righteousness in the universe and that is God's. Before we get
through, I want you to see this fact of the impossibility of any man
or woman, however moral, however religious, however wonderful, however good they may think they are, the impossibility of
their standing in the presence of God who is righteous unless they
have a righteousness that is equal to His.

Paul begins to unfold the gospel, the good news from God, that
God's righteousness is to be put to the account of the one who
puts his trust in the Lord Jesus. In Philippians 3, Paul could say

concerning the righteousness which is in the law that he was "blameless," but he was lost. Then he says, having caught a glimpse of God's righteousness in Christ, that everything else fades out of the picture and that he wants to "be found in him, not having mine own righteousness"—that is, what he thought was wonderful—but to be found in Him, having Christ's righteousness.

Do you realize the utter folly and futility of religion? Every religion informs us what we should do. The gospel of God's grace tells us what God has done. He wants us to come with our sin, our shame, our unrighteousness, just as we are. By our simple trust in Him, by putting our trust in the Savior Jesus Christ, He pronounces us righteous.

I love the testimony of John Bunyan, that cursing tinker who wrote *Pilgrim's Progress* and *Grace Abounding to the Chief of Sinners*. That dear old John Bunyan had been cursing everyone, and the Lord convicted him of his condition. With his conscience pricked, he realized that only in Christ could he be found acceptable, only in Christ did he have righteousness. And he shouted, "Praise the Lord! My righteousness is at the right hand of God where my good works can't help it and my bad works can't hurt it."

Christ is our righteousness! It's not the one who is good or religious, but it is the soul who will simply put his or her trust in the Lord Jesus that God pronounces righteous. It's not an experience. It's not coming to what God does in me. Get this clear in your mind. It is not what God does *in* me. It is what God has done *for* me. If we do not have God's righteousness, then, my friend, we haven't anything. Everything else fails.

Where is this righteousness of God manifested? Where is it revealed? It has been unveiled for us in only one place—in Jesus Christ. In this good news from God, He pronounces righteous the one who puts his trust in the Savior.

This righteousness of God is witnessed by the law and the prophets. Let me remind you, for example, of Jeremiah 23:6 where, when our Lord returns to the kingdom, He is going to be called "the Lord Our Righteousness." The whole nation is going to come to the realization that Jesus Christ is its righteousness. Isaiah 53:11 says, "By his knowledge shall my righteous servant justify many." The Righteous One shall declare righteous the many who believe, for this righteousness of God is received on only one ground, the ground of faith—"unto all and upon all them that believe."

The righteousness of God was mine the moment I accepted Christ as Savior. From the moment I became a Christian and came into right relationship with Jesus Christ by simple faith, from that very moment to this present moment and through eternity, I'm going to stand before God in all the righteousness of Christ.

Some of you may say, "Mr. Mitchell, aren't you going too far?" My friend, how clearly can God put it? Jesus Christ became what I was—sin—that I might become what He is—righteousness. There never has been a person who stood before God righteous—justified—apart from Christ.

The next question is raised in verse 23: But who needs this righteousness?

All Men Need This Righteousness (3:23)

> **3:23.** *For all have sinned, and come short of the glory of God.*

What is God's measurement? We have all sinned and fallen short of His *glory* or righteousness. You can't come into the presence of the blazing glory and omnipotent righteousness of God. The moment you catch a glimpse of the eternal glory of God, my friend, you will be glad to get out of His presence. No one can come into God's presence unless we come His way—in Jesus Christ. We all need this righteousness. This is God's yardstick. The gospel is a display of the righteousness and glory of God.

This Righteousness Is Given Freely (3:24)

> **3:24.** *Being justified freely by his grace through the redemption that is in Christ Jesus.*

Given freely. Don't you like that? If God had put a cost on it, nobody would have been saved. And if He had, I am sure I couldn't have paid the cost, nor could you. If God had said to us, "Walk on your knees to the nearest mountain, and when you get to the top, I'm going to give you eternal life," believe me, we would all be heading for the high country.

I'm so glad He didn't do that. A lot of folks would fall by the wayside. No, this righteousness is given *freely*, which means it is given without a cause. The same word is used in John 15:25 where the Lord Jesus said "that [it] is written in their law, They hated me without a cause." There was no reason why they should hate Him. It was just envy and jealousy. It's the same word— "being justified freely, without a cause." There is no cause in me why God should do it. The cause is in Him. It costs me nothing to be saved. I cost Him everything; and, my, what a cost.

I was involved with the leaders of the counseling program for a Billy Graham crusade years ago. We were working out a series of lessons for counselor training, and I raised the question in our committee meeting, "Shall we put something in this about justification so that, when we deal with those who are hungry for the Lord, we will not only bring them to the saving knowledge of Christ, we will also tell them what they have in Christ—that they're forgiven every trespass, that they're redeemed, that they're children of God, and that they have life eternal?" I wanted to know what they were going to do about justification.

A gentleman on the committee who didn't agree with me on doctrine (that's why I raised the question) said, "Why, of course, Dr. Mitchell, we all believe in that."

So I asked, "And what do you believe justification is?"

He said, "Don't you know?"

I said, "Yes. Do you know?"

"Oh, yes," he said, "justification means that we stand before God just as if we had never sinned."

That's the common definition of justification, but it's inaccurate because it's only partially true. More accurately, justification is a pronouncement from God that the sinner who puts his trust in the Lord Jesus is righteous. Justification is a positive thing! God says, "I put to your account my righteousness." The holy, righteous God not only sees us with our sin, but He sees us absolutely righteous in His Son. Oh, I hope we get hold of this fact.

You take that simple verse, "Therefore, being justified by faith"—we have what?—"we have peace with God." You couldn't have peace with God if you weren't righteous.

We have seen darkness and condemnation in the first three chapters of Romans, but I want you to see some of the glory. If it ever gets hold of your heart, my Christian friend, you will never again be the same.

Paul said, "When I saw him in his righteousness and when I saw that his righteousness would be put to my account, I counted all things lost—the things that were gain to me, the things I counted wonderful—I counted them but the garbage of the streets." Why? "That I might be found in him, having his righteousness." It's a complete reversal of value. All men need righteousness, and anyone who puts his trust in the Savior is pronounced righteous.

I spoke with a man who had been religious most of his life, and he wanted to know if he was saved. I gave him some Scripture, and he said that he'd heard that, but he wasn't sure he was saved. After talking about it some more, I finally said, "Do you know what you're doing? You're questioning the character of God. I just read you a verse and you don't believe it."

"I do believe it," he said.

"Who said it?"

"God."

"There are no ifs, ands, or buts in there," I said. "If God says it, believe it!" And it was as if someone had removed the blindness from his eyes. I could just see his eyes brighten, and he said, "Dr. Mitchell, I'm saved!"

"Is that because you feel it?"

"God says it," he said. "And if God says I'm righteous in His sight, who am I to question God?"

It's high time we Christians got down to bed-rock on this. When Jesus Christ died, we died. When He was buried, we were buried. The Savior who died for me on the cross satisfied God.

God must act either in grace or He must act in judgment. Which would you rather have? God has acted toward the human race in grace. We didn't love Him, but He loved us. He sent His only begotten Son into the world to be a sacrifice, to put away our sins, to make it possible for Him to pronounce us righteous, and to free His hands to take sinners—ungodly, unrighteous men and women—and make us the sons of the living God in all the righteousness of Christ.

My friend, what a Savior! What a Savior! No wonder the hymn writer says,

> I need no other argument,
> I need no other plea;
> It is enough that Jesus died,
> And that He died for me.

He died for you and me and rose again, guaranteeing this salvation we have in Christ.

I wish you'd read and reread this passage until it gets ahold of your very being. It was the first great truth that got ahold of my heart. When I was saved, I came into contact with a little bald-headed barber in Calgary, Alberta. (I don't know why a barber should be bald-headed.) This dear brother never had gone to school in his life. He had been saved out of a life of alcoholism and had moved from New York to Calgary to get away from his old habits and friends. And the Lord wonderfully transformed him. All he knew and all I heard for the six months I was with him was Romans 3:21-31.

I said to him one day, "Heddy, don't you know any other Scripture besides this?"

He said, "I know a few. I've learned to read a few. But I'm not gonna give you up until you know Romans 3!"

"Well," I said, "I know it backwards and forwards."

"Yes, you know the Scripture, but you don't know its truth."

After I'd been with that barber for a year, I started doing some preaching. A week of meetings had been announced, and I thought the fellow who announced the meeting was going to be the speaker. But he took the train and beat it and left the meeting in my hands. I had to keep one jump ahead of the people so I began to teach the Book of Romans, and I taught Romans every night that week.

When I got to Romans 3, I spent all day and night reading passages on justification and righteousness. And when I stood up to speak on Sunday afternoon, I declared that I have a righteousness that is the righteousness of God. There was another preacher in the audience, and he walked out and announced all over town that this young fellow Mitchell was declaring that he was God. But I didn't say that.

I can still see the man who was in charge of that work, sitting in the front seat with his mouth open. He was horrified.

I looked at him and said, "Did I say something wrong? When I say that I have the righteousness of God, am I wrong?" And out of my mouth came Scripture reference after Scripture reference on justification and righteousness. I said, "Please don't judge till you read them all." And I closed the meeting and walked out. I didn't stay because I was scared stiff. I didn't know what I had done. I was in my innocence. I wasn't a preacher. I wasn't raised in churches. I didn't know anything about it except what I was reading in the book of Romans.

The next Sunday afternoon in the middle of the testimony meeting, this same dear man got up and said, "Last Sunday afternoon, when our young brother spoke about justification and righteousness, I thought something had gone wrong with his head. He was making some drastic statements. But," he said, "it's true!"

I didn't even get a chance to preach that afternoon. He opened his mouth and spoke a whole hour on the righteousness of God which believers in Jesus Christ have.

My friend, justification is not just an experience. Some say that justification is having your sins forgiven. It isn't. Justification is

God pronouncing righteous the man who believes in Christ. The believer has the righteousness of God put to his account.

Continuing on in verse 24, we are "justified freely by his grace through the *redemption* that is in Christ Jesus." Underlying all of justification is the great doctrine of redemption. "To redeem" means to purchase for the purpose of setting free. In Matthew 20:28, Jesus said, "Even as the Son of man came not to be ministered unto, but to minister, and to give his life a ransom for many." Romans 7:14 declares that we were "sold under sin." You and I were slaves in a slave market. We were slaves of sin. Sin was our master, and when Jesus Christ came, He paid the price to deliver us from the markets of sin. We have been emancipated from sin as a master. We have been set free.

In 1 Peter 1:18-19, Peter writes, "Forasmuch as ye know that ye were not redeemed with corruptible things, as silver and gold . . . but with the precious blood of Christ, as of a lamb without blemish and without spot." In Revelation 5:9, the heavenly hosts are singing and praising God. And what do you think is the theme of their song? "For thou . . . hast redeemed us to God by thy blood out of every kindred, and tongue, and people, and nation."

We are not saved by what Christ is doing *in* us. We are saved on the ground of what Christ did *for* us at the cross. His life was a ransom. He bought us from the slave markets, and it cost everything to redeem you and me. By His grace we're redeemed freely without any charge.

"But what if I lose my redemption?"

My friend, you can't do that. Hebrews 9:12 says, "By his own blood He entered in once into the holy place, having obtained eternal redemption for us." He didn't buy our redemption for a year or ten years. He bought you and me for himself forever. And if He bought us with His own blood, isn't He going to take care of us? Aren't we His purchased possession? Isn't that an amazing thing? Those who are trusting the Savior ought to be filled with continual joy and thanksgiving to God.

I can't help but add this to it. He has delivered us from three tremendous things. He loosed us *from sin and the grave*. Titus 2:14

declares, "Who gave himself for us, that he might redeem us from [out of] all iniquity, and purify unto himself a peculiar people, zealous of good works."

He also ransomed us *from the curse of the law*. Galatians 3:13 says, "Christ hath redeemed us from the curse of the law, being made a curse for us: for it is written, Cursed is everyone that hangeth on a tree." Aren't you glad He ransomed you from the curse of the law? And Galatians 4:4-5 says, "But when the fullness of the time was come, God sent forth his Son, made of a woman, made under the law"—for what purpose?—"to redeem [loose] them that were under the law." We are loosed not only from the law's curse but also from the law itself.

He also redeemed us *from this present evil world*. Galatians 1:4 says, "Who gave himself for our sins, that he might deliver [loose] us from this present evil world." He ransomed us not only from sin and the grave and from the curse of the law, but He loosed us from this present evil world.

God has made the provision in Jesus Christ whereby we can be fit for the presence of God. This is redemption. God has set men free from sin, from the law and its curse, from this present evil world through the precious blood of Christ. He gave himself a ransom for you and for me. This is the basis of our righteousness.

Romans 3:24 declares that we have been made righteous freely without a cause. It cost God everything; it cost us nothing. Its source is grace, and it is through the redemption that is in Christ Jesus. He purchased us for the purpose of setting us free.

"Justification" means that God pronounces righteous the sinner who puts his trust in the Lord Jesus. "Redemption" means that we have been set free by the payment of a price, the precious work of Christ at the cross.

This Righteousness Is Displayed at Calvary (3:25-26)

We come to a third word in verse 25, the word *propitiation*.

> **3:25a.** *Whom God hath set forth to be a propitiation through faith in his blood.*

Both verses 25 and 26 tell us where the righteousness of God was displayed—at the cross of Calvary. God set forth His Son as a sacrifice which satisfies Him. Isaiah 53:11 says, "He shall see of the travail of his soul, and shall be satisfied." Propitiation is a divine satisfaction. When Jesus Christ died on the cross, He vindicated, He satisfied the holy, righteous character of God. This is what the cross means to God. This is the most important part of the work of Christ. What's important is not what man sees. It's what God sees.

When you and I think of the cross, we think of Christ's being a Savior, giving His life a ransom, dying on the cross for us sinners. We think about what we receive from it. Did you ever stop to think that God has more involved in the work of Christ at the cross than you and I do? When Christ died on the cross, He did not die to secure the righteousness of man; He died to reveal and to vindicate the righteousness of God. The issue is not how to fit man for the presence of God. The question is how can you bring a holy, righteous, sovereign, eternal God down to man whereby man can be fitted to come into relationship and fellowship with God.

Something must be done before a man can be fitted for the presence of God. And we find this wonderful truth in this doctrine of propitiation.

How can God remain righteous and yet declare ungodly sinners righteous? At the cross, Jesus Christ met all the demands of God's character and justice. Since God is perfectly satisfied with the work of His Son, He is also satisfied with those who put their trust in the Son. Christ satisfied the righteous character of God. He made it possible for God to show mercy to sinful man. It is not that man is satisfied with the work of Christ. God is satisfied. The barrier is gone; access is ours. There is a throne of grace to which we can come, and Christ need never die again. God set Him forth "to be a propitiation through faith in his blood."

3:25b. *To declare his righteousness for the remission of sins that are past, through the forbearance of God.*

When sin entered the human race (Genesis 3), God already had planned a Redeemer. From the time Adam sinned right through until Jesus died on the cross, God looked at man through His Son, the Lamb slain before the foundation of the world.

How do you think the Old Testament saints were saved? They had been taught from Genesis 3 and following that they were to put their trust in the One who would come, the Heavenly Seed, God's Lamb, who would die to remove their sin. God covered their sins. He saved men and women in the Old Testament on the ground that His Son would come to put away those sins.

When Christ died on the cross, He did it because of His Father. He did it to vindicate the righteousness of God, as you have it in verse 26:

3:26. *To declare, I say, at this time his righteousness: that he might be just, and the justifier of him which believeth in Jesus.*

How could God in His righteousness manifest mercy to sinners who have no righteousness? Jesus Christ came and put away our sin. He vindicated the righteous character of God and freed God to come down to man. No wonder we sing,

Amazing grace—how sweet the sound—
That saved a wretch like me!
I once was lost but now am found,
Was blind but now I see.

I need no other argument,
I need no other plea;
It is enough that Jesus died,
And that He died for me.

If God is perfectly satisfied with the work of His Son, are you? Paul could say in Hebrews 4:16, "Let us therefore come boldly unto the throne of grace, that we may obtain mercy, and find grace to help in time of need."

My friend, God's heart is opened up to us. All the misunderstanding from Adam down has been cleared. That's why Paul could say to the philosophical Athenians in Acts 17:30, "The times of this ignorance God winked at." God let the nations go their own way to do what they wanted to do. But now, something has happened. Jesus Christ has died and satisfied the holy character of God. And God today is willing to save any and all who come to Him.

As 1 John 4 says, "Herein is love, not that we loved God, but that He loved us, and sent his . . . only begotten Son into the world, that we might live through him." And John repeats it in verse 10 with this change, that God "sent his Son to be the propitiation for our sins." In other words, God transforms the judgment throne into a mercy throne—from a judgment seat to a mercy seat.

The law of God said men must die. But in the Most Holy Place in the tabernacle, behind the curtain, was the mercy seat. Every year on the Day of Atonement, the high priest came in and sprinkled that mercy seat with blood, and for another year, God looked upon the people of Israel through the blood of the mercy seat.

Why doesn't God today judge the world? Why doesn't God blot man out for his rebellion? for his corruption? for his lawlessness? for his sin? for his vileness? Why doesn't God do something?

My friend, we ought to be thankful that "the Lord is not slack concerning his promise as some men count slackness; but is longsuffering to us-ward, not willing that any should perish, but that all should come to repentance." You see, without the death of Christ, justification, salvation and redemption would have been impossible. But, because He died, we live. His very righteousness is put to our account.

Someone is going to ask, "How can I receive this righteousness?" And so we come to verses 27 through the end of the chapter.

It Is Received by Faith (3:27-31)

> **3:27-28.** *Where is boasting then? It is excluded. By what law? of works? Nay: but by the law of faith. Therefore we conclude that a man is justified by faith without the deeds of the law.*

All human boasting is gone. God is satisfied with the work of His Son, and I manifest my satisfaction by putting my trust in Him. Ephesians 2:8-9 says, "For by grace are ye saved through faith; and that not of yourselves: it is the gift of God: not of works, lest any man should boast." In John 14:6, Jesus could say, "I am the way, the truth, and the life: no man cometh unto the Father, but by me." And 1 Corinthians 1:29-31 says "that no flesh should glory in his presence. But of him are ye in Christ Jesus, who of God is made unto us wisdom, and righteousness, and sanctification, and redemption: That, according as it is written, He that glorieth, let him glory in the Lord."

Salvation is absolutely apart from works. It is apart from the law entirely. Listen to it:

> **3:29-30.** *Is he the God of the Jews only? is he not also of the Gentiles? Yes, of the Gentiles also: seeing it is one God, which shall justify the circumcision by faith, and uncircumcision through faith.*

Why, of course, there's only one way of salvation. If all men are sinners and there is only one God, how many ways of salvation will He have? Just one.

Paul rules out the law and circumcision and works of man as having any part in it at all. So it is received only on one ground, on the ground of faith. And the law is upheld:

> **3:31.** *Do we then make void the law through faith? God forbid: yea, we establish the law.*

We don't cancel out the law. We were slain. We died. In Christ all the demands of the law were met for us, and the only way the law can be met is by death.

There is no mercy in law. We acknowledge the demands of the law. But, my friend, it is our Savior only who met all the demands of the law. We are set free so that the law doesn't have a word to say. We are saved apart from works and everything else by putting our trust in the One who died for you and for me.

And God is satisfied.

Romans 4

Romans 3 says in essence, "How can a righteous God pronounce guilty sinners righteous?"

The righteousness of God was displayed at the cross. When our Savior died, He vindicated the righteousness of God; that is, He satisfied all the divine character of God for you and for me. Man could not provide one thing. God provided the remedy. It is received in only one way and that's through faith, not works. He justifies those who believe. He doesn't justify anyone else. Hence, all human boasting is excluded.

Can a person be justified other than by simple faith in the Lord Jesus Christ? The apostle Paul rules out the law and circumcision as having any part. Does faith make void the law? No, says Paul, we establish the law by the execution of the penalty. All the law's demands were met when Jesus died for you and for me.

The question is raised at the end of chapter 3, "Do we have the right kind of faith?" Paul concludes that the only way one can be fitted for the presence of God is on the ground of grace through faith. In chapter 3, God declares righteous not the saints who believe but the sinners who believe. We do not change from being ungodly to godly and then believe. God takes men and women wherever they are, in whatever condition they are, however low they may be, however much they have sinned. And the moment they put their trust in Jesus Christ as their Savior, God pronounces them righteous.

Now in chapter 4, Paul presses justification home and uses three examples. In the first five verses, he takes up Abraham, the father of those who believe. The emphasis here is on faith without works. Then in verses 6 to 8, he takes up David, and the emphasis is not on faith but on righteousness apart from works. In verses 9 to 13, he emphasizes that righteousness is without ceremonies or ordinances. Then he ends the chapter by referring back to Abraham as an example of faith.

In the first sixteen verses, the apostle proves to us that from Adam right down to the cross nobody has ever stood justified before God except by faith—never on the ground of works, never on the ground of ceremonies. In the first five verses, we have Abraham, the father of all believers. What kind of faith did he have?

THE SAMPLE FAITH (4:1-25)

The Righteousness of God Is by Faith Alone (4:1-5)

> **4:1-2.** *What shall we say then that Abraham our father, as pertaining to the flesh, hath found? For if Abraham were justified by works, he hath whereof to glory; but not before God.*

Galatians 3:7 tells us that "they which are of faith, the same are the children of Abraham." In John 8:37,39 the Jewish leaders said, "We have Abraham for our father." And the Lord answered, "I know that ye are Abraham's seed; but . . . if ye were Abraham's children, ye would do the works of Abraham." In other words, "You would believe me."

Abraham is an illustration of how one is justified. He found that all that the flesh stood for could not stand before the presence of God. If it were by works, he would be able to glory in what he had done. Can you imagine what heaven would be like if men got there by their good works? Why, they would be boasting all through eternity about what they had done. They wouldn't glorify God at all. It's not me-plus-Jesus. It's not Jesus-plus-me. He did the whole thing. He satisfied God, and we are the recipients of His wonderful grace. Justification before God can never be on the ground of works.

> **4:3.** *For what saith the scripture? Abraham believed God, and it was counted unto him for righteousness.*

Quite often someone says to me, "But, Mr. Mitchell, there must be a conflict here. In Romans, Abraham is justified by faith without works. In the Book of James, chapter 2, Abraham is justified by his works. Which one is right?"

They're both right. In Romans we have the root of the matter; in James we have the fruit. In Romans we stand before God, hence we need faith. In James we stand before men, hence we need works. In Genesis 15:6 (the passage Paul quotes in verse 3) we see the ungodly saved. In James 2 we see the godly man tested. In one, you have faith alone; in the other, you have the works of faith.

Lest someone misunderstand me, even in James the writer is not talking about works of the law or works of the flesh. He is talking about the works of faith. I can't see your faith. God sees your faith and He knows whether it is real or not. All I can go by is your works. The life of faith is a life of walking in fellowship with God. If I do not see any manifestation of a godly life in you and someone asks me if you are a Christian, I must say, "I don't know. He may be. He says he is, but I don't know because I do not see the works of faith in his life." But when I see one who is walking before God, seeking to please Him, and you ask me if that fellow is saved, I say, "Why, sure. I see his faith manifested by his works."

Abraham did just one thing. He believed God. When was he justified? When he believed God. It was not when he worked, but when he believed.

> **4:4-5.** *Now to him that worketh is the reward not reckoned of grace, but of debt. But to him that worketh not,*

but believeth on him that justifieth the ungodly, his
faith is counted for righteousness.

Paul gives us here the principle of works and the principle of grace. One is an obligation, a debt; the other is of grace and the kindness of unmerited favor. You have the working method versus the believing method. You work for a man and he pays you your wages. It's not a gift, it's a debt. "But to him that worketh not, but believeth on him that justifieth the ungodly, his faith is counted for righteousness." It was the faith of the ungodly man that was counted for righteousness. God's very righteousness reaches right down to men in whatever state they are as they accept the Lord Jesus Christ as Savior. It's not changing an ungodly man into a godly man who will believe. It's the ungodly man who believes and becomes a godly man.

Some people say, "If I were only better." No, God doesn't say, "When you get better and believe, I'll take you." You have to be saved first and then you become better. Let's put this straight. It's by faith A-L-O-N-E, not faith plus anything else. It is just faith in the Lord Jesus Christ.

The Righteousness of God Is without Works (4:6-8)

Paul now uses David to illustrate the blessedness of righteousness by faith. When he used Abraham, he was stressing the question of faith; with David he stresses that it is without works.

4:6-8. *Even as David also describeth the blessedness of the man, unto whom God imputeth righteousness without works, Saying, Blessed are they whose iniquities are forgiven, and whose sins are covered. Blessed is the man to whom the Lord will not impute sin.*

Please mark this passage. Paul is dealing with the blessedness, the joy that a person has in the forgiveness that is perfect, that is divine, that is eternal. David, filled with joy in Psalm 32:2, writes,

"Blessed is the man unto whom the Lord imputeth not iniquity [sin]."

For God not to impute sin is to impute righteousness. May I change it around? When you and I put our faith in the Savior, He counts us righteous and He will never under any consideration impute sin. God is revealing His character as the righteous One in not imputing sin to those who believe and put their trust in His Son.

Here is an amazing thing. The enemies of the Word of God make a joke of David and Bathsheba. They hate the God of David. They prefer the sin of David with Bathsheba to a righteous God who demands judgment. And David, under the judgment of God, comes before him in repentance and confession. God forgives his sin and David is filled with the joy and the blessedness of a forgiveness that's real, that's eternal, that's divine.

That didn't free David from judgment. The child died. Amnon was killed. Absalom was killed. Adonijah was killed. The sin of David went through his family. He had nothing to present to God but sin. He stood before Him in his shame. As he could say in that thirty-second Psalm, the hand of God "was heavy upon me: my moisture [tears] is turned into the drought of summer." He went through hell for a whole year until Nathan came and opened his heart. And when David saw the sinfulness, the blackness, the awfulness of his own heart, he bowed in repentance and shame before God in confession.

What work could David bring? What work can you bring? I'm afraid too many of us are like David in that we condemn the sin we see in others and not the sin in ourselves. Yet the marvel of it, the wonder of it that the moment a sinner comes into the presence of God, confesses his sinfulness, repents, and in simple faith puts his trust in Jesus Christ without works of any kind, God imputes righteousness!

"But Mr. Mitchell," you say, "that's too strong." Is it? My friend, I'm dealing with a foundational truth. God in infinite, wonderful grace through His blessed Son takes the ungodly, the sinner,

the outcast and pronounces him righteous without works when he
puts his trust in the Savior. "Blessed is the man unto whom the
Lord imputeth not iniquity." What a joy! What a wonderful thing
that you and I can come into the presence of a righteous, holy
God. And as we stand in His presence, we have that joy of knowing that the righteous God will never again impute sin to the one
who puts his trust in His Son. That's the good news from God.

I have met people who are afraid to come into the presence of
God. They say, "But I've been such a sinner. I've failed so much."

My friend, nobody will ever see your sins or your failures when
you get to heaven. That's why I like Hebrews 11. Did you ever
notice that not a word is said about the failures of all those Old
Testament worthies? Did Abraham fail God? Yes, but you don't
find it in Hebrews 11. Did David fail God? Yes, but you don't find
it in Hebrews 11. Did Moses fail God? He certainly did, but you
don't find it in Hebrews 11.

Just before our Lord went to the cross, He said to His Father, "I
have given these men the Word you have given Me and they have
kept Your Word." There is not a word about the fact that they
were going to run away, that they were going to deny Him. When
Jesus stands before His Father and prays for His disciples, not a
thing is said about failure or weaknesses. Oh, what a salvation is
this that you and I can come into the very presence of God in
Christ Jesus and know that we stand before Him in all His righteousness and that every sin is forgiven, put away, and forgotten.

JUSTIFICATION IS WITHOUT CEREMONIES (4:9-16)

Paul has the Jewish people in mind in this section, but it also
applies to the "churchianity" of our day. We have a number of
professing Christians who make a great deal of ordinances and
ceremonies. Though they see there is no value to these when it
comes to salvation, they stress them so much that they take to
themselves some value that is not there. If we trust an ordinance,
we are not trusting the Son of God.

4:9-12. *Cometh this blessedness then upon the circumcision only, or upon the uncircumcision also? for we say that faith was reckoned to Abraham for righteousness. How was it then reckoned? when he was in circumcision, or in uncircumcision? Not in circumcision, but in uncircumcision. And he received the sign of circumcision, a seal of the righteousness of the faith which he had yet being uncircumcised: that he might be the father of all them that believe, though they be not circumcised; that righteousness might be imputed unto them also: and the father of circumcision to them who are not of the circumcision only, but who also walk in the steps of that faith of our father Abraham, which he had being yet uncircumcised.*

When was Abraham justified? He was justified fourteen years before he was circumcised. You see what Paul is after? The Jew has divided the human race into two groups, saying, "We are of the circumcision. Everybody else is of the uncircumcision. We are God's people, and the rest are outside of God's covenant."

Circumcision was a sign to Abraham of his union and relationship to the Living God, that he was separated unto God, that his God was Jehovah. He had been called out by the God of glory, out of idolatry in Ur of the Chaldees. Now he could say, "In my being I have a sign, given to me by God, that I belong to him." It is a sign of his separation from the world unto God. That's all it is—an outward sign to the world and to Abraham that he was justified by faith in God.

The blessings that came upon the Jewish race were not through the faith of a circumcised man but through the faith of an uncircumcised man. That is, the blessings that came upon the Jewish race were through the faith of one who was declared righteous while he was a Gentile. Indeed, if the Jews are going to be saved at all, they have to come the Gentile way—that is, by faith.

In Acts 15 some Jews who were Christians wanted the Gentiles to come to Christ through Judaism. They wanted the Gentiles to be circumcised, to keep the law. Both Peter and James withstood that, and so did Paul. Peter said, "Even we Jews have to be saved the same way as the Gentiles." How's that? By faith. And here in Romans, Paul is insisting that no ordinance will ever take the place of Christ's work for us.

It's an amazing thing how much merit we in professing Christendom put in ordinances and ceremony, whether it be baptism or communion or whatever it may be. But we are not saved by baptism or by observing communion. Of course, I'm not opposed to these ordinances, but the moment you add the least thing to salvation, however precious that thing is to you, you add to the work of Christ. At that moment you ruin God's good news.

Paul says in Galatians 1:8-9 that the curse, the anathema of God, is upon anyone who brings to you any other message than this. No religious observances of any kind can add or take away from the work of Christ. No soul was ever saved by faith in Christ plus any work or any ceremony of any kind.

"But," you say, "baptism is not a work." Well, what is it if it's not a work? It's something you do, and what you do is works. Baptism is a sign to the world of your separation unto God. It's a sign of your testimony that you are trusting in what Jesus Christ did in His death and burial and resurrection. To those who believe, it is a sign that you have received the Spirit of God. But baptism does not add one iota to your salvation in Christ. Christ is a perfect, complete, eternal Savior. If you try to add to the work of Christ, you spoil the gospel. It is no longer good news.

Paul insists that justification is without works, by faith, and without ceremonies. No ordinance of any kind will ever take the place of the work of Christ.

In verses 13 to 16 we find God's promise to Abraham that he would be the heir of the world on one ground, the ground of faith:

> **4:13-16.** *For the promise, that he should be the heir of the world, was not to Abraham, or to his seed, through the law, but through the righteousness of faith. For if*

*they which are of the law be heirs, faith is made void,
and the promise made of none effect because the law
worketh wrath: for where no law is, there is no transgression. Therefore it is of faith, that it might be by
grace; to the end the promise might be sure to all the
seed; not to that only which is of the law, but to that
also which is of the faith of Abraham; who is the father
of us all.*

This dear man Abraham was called out from Ur of the
Chaldees, from the house of idolatry. He went out not knowing
where he went, and step by step, there came to his heart the revelation of God. One day, when God said, "Behold the stars of heaven;
so shall thy seed be," he believed God and it was accounted to
him for righteousness. Galatians 3:16 says that seed was Christ.
When his faith was coupled with Christ, he was justified.

But God went beyond that and declared to him an inheritance
of the whole world. God had made Adam and had given him
dominion over all the works of his hands. Sin came in and Adam
lost the whole business. God found a man He called His friend, a
man who walked with Him in all his tests and trials, in all his
accomplishments and failures. And Abraham believed God. He
believed God in spite of everything.

And God said, "I've found my man. I've found the one through
whom my Son shall come. I've found the one to whom I'm going
to give the whole world. He's the heir of the world through faith."

Go beyond this question of justification for a moment. The
Jews said, "Abraham is our Father. We are God's people. We are
going to rule the world. We are going to be the leading nation of
the world." They could go back to the Old Testament to prove
that. Did Zechariah not say, "The time is coming when ten men
from every nation from under heaven will lay hold of the skirt of
him that is a Jew and say, 'We are going to go with you' "? Does
it not say in Isaiah that men shall call Jews the priests of God, the
ministers of God? Does it not say that the Word of God shall go

forth from Jerusalem and all the nations of the earth shall be under
His dominion?

Paul says, "Yes, but don't forget that this promise that Abraham
would be the heir of the world, this in which you Jews are boasting, was not received through the law or through works or through
ceremonies. It was received by faith."

Then, in verses 13 and 14 he makes this amazing statement, "If
it is by works, then God cannot fulfill his promises." If it is by
works, if it's by the law, the Jews have broken that law. They do
not qualify. The Gentiles are outside the pale of the law, hence
they cannot qualify. If the Jews and the Gentiles cannot qualify,
then God can't keep His Word. Hence it must be by faith so that
the promise might be made sure to the seed.

God's promise that Abraham would be the heir of the world
was not on the ground of the law because he didn't have the law.
It was not on the ground of works. It was not on the ground of
ceremonies, but on the ground of one thing—faith. Abraham
became the heir of the world through faith. And this is ever the
divine mode of blessing.

Nothing pleases the Lord more than for people to believe Him.
It rejoices the heart of God when you dare to believe what He says
is true, whether you feel it or you don't feel it.

Let me paraphrase what it says in verses 14 to 16: "If those
who are of the law are heirs, then there is no need for faith, and
the promise is no good because the law works wrath. For where
there is no law, there is no transgression. Therefore it is by faith so
that it might be by grace that the promise may be sure for all the seed."

If it's by the law, if it's by the works of the law, then there is no
need for a promise. Nobody can receive the promise if it is on the
ground of the law because nobody can keep the law. The Jews
didn't keep it; the Gentiles didn't have it. Hence, there would be
no heirs. The law just shuts everybody up.

So verse 16 says, "Therefore it is of faith, that it might be by
grace; to the end that the promise might be sure . . ." Aren't you
glad for that? He makes the thing sure to all—Jew and Gentile—

who are of the faith of Abraham. In other words, Abraham is our example of faith. He dared to believe God in spite of everything else. He didn't add one iota of works to it.

So it is with us. We are declared righteous by faith. It is without works and it is without ceremonies. We have every sin forgiven. For God not to impute sin is to impute righteousness. He is not going to impute sin to us at any time. And we become the heir of the world through faith.

In addition, Paul says this promise has been made *sure* (v. 16). We have this confidence because God has done it. If this were by works—religious works, moral works—we would never be sure we had done enough. We would never have peace. We would never have assurance. No, to make the thing sure, God puts it entirely on the ground of His grace.

There is one word in verse 15 I must touch on since we have been discussing the question of works and the question of the law. That word is *wrath*—"because the law worketh wrath."

Someone is bound to ask, "Then why in the world did God give the Jew the law of Moses? What's its purpose?"

Let me give you a few reasons. First, the law was given to make sin exceedingly sinful. That is, the law was given to give a distinctive character to sin. Where no law is, there is no transgression or missing the mark. "I had not known sin," says Paul in Romans 7, "until the law said, 'Thou shalt not covet'; and that which I thought was going to give me life, behold it brought death." The law is like a looking glass, says James, showing us where all the dirt is and what we look like.

Second, the law is the strength of sin. The law is not the strength of righteousness. The law is not the strength of goodness. The law is the strength of sin (1 Corinthians 15:56-57). Romans 6:14 tells us, "Sin shall not have dominion over you." Why? Because you are not under the law but under grace. You put men under the law, my friend, and you put them under the dominion of sin. You can't separate the law and sin. The law was given to show us what sin really is. It was never given to save.

Third, the law was given to bring us to Christ (Galatians 3:24). The law is effective only as it drives the sinner to the Savior. The law was our schoolmaster to bring us to Christ. And having come to Christ, says the apostle Paul, we are no longer under the school-master.

What does the law do then?

First, the law demands perfection. James 2:10 says, "He that breaketh the law in one point is guilty of all." Not much chance, is there? Even if a man could live to a ripe old age without breaking the law, and then one day he breaks the law just once—too bad, he is under the sentence of death. The law demands perfection.

"Why, Mr. Mitchell," you say, "no man is perfect except Jesus Christ."

That's right, and the law demands perfection. Listen to Galatians 3:10: "Cursed is every one that continueth not in all things which are written in the book of the law to do them." They were obligated to do the whole law, not just part of it. The law doesn't say, if you do the best you can, you will have some mercy. The law doesn't have any mercy to give you.

The second thing the law does is bring wrath (4:15). It doesn't bring salvation. It doesn't bring peace. It doesn't bring justification. It doesn't give you forgiveness. The law brings wrath.

Third, the law is a ministration of death. You have this in 2 Corinthians 3:7-18 and in Romans 7:5, 12-13. The law says you must die. And Paul says, "That which I thought was going to give me life, behold it brought death."

The fourth thing the law can do is curse. We have already mentioned that in Galatians 3:10-13. It curses whom? "Those who continue not in all things which are written in the book of the law to do them." Man doesn't believe that. He just goes on trying to keep the law to gain favor with God. He doesn't believe the law curses.

Can't the law do anything? No. The law cannot save you, the law cannot give life, the law cannot perfect God's people, it cannot fit men for the presence of God.

When you and I accept the Savior, we are saved apart from the law entirely—we are outside its jurisdiction. The law has no authority to save you or to help you or to forgive you. And the moment you and I, as sinners, whether Jews or Gentiles, put ourselves under the law, then we have to face the fact: "Cursed is everyone that continueth not in all things which are written in the book of the law to do them." All it can do is to curse. Thank God, we are delivered from the law and its curse, as Galatians 3:13 says: "Christ hath redeemed us from the curse of the law being made a curse for us: for it is written, 'Cursed is everyone that hangeth on a tree.' "

We are delivered from the curse of the law, and we are also delivered from its authority. In the fullness of time, God sent forth His Son, born of a woman, born under the law, so that He might free us from the law and all that pertains to it, and "that we might receive the adoption of sons" (Galatians 4:5).

My friend, either Christ is sufficient to save us and keep us or He is not a Savior at all. It's about time we Christians understood that when Jesus Christ came, He absolutely and perfectly completed the work of redemption. The resurrection is the guarantee of it. For one who professes Christ as Savior to go back under the law, even as a rule of life, is to deny the sufficiency of the work of Christ. You put yourself under the curse and you fall from grace (Galatians 5:4).

Indeed, the death of Christ has forever severed the relationship between the believer and the law. If we turn from the Levitical priesthood of the Old Testament to Christ, then we must turn from the covenant of law to the covenant of grace (Hebrews 7-8).

But how do we know when we have the right kind of faith? What is justifying faith? Verses 17 to 25 give us the answer.

IT IS FAITH IN THE GOD OF RESURRECTION (4:17-25)

Abraham is given to us as an example, the father of those who believe. In Luke 19 Jesus paid a visit to Zaccheus, and when His visit was through, He said, "This day is salvation come to this house, forsomuch as he also is a son of Abraham." What did Abraham do? Abraham believed in the God who made alive, who quickened the dead. He believed in the God of resurrection.

> **4:17-25.** *(As it is written, I have made thee a father of many nations,) before him whom he believed, even God, who quickeneth the dead, and calleth those things which be not as though they were. Who against hope believed in hope, that he might become the father of many nations, according to that which was spoken, So shall thy seed be. And being not weak in faith, he considered not his own body now dead, when he was about an hundred years old, neither yet the deadness of Sarah's womb: He staggered not at the promise of God through unbelief; but was strong in faith, giving glory to God; and being fully persuaded that, what he had promised, he was able also to perform. And therefore it was imputed to him for righteousness. Now it was not written for his sake alone, that it was imputed to him, But for us also, to whom it shall be imputed, if we believe on him that raised up Jesus our Lord from the dead; who was delivered for our offenses, and was raised again for our justification.*

The great thing about Abraham was that he believed what God said. When God said, "I'm going to make your seed like the stars of heaven; you are going to have an heir," Abraham believed God in spite of his body. Though conscious of a physical impossibility, he rose above it in faith and believed he was going to have a boy. "Whatever the circumstances, whatever anybody else says, I am going to believe in God." He didn't waver one little bit. He dared to believe God because God had spoken. He believed beyond the physical in a God who could keep His Word.

Friend, do you? Abraham's faith was credited to him as righteousness, and we must have this same kind of faith. We must have faith in Him who raised Jesus our Lord from the dead. The same God who raised Jesus from the dead quickened the "dead" body of Abraham so that he could have a son.

The apostle Peter says, "Blessed be the God and Father of our Lord Jesus Christ, which according to his abundant mercy hath begotten us again unto a [living] hope by the resurrection of Jesus Christ from the dead. . . . Who by him do believe in God, that raised him up from the dead, and gave him glory; that your faith and hope might be in God" (1 Peter 1:3, 21).

The disciples and even the Lord himself never spoke of the cross without resurrection. The cross was a tragedy apart from resurrection. The blessing of justification is secured by the resurrection of Jesus Christ from the dead. He was delivered up because of our offenses, yours and mine. He bore your sins and my sins. He bore the penalty. How do I know He put them away? God raised Him from the dead. That's why, when you come to the Book of Acts, the apostles proclaim nearly thirty times the resurrection of Jesus Christ from the dead.

If there is no resurrection, there is no salvation. But if He was raised from the dead, then His work at the cross absolutely, perfectly satisfied God. The resurrection is God's personal proof to you that Jesus Christ has put away your sins. He has satisfied God. God is now free to take anyone who puts his trust in the Savior and not only forgive his sins, but also cover him with the righteousness of Christ.

Let me give you a little Bible study.

We are justified *by God* (Romans 3). This is the source of our justification. We are justified *by grace*, as Romans 3:24 says, "Being justified freely by his grace." That's the principle of it. We are justified *by faith*, as Romans 5:1 says, "Therefore being justified by faith, we have peace with God." This is the method of receiving justification. And then we are justified *by His blood*, and this is the ground of justification. Romans 5:9 says, "Much more then, being now justified by his blood, we shall be saved from wrath through him." And *resurrection* is the proof of it. That's what you have here in Romans 4:25—"He was raised again for our justification." As 1 Corinthians 15:17 says, "If Christ be not raised [from the dead]," we haven't anything. We just haven't anything.

In chapter 3:21-31, we found that justification is by faith, and in chapter 4 we have been dealing with what this faith is. What is justifying faith? We are justified by faith without works, without ceremonies, without the law. We are justified by faith in the God of resurrection. The very foundation of our Christian faith is based upon not only the death of Jesus Christ but also the resurrection. "If Christ be not raised [from the dead] . . . ye are yet in your sins. . . . we are of all men most miserable" (1 Corinthians 15:17,19).

"All right, Mr. Mitchell, I believe in the God of resurrection. I believe that God raised Jesus Christ from the dead. And I believe that this One who bore my sins put them away. God raised Him from the dead as the guarantee that He is satisfied with that work. But what if I lose my faith? Is that possible?"

Lose your faith? Is it possible for a real Christian, one who has trusted the Savior, to lose his faith?

The answer to that question is given to us in Romans 5:1-11. In our next chapter we will take up this guarantee—the guarantee of faith. Faith in the God of resurrection cannot be destroyed.

Romans 5

Let me give you a bird's-eye picture of what's ahead in chapters 5 through 8. In chapter 5, the death of Jesus Christ severs the relationship between the believer and Adam's race, and it severs the believer from the bondage of death. In chapter 6, the death of Christ severs the believer from the dominion of sin as a master, as the principle of operation in his life. In chapter 7, the death of Christ severs the believer from any relationship to the law. And then in chapter 8, we learn what it means to the believer to be in Christ Jesus. That chapter starts with no condemnation and ends with no separation.

THE GUARANTEE OF FAITH (5:1-11)

In the first five verses of chapter 5, Paul assures us that the tests and trials of life do not destroy faith. And then in verses 6-11, he tells us faith is never destroyed because it is guaranteed by the love of God. Faith can never be destroyed because tests only purify it.

Faith Is Never Destroyed by Tests (5:1-5)

5:1. *Therefore being justified by faith [being declared righteous by faith], we have peace with God through our Lord Jesus Christ.*

In verse 1, our faith is a past, settled thing. God has declared us righteous. In the first part of verse 2, we have a present experience, and then we have our future experience at the end of the verse:

5:2. *By whom also we have access by faith into this grace wherein we stand, and rejoice in hope of the glory of God.*

It is then that we shall see the culmination of the purpose of God in redeeming men and women by simple faith in His Son.

Every message from God to man starts on the ground of peace—God's "fear not." When Gabriel comes, when the angels come, when God comes in the Old Testament and comforts the hearts of men, the first thing mentioned is peace. Now, because of Christ, there's no longer any enmity between God and us. There's no longer a barrier between us. There's no longer sin between us. God sees us in His Son, absolutely righteous.

All that was between God and you and me has been put away by the work of our Savior at the cross of Calvary. We have peace with God. God is perfectly satisfied with what His Son has done. And can I put it this way? God is at perfect rest concerning His people. Hence we can have peace. God looks at Christ, not at our failures. He sees us as righteous in His Son, and this gives us peace.

In the second verse, we have access—access by faith. It is not something we are brought into; it is something we are already in. It is not something for the future; it is a simple fact for now. "We have access by faith into this grace wherein we stand." Having been justified, having been declared righteous, we have our access; we are already in this grace. In Christ we have a new and living way whereby we come into the very presence of God at any time, under any circumstance. God is not looking at my failures. He's looking at His Son when He sees you and me.

I remember a friend of mine, a preacher of the gospel, who just loved to preach. He was a good preacher and a fine teacher, and when he would preach on the coming of the Lord, he would get so blessed it was as if he had one foot in heaven already. But he wasn't sure he would be saved tomorrow.

You've met those folk, haven't you? They're saved today, and they hope the Lord will come before tomorrow comes so they won't fail God lest they be lost.

One day, I said to him, "I just love to hear you preach on the coming of the Lord."

He said, "Brother Jack, I just love to preach it, too."

I said, "I don't know why you should love to preach it because you're so inconsistent. You are rejoicing in the hope of the glory of God, but you're scared stiff you won't be saved tomorrow. He might come tomorrow when you're not saved. Why do you rejoice today when you don't know if you'll be there tomorrow?"

He got a peculiar look on his face and said, "Now I am in a predicament. What shall I preach? I'm going to give up one or the other."

I said, "Why don't you get straightened out on what Christ has done for you on the cross? I suggest that you get into the book of Romans and get straightened out a wee bit."

We rejoice in the hope of the glory of God. Look at these three things: we have peace with God, we have our access into this grace, and we look forward to the future—we rejoice in the hope of the glory of God. What a folly to rejoice in the glory of God if you are not sure you're going to be there to see it.

That marvelous day is coming when God is going to reveal to all created intelligences in the whole universe who His children are. He's going to be glorified in them and they in Him. That's what Paul means in Romans 8:18 when he says, "For I reckon that the sufferings of this present time are not worthy to be compared with the glory which shall be revealed in us." In 2 Corinthians 4:17, he says, "For our light affliction, which is but for a moment, worketh for us a far more exceeding and eternal weight of glory." And Colossians 3:4 says, "When Christ, who is our life, shall appear, then shall ye also appear with him in glory." I could go on.

Did you ever get a taste of the glory? If not, you have missed something. There isn't a thing on the face of the earth that could buy it. The world doesn't know a thing about it. It's a little touch of the glory, of coming into the presence of God where you get a taste of the glory of Him who is our Savior and everything else fades out of the picture. Nothing down here is worth looking at. That's what Paul meant in Philippians 3, when he saw the Lord in His righteousness, and he said, "I count everything, everything but loss for the excellency of the knowledge of Christ Jesus my Lord. I am willing to suffer the loss of all things just to know him, just to see him, to be found in him, in his righteousness."

Let's get our hearts occupied with our wonderful God and our wonderful Savior, who has made such a marvelous provision, who has declared us righteous, who grants us peace, who stands us in this grace forever, who gives us access into His presence and into His grace. Let us rejoice in hope of the glory of God.

"Oh, but Mr. Mitchell, if you only knew what tests and trials I go through. If you only knew my circumstances." Listen to what Paul says:

> **5:3-5.** *And not only so, but we glory in tribulations also: knowing that tribulation worketh patience; and patience, experience; and experience, hope: and hope maketh not ashamed; because the love of God is shed abroad in our hearts by the Holy Ghost which is given unto us.*

Here's a wonderful thing. In verse 2, we rejoice in hope of the glory of God. That's future. Today, we glory in our tribulations.

Pardon me, I think I should read verse 3 the way most people would like it to read: "Not only so, but we growl in our tribulations also, knowing that tribulations disturb me; and, when I am so disturbed, I am not worth living with."

Is that what the Book says? Of course not. But this is the way some people think it reads. No. We not only rejoice in hope of the glory of God, but we rejoice—we glory—in tribulations also.

Paul is saying that faith is never destroyed by tests. In fact, if you go to 1 Peter 1:6-8, you will find that faith is indestructible. Peter speaks of the numerous temptations that have come upon the earth to try you, "That the trial of your faith, being much more precious than of gold that perisheth, though it be tried with fire, might be found unto praise and honour and glory at the appearing of Jesus Christ: Whom having not seen, ye love." Faith is purified by tests. It is never destroyed by tests.

God always limits the tests. He will not test you beyond what you are able to endure, but will, with the temptation, open the way of escape that you may be able to bear it. Everyone of us has temptations and trials.

You may think, "I have so many tests and trials that nobody goes through what I go through." Oh? Listen, my friend. You can always find somebody who is in a hotter, tighter place than you are.

I met a man years ago who had been on his back eight or ten years, and he suffered excruciating pain. The doctor told me he should have been dead six or eight times, according to medical science. I saw that fellow with sores from the top of his head to the soles of his feet, inside and outside, and he never complained.

One day I took a missionary to see him, and when we came out of that sickroom, he said, "Mr. Mitchell, that room is a service station. I thought when I went in there that I would go to cheer him up and help him. Instead, he helped me. Why, that fellow is living so close to God that he is just full of the love of the Savior."

Off and on I used to go to see my friend, and I'd forget about all my trials and my little aches and pains, whatever they were. We feel so sorry for ourselves, so self-sympathetic. You know that most of us do. Here was a man just glorying in his infirmities. He was living continually in anticipation of the coming of the Lord. He said to me, "Dr. Mitchell, I'm going to beat you to glory. Think of it! I'm going to get there ahead of you so that, when you come, I'll be there to greet you and I'll not have this old body that I have today." Here was a man living in the presence of God, radiating the sweetness and the love and the aroma of Christ in spite of his suffering.

Faith is never destroyed by tests. Faith is purified by tests. Faith is indestructible.

By the way, God did not promise to deliver us from the tests, but to bring us through the tests. He is always with us in the tests, as Hebrews 13:5 says: "I will never leave thee nor forsake thee." Anyone will be encouraged with that. Read the third chapter of Daniel about the three Hebrew children who were in the fiery furnace. God was with them in that furnace.

Yes, but someone says to me, "I've had more tests and trials since I became a Christian than I ever had before."

Why, sure. You ought to expect that. Before you were a Christian, you didn't have any enemies. Now that you've taken Christ as your Savior, you have the world, the flesh, and the devil opposed to you. You can expect tests. That's how faith grows. That's how faith becomes strong, but it's never destroyed.

Other people tell me, "God doesn't test me like He does Mrs. So-and-so. She always has problems and tests and trials, and I don't."

I wouldn't glory in that too much if I were you. It may be the Lord can't trust you with tests and trials. Not everyone can go through tests and afflictions and sorrows without breaking down. God knows whom He can test, whom He can try.

Many years ago I worked in the machine shops. Sometimes we had to make bearings for some of the farmers' machinery, and we would take old babbitt, put it in a pot, and put the pot in the forge. We would melt the babbitt down and begin to skim it. We wanted to make a good bearing; we didn't want any refuse in it. So, as the metal came to a boil, on the top of the metal would be all the stuff you couldn't use—stuff that would hinder a good bearing. We kept skimming it off until we saw the blues and the greens and the yellows on top of the metal. There was no more scum there. Then we poured out the metal and we had a good bearing.

Now, faith is put in the crucible, not to be destroyed but to skim off the stuff that you don't want, stuff that is a hindrance to your walk with God or to your service or to your growth in the grace of God. We are down here in school and our faith must be tested and tried and purified.

Paul says we glory in tribulations because "tribulation worketh patience; patience, experience; and experience, hope." Each time we have a test, something is added to our faith, not subtracted. Oh, the wonderful thing! From tribulation to patience to experience to hope. Not only our faith but also our hope is strengthened through tests.

Paul says about this hope that it "maketh not ashamed because the love of God is shed abroad in our hearts by the Holy [Spirit] which was given unto us." Here you have the eternal, abiding, wonderful love of God shed abroad in our hearts by the Holy Spirit. This is the first time in the book of Romans that the Holy Spirit is mentioned (He is not mentioned again until chapter 8), but here we find that the Spirit of God is the agent of God's love to us. The Spirit of God assures us of God's divine love for His people.

It is the love of an eternal God, a love that never fades, a love that is always sure, a love that is eternal. Just like you find in Jeremiah 31:3, "Yea, I have loved thee with an everlasting love."

GOD'S LOVE GUARANTEES OUR FAITH (5:6-11)

God's love—His eternal, wonderful, unchanging love—guarantees the faith of His people. This love of God is shed abroad in our hearts, and the more the Spirit of God controls your life and my life, the more God's love is manifested to people. It is divine love, and it's an amazing thing—you can love people you've hated.

I've heard people say, "I love so-and-so, but I don't like him." That's not a good statement. If we Christians can't manifest genuine love, there is something wrong with what we believe. If you and I are indwelt by the Spirit of God, then we can go to that Christian we have something against and swallow our pride and try to make things straight. This is love, and the first thing you know, you will be surprised how lovely that person is. It's amazing how a little manifestation of love to the other fellow—divine love manifested in you and me—will change him. The one you thought you didn't like turns out to be a wonderful person.

This love of God, which has been shed abroad in our hearts by the Holy Spirit, guarantees our faith:

> **5:6-11.** *For when we were yet without strength, in due time Christ died for the ungodly. For scarcely for a righteous man will one die: yet peradventure for a good man some would even dare to die. But God commendeth his love toward us, in that, while we were yet sinners, Christ died for us. Much more then, being now justified by his blood, we shall be saved from wrath through him. For if, when we were enemies, we were reconciled to God by the death of his Son, much more, being reconciled, we shall be saved by his life. And not only so, but we also joy in God through our Lord Jesus Christ, by whom we have now received the atonement [reconciliation].*

Verse 5 is the door to verses 6 through 11. The love of God has been shed abroad in our hearts, and it is the guarantee of our faith—not our love for Him but His love for us. If your faith and my faith were guaranteed by our love for Him, brother, I don't know whether or not I would have much peace. Would you? Let's be realistic about it. If my faith is to be guaranteed by my love for the Savior and I grow cold or indifferent, does that mean I lose my faith too? Oh, no.

His love guarantees your faith. When did God start to love you and me? Verse 6: "When we were yet without strength . . . Christ died for the ungodly." Verse 8: "God commendeth his love toward us, in that, while we were yet sinners, Christ died for us." Verse 10: "For, when we were enemies, we were reconciled to God by the death of his Son."

Notice the condition you and I were in when the Lord loved us and manifested that love by dying for us. We were without strength, we were ungodly, we were yet sinners and still active in our sins, we were enemies of God. In spite of our spiritual and moral bankruptcy, He demonstrated His love to us and gave us heaven's best.

I'll tell you, my friend, the death of the sinless Son of God gives full proof of God's eternal love for you and for me.

Man must have a motive for his love, but God doesn't. His motive was in Himself.

Sometimes people say, "If only I were a better man, I could accept the Savior." No, God didn't die for better men. God didn't die for good people. God didn't die for religious people either. God died for sinners. You and I have to take our place as sinners needing a Savior. It's when we see our lost condition that we come to the Savior and receive the divine provision for our need.

Look again at 1 John 4:10: "Herein is love, not that we loved God, but that he loved us, and sent his Son to be the propitiation for our sins." He loved us when we were helpless, ungodly sinners. We were opposed to God, we were enemies of God, and He still loved us.

This blessed love of God, this divine love which provided a Savior, guarantees your faith. If God declared me righteous when I was ungodly, what will He not do for me now that I am righteous in His Son? Much more! Much more! If God loved me enough to reconcile me to Himself when I was His enemy, what will He not do now that I am His child? "Much more, being reconciled, I shall be saved by His life."

What I am trying to get.to your heart, friend—and forgive me if I repeat it—is that if God loved us enough to die for us when we were ungodly and helpless and enemies, loved us enough to save us, to give us faith to believe in His Son, to draw us to Himself and to bring us nigh by the blood of His Son, what will He not do for us now that we are His children? What will He not do for us now that we are righteous in His Son? What will He not do for us now, having forgiven us every trespass?

Oh, how wonderful it is to know that we have a place of certainty, a place of assurance. We are the objects of God's love! The marvel of it all—that ungodly, helpless, hopeless enemies could be so transformed that we become special objects of the affection and devotion of the living God. Who wouldn't put his trust in such a Savior?

Paul doesn't stop there: "Much more, being reconciled, we shall be saved *by his life*" (v. 10). What life? Not His life on earth, surely. No, His life now, His present life. Not only does He love us and guarantee that our faith will continue, but His present life in heaven guarantees it. Take Hebrews 7:25, "Wherefore he is able also to save them to the uttermost that come unto God by him, seeing he ever liveth to make intercession for them." Or take 1 John 2:1-2: "My little children, these things write I unto you, that ye sin not. And if any man sin, we have an advocate with the Father, Jesus Christ the righteous."

We have One pleading our cause. Way back in the Old Testament, Job cried out, "Oh, that I had somebody who could put his hand on God and put his hand on me and bring us together." This is what God has done. He has made the provision for Jesus Christ to be our Mediator and then to be our Advocate. Jesus has put His hand on God and He has put His hand on us. He has brought us together into union with Himself, and He advocates our case. We are down here in frailty and sometimes in failure, and He never tires of praying for us.

He guarantees our faith. He guarantees our life in Himself. He guarantees our forgiveness because He ever lives to make intercession for us. His work on the cross guarantees justification, forgiveness, relationship. His work on the throne guarantees our faith and guarantees that we will stand before God in all the perfection and all the beauty of Christ. Oh, what a Savior we have! What a God we have!

We find furthermore in verse 11 that not only has He made reconciliation for His enemies, but we, having become His children, now revel in the reconciliation.

What do we mean by reconciliation? God has made peace for sinners. We were alienated, enemies in our minds by wicked works; and God at the cross made peace for us. He removed the barrier. Now, by simple faith, when we take Christ as our Savior, we enjoy our reconciliation in Christ.

In chapter 3, our mouths were shut. We stood before God guilty. Now in chapter 5, every believer's mouth is open. We rejoice in the glory of God. We glory in tribulation and we rejoice because we now have received the reconciliation. Oh, what a wonderful thing.

Friend, we need to be filled with joy and rejoicing because we have an all-sufficient, wonderful Savior. Isn't it wonderful to become the objects of divine love of such a God who loves us with an everlasting, perfect love?

GOD'S WAY OF SANCTIFYING SAINTS (5:12-8:39)

Now we come to the second main division of Romans. The first division was God's way of declaring righteous the ungodly who believe in Jesus Christ. Now we have the second: God's way of sanctifying saints. Having taught the great doctrine of justification, Paul prepares to enter into the sphere of sanctification. We are going to find, as we finish chapter 5, that this means more than forgiveness. It means more than being declared righteous. It means the impartation of a new life.

In chapter 5, we are delivered from Adam's race, which is under the sentence of death. The ground of that deliverance is the death and resurrection of Jesus Christ. In chapter 6, we are delivered from sin as a master, as a principle of operation in our lives. This is also on the ground of the death of our Savior. In chapter 7, we are delivered from the law as a rule of life and from its bondage. This is always on the ground of the death and resurrection of Christ. When we come to chapter 8, we are in Christ Jesus. And what safer place can we be than there?

DELIVERANCE FROM DEATH (5:12-21)

In the last half of chapter 5, Paul discusses what we were in Adam and what we are now in Christ. He is talking about two Adams and two races of people. We are either in Adam or we are in Christ. Death reigns in Adam, and the whole human family has been affected by it.

Death Reigns

5:12-14. *Wherefore, as by one man sin entered into the world, and death by sin; and so death passed upon all men, for that all have sinned (For until the law, sin was in the world: but sin is not imputed when there is no law. Nevertheless death reigned from Adam to Moses, even over them that had not sinned after the similitude of Adam's transgression who is the figure of him that was to come.*

When Adam sinned, death came in and affected the whole race. Sin was here. You can't get away from the fact of sin. What caused the flood? Sin. What caused the Tower of Babel and the dispersion upon the earth? Sin. What caused God to confound their language? Sin. This sin occurred before the law was given, but sin and death were here nevertheless. Wherever you find death, you find sin. Romans 6:23 says, "For the wages of sin is death;" and, wherever you turn, you find sin and death together.

Having been a pastor for a great many years, I believe one of the hardest things I ever had to go through was the death of a precious baby. Here is a young couple that has been wanting a baby. Then they have one, and the baby dies. When it lives four or five months, it is harder yet. Why does it die? Because it was born into a human race where death reigns.

My friend, you can't get away from it. Death reigns. And the only way you will ever be freed from death is to be in Jesus Christ.

"But Mr. Mitchell," you say, "Christians die."

No, Christians don't die. Christians have eternal life, resurrection life. They may put our bodies in the grave, our bodies may go back to dust, but we still live. We go right into the presence of the Lord. The apostle Paul taught that "to be absent from the body is to be present with the Lord." We have hope.

All the philosophies of men end in death with no hope. When Jesus Christ bore our sin, He was raised again from the dead to give hope. He brought into being a new race of people over whom death does not reign. All over the world death reigns, whether rich or poor, slave or free, religious or irreligious. But God in His wonderful love and grace has made provision whereby we can be delivered from death.

Jesus said, "If a man keep my saying, he shall never see death." He said in John 14:19, "Because I live, ye shall live also." We are just as sure of it as we are that Jesus Christ was raised from the dead. The Lord Jesus said to the people of His day, and He says it to you and me: "He that . . . believeth on him that sent me, hath everlasting life, and shall not come into condemnation; but is passed from death unto life" (John 5:24).

Whether you want to believe it or not, these verses are true. "Wherefore, as by one man sin entered into the world, and death by sin; and so death passed upon all men, for that all have sinned."

How can Christians be sanctified and live a life pleasing to God? First, God must take us out of Adam's race where death reigns. Remember, Adam's one sin brought ruin to the human race. We have to face this issue. I have sinned, and the penalty of sin is death. How will I get free?

From verses 15 to 19, Paul says that Christ's one act on the cross brought justification of life. When God justifies a man, He communicates a new life—a life that is not contaminated, a life over which death has no power. When sinners accept God's precious Son as their Savior, they are born from above, they are born into a new family, they are born into a new race where death doesn't cast a shadow. When Jesus Christ saves a man, He not only forgives his sin, He not only covers him with His own righteousness, but He also imparts to him a new life—a new life and a new nature. This is what the apostle Peter means when he says, "By these exceeding great and precious promises we become partakers of a divine nature," belonging to a new race, a new family. Death reigns in the old family of Adam because of sin. Now we have been translated out of Adam's race into a new race and death doesn't even cast a shadow. This is the first step in the deliverance from sin.

Christ's Act at the Cross Brought Justification of Life (5:16-19)

5:15. *But not as the offence, so also is the free gift. For if through the offence of one many be dead, much more the grace of God, and the gift by grace, which is by one man, Jesus Christ, hath abounded unto many.*

All in Adam are dead because of Adam's sin. All in Christ receive the gift of grace by Jesus Christ.

5:16-19. *And not as it was by one that sinned, so is the gift: for the judgment was by one to condemnation, but the free gift is of many offences unto justification. For if by one man's offence death reigned by one; much more they which receive abundance of grace and of the gift of righteousness shall reign in life by one, Jesus Christ.) Therefore as by the offence of one judgment came upon all men to condemnation; even so by the righteousness of one the free gift came upon all men unto justification of life. For as by one man's disobedience many were made sinners, so by the obedience of one shall many be made righteous. Moreover the law entered, that the offence might abound. But where sin abounded, grace did much more abound: that as sin hath reigned unto death, even so might grace reign through righteousness unto eternal life by Jesus Christ our Lord.*

There are those who teach universal salvation on the ground of this passage. They say that eventually everybody is going to be saved. Paul says, "By one man's disobedience all were made sinners. By the obedience of one shall all be made righteous." So they say that, in Adam, death reigned over the whole human race without exception; therefore, in Christ all shall be made righteous. But they fail to realize what the apostle is writing. We are under death because we are in Adam. But to be righteous you have to be in Christ.

Paul is not teaching universal salvation. He is making a contrast between two races of people. You are either in Adam or you are in Christ. And there are seven things you should know concerning your position in Adam and seven things regarding your position in Christ:

1. By the offense of one, many (all) are dead in Adam. In Christ, the gift of grace has abounded to many (v. 15).
2. Judgment followed the one man's sin and brought condemnation. But the free gift justifies those who have many offenses against them (v. 16).
3. Death reigned through the one man, Adam. Those in Christ shall reign in life by the one man, Jesus Christ (v. 17).
4. By one offense, judgment came to all. In Christ, the righteousness of One has brought justification to all (v. 18).
5. By one man's disobedience, all were made sinners. By the obedience of Christ, all were made righteous in Him (v. 19).
6. Where sin abounds, grace much more abounds. In Adam, sin abounds; in Christ, grace much more abounds (v. 20).
7. Sin reigns unto death. In Christ, grace reigns through righteousness unto eternal life (v. 21).

Those seven things are true of everybody in Adam whether you are good, bad, indifferent, moral, immoral, whatever you are.

Since you are born in Adam, you are under the sentence of death, you are under condemnation. You are a sinner, and death reigns over you. Sin abounds, and sin reigns unto death for all who are in Adam.

If we are in Christ, the gift of grace has abounded toward us. By the righteousness of the One, we are justified. By His obedience, we are made righteous. This is true of all in Christ, whether we are a strong or a weak or a stumbling Christian. Everyone in this new race stands before God righteous, without sin, having eternal life.

You might find some who do not believe in the Savior but yet live a good, moral, and possibly a better life than Christians you know. But it is not a question of walk here. The main issue is, are you in Adam or are you in Christ? You needn't stay in Adam under sin, under the bondage of death, under the wrath of God. You can be in Christ.

The Bible says, "Where sin abounded, grace did much more abound." Notice the "much more." There are several in this chapter alone: "Much more then, being now justified by his blood"; "much more, being reconciled, we shall be saved by his life"; "much more the grace of God"; and "much more they which receive the abundance of grace and of the gift of righteousness shall reign in life by one, Jesus Christ."

In other words, my friend, when you and I accepted the Lord Jesus Christ as Savior, regardless of our background, of our life, whether it was much in sin or not, the grace of God reached right down where we were. And where were we? We were dead in trespasses and sin. And right where we were, He picked us up and redeemed us and justified us and imparted to us new life.

That's why I read in 2 Corinthians 5:17, "If any man be in Christ [this Head of a new race], he is a new creature: old things are passed away; behold, all things are become new."

Isn't that wonderful!

Romans 6

The sixth chapter of Romans is full of foundational truth, not about sins, not about forgiveness or justification, but about deliverance from sin as a master.

DELIVERANCE FROM SIN (6:1-23)

Paul raised this issue in chapter 5 by saying, "Where sin abounded, grace did much more abound."

"Then, Paul," we might say, "if grace super-abounds wherever sin is, let us sin that grace may abound." So he raises the question and answers it early on in chapter 6.

We Are Delivered from Sin as a Place (6:1-11)

6:1-2. *What shall we say then? Shall we continue in sin, that grace may abound? God forbid. How shall we, that are dead to sin, live any longer therein?*

Sin is a tyrant. You can't afford, Christian friend, to play with sin. You say, "Well, Mr. Mitchell, I wouldn't lie. I wouldn't steal. I wouldn't get drunk. I wouldn't do this or that."

I'm not talking about sins. I'm talking about sin as a whole, sin that dominates your life, sin that forces you to obey its whims. It is an amazing thing, the confusion in a great many Christians' minds concerning victory or deliverance from sin as a master. Some go to a spiritual life or a victorious life conference or they go somewhere to get sanctified. Some say you have to receive the baptism of the Spirit. Others have various doctrines. But all, basically, are trying to do one thing. They want to get free from sin as a master. "How can I glorify God in my life when I am so frail and weak?" they ask.

We have a body that is not yet redeemed. Our salvation is not yet complete in our experience. It is true we have been forgiven and justified, and as far as God is concerned, He sees us glorified in His Son. Those facts are true, but you don't experience facts. You experience life. Facts are to be believed; the life is to be lived. Many Christians, having come into contact with the Savior, loving the Lord Jesus and wanting to please Him, find that sometimes the more they try to please the Lord, the more they fail. And I know I'm talking to a lot of folk who know this through experience.

The more we try to live a holy life, the more we do things we don't want to do. So we try to formulate a way whereby we can be delivered from the power of sin in our life. But our bodies are not yet redeemed, and we experience desires and lusts whether we want to acknowledge them or not. Christians do sin.

How can I find deliverance? I'm yearning for a life that is pleasing to God. I want to be like the Savior, who said, "I do always the things that please Him." But the more I try, the worse it gets. So we try in the energy of the flesh. We keep our chins up. We try by willpower. We say, "I'm not going to do that thing again. It's dishonoring to the Lord. It's sin, and I'm not going to do it again."

And we confess our sin to the Lord and turn right around and do it all over again. That's because we are trying by the energy of the flesh, and there is no deliverance that way. There is only one way of deliverance and that is God's way. He wants us to trust Him for the deliverance. God wants us to let Him do it. It's a question of our yielding ourselves to Him.

"I know He saved me from the guilt of sin and the penalty of sin," you say, "but what about the power of sin?"

Being saved from the power of sin calls for a daily walk with God, a daily walk that is pleasing to Him where it is none of self but all of Him. Some people try to conquer sin by crucifying self. They are talking about an impossibility. The Lord Jesus did not crucify himself; others crucified Him. The Bible does not teach self-crucifixion.

"Doesn't the Bible say some place that we are to take up our cross and follow Him?"

Yes, but what is the cross? Christ must come before self, that's true; but that's not self-crucifixion. Galatians 2:20 says, "We were crucified with Christ." That's past. If I talk about crucifying self, then I must be on the other side of the cross. We are on the resurrection side. Colossians 3:1 says, "If ye then be risen with Christ, seek those things which are above."

Others teach that we die daily to sin. There's no such Scripture about that either. In 1 Corinthians 15:31-32 Paul says, "If [for merely human reasons] I have fought with beasts at Ephesus, what's the advantage of it if the dead are not raised? Behold I die daily." Paul was living in daily expectation of martyrdom. That's why he could say, "What is the advantage of being a martyr if there is no resurrection? I die daily." And he says in Romans 8:36, "we are accounted as sheep for the slaughter."

We are dead to sin. Our history as sinners came to an end at the cross. This is not something you feel or experience. This is a fact, and facts, I repeat, are to be believed. But before I can experience this life in Christ, this being freed from sin as a master, I must acknowledge by faith that what God says is true—that when Christ died, you and I died. We are new men, new women in Christ.

Now, Romans 6 contains four basic instructions. First, we are to know the facts. Let's not be ignorant of the facts of what God says is true. Second, we are to acknowledge, to reckon the facts to be true. Third, we are to yield our bodies to Him so that He can work through us. And fourth, we are to walk pleasing to the Lord. That's what He wants.

As we go more deeply into this chapter, I hope you will read it and reread it. Yes, there is a great deal of confusion about being delivered from the power of sin in our daily walk, but God has a way, and His way is best. Let us learn the facts, believe them to be true, and act upon them by yielding our members to Him.

> **6:3-4.** *Know ye not, that so many of us as were baptized into Jesus Christ were baptized into his death? Therefore we are buried with him by baptism into death: that like as Christ was raised up from the dead by the glory of the Father, even so we also should walk in newness of life.*

I'm going to say this again. We are not dealing with your experience or my experience. We're dealing with a fact. God has declared that when Christ died, you and I were joined to Him. We were baptized into His death. When He was buried, we were buried. And when He came forth in resurrection, we too came forth, identified with the risen and glorified Christ. It's the end of you and me as far as our history as sinners. God has declared that when a sinner accepts the Savior, he is not only forgiven his sin and delivered from the control of Adam's race where death reigns (hence he has eternal life), but he is joined to the Savior in resurrection. We are joined to the Man at God's right hand.

Paul affirms this fact in other passages, such as Colossians 3:1-3 and 2 Corinthians 5:13-17. In Galatians 2:20 he says, "I have been crucified with Christ. I no longer live, but Christ lives within me." These verbs are in the past tense. We died. We are not dying, but we died. It is a finished transaction. As long as a person is dying, there's still hope. But if death comes in, that's the end.

Are you dying to sin or have you died to sin? The Book says you died to sin, and if you have died, then Colossians 3:1 says you have risen with Him. We were identified with Christ, not only in His death and burial, but also in His resurrection. I have met men, even teachers, who glory that they died with Christ and then they came full stop. We not only died with Christ, but we were raised with Christ. Not only are we dead to sin, but we have a new life to live for God.

You have the two aspects. Your past life as a sinner came to an end. You are now one of God's children, one of the saints. That's why, when you come to the end of Romans, you are exhorted to be saintly in your life. I am a saint by calling, but I should be saintly in my life. All Christians are saints, but they do not all walk as becomes saints.

We are dealing in Romans 6 with a positional truth. When we come to chapters 12 through 16, we have the experiential side of the picture. But it's no use talking about our experience until we get the facts about what God says we are.

> **6:5-6.** *For if we have been planted together in the likeness of his death, we shall be also in the likeness of his resurrection: knowing this, that our old man is crucified with him, that the body of sin might be destroyed, that henceforth we should not serve sin.*

Dead people don't break the law. They don't sin. They are dead. God says when you and I accepted the Savior, we were joined to Jesus Christ; when He died, He died not only for your sins but He died for you. He died not only for our acts but for the "actors", not only for the guilt but for the guilty.

Since Christ died for you and not just for your sins, then that's the end of you. You and I were the ones who should have been crucified. We were the ones who had transgressed against the law of God. We were the sinners, and God says "the wages of sin is death." Either we die or somebody else dies. Christ died in our stead. We were identified with Him—we were joined with Him when He died. God saw you and me in His Son hanging on the cross and in the grave. And when He rose from the dead, we were joined to a risen Christ.

In verses 3 to 5, is Paul talking about the rite of water baptism?

No, of course not. No rite can put me into Christ and join me to Christ in His death, burial, and resurrection. It is an act of God for everyone who receives His Son as Savior.

If you want to give witness to this fact by water baptism, that's between you and the Lord. If you want to show forth in this way your identification with Christ in His death, burial, and resurrection, then you are still to walk in newness of life. Sometimes I jokingly tell people I am about to baptize, "If I thought for one moment that you are not going to glorify the Lord in your life, I would put you under the water and keep you there!" If I am going to witness that I am joined to a risen Christ by some rite or ceremony, then my life ought to reflect that. My life ought to show forth that I am a new man, a new woman in Christ.

The moment a sinner receives the Lord Jesus Christ as Savior, he puts on Christ. He becomes a member of the body of Christ. He is baptized into the body of Christ by the Spirit. He is joined to the eternal Son of God. Paul here is stressing that, when Christ died, you died. It is an act of God. It joins us to the Son of God in His work at the cross, in His burial and in His resurrection.

Beginning in verse 6, Paul continues this question of identification. Remember, he wants you to know the facts and to reckon the facts to be true. And he wants you to yield your body to God. That's what we find as we continue through the chapter.

> **6:6-7.** *Knowing this, that our old man is crucified with him, that the body of sin might be destroyed, that henceforth we should not serve sin. For he that is dead is freed from sin.*

When Paul says the body of sin might be "destroyed," he does not mean "annihilated." The meaning here is to render powerless, just as our Lord by His death destroyed or rendered powerless "him that had the power of death, that is, the devil" (Hebrews 2:14-15). With this in mind, Romans 6:6 says: "Knowing this, that our old man (all that we were in Adam) is crucified with him, that the body of sin might be destroyed, that henceforth we should not serve sin." Sin is no longer our master. He that has died is freed, liberated, from his old master, sin. We have a new master, Jesus Christ.

The man outside of Christ is still under the authority and power of sin. Sin is his master. He may deny this (and sometimes we Christians are amazed at the good that sinners will do), but sin is still his master. That's where he lives—in sin.

Most Christians know that the death of Christ has severed their relationship to sin. They have been forgiven their transgressions, and they will never again see their sins. They believe that Christ put away their sins "by the sacrifice of himself" (Hebrews 9:26; 1 John 3:5,8). Sin has lost its authority, its power over us. Death has taken us out from under its reign, and we are now on resurrection ground. We are joined to a risen Christ. He that has died is freed from sin.

> **6:8.** *Now if we be dead with Christ, we believe that we shall also live with him.*

If I acknowledge that when Christ died, I died, then I believe I am going to live with Him, being joined to the risen Savior. It's a funny thing about us Christians. I ask the average Christian, "Do you believe you live with Christ."

"Oh, yes."

"Do you believe you are going to spend eternity with Christ?"

"Oh, yes."

"Do you believe Christ has put away your sins?"

"Oh, yes."

"Do you believe that you died to sin once?"

"Now, wait a minute. My experience doesn't say that."

I didn't ask what your experience says. I'm talking about a fact. He that has died is freed from sin. He that is dead will live with Him.

> **6:9-10.** *Knowing that Christ, being raised from the dead, dieth no more; death hath no more dominion*

over him. For in that he died, he died unto sin once:
but in that he liveth, he liveth unto God.

You say, "Well, Mr. Mitchell, I know that Christ died unto sin once." And so did you. Paul's not talking about your failures. He's talking about sin being a master, a tyrant. Don't you forget that—sin is a tyrant.

I know it's hard to absorb these verses because as soon as I talk this way, you immediately look at yourself. You see your failures and your frailties instead of daring to believe what God says. Do you believe what it says here? He that has died is free from sin?

"Well, Mr. Mitchell, I sin."

But he that has died is freed from sin as his master. This is a fact.

"But I'm not freed from sin," you say. "That's true about Jesus, but not about me."

Let me attack this from a different angle. Is Jesus Christ, the Living Son of God, through with sin?

"Oh, yes!"

When did that take place?

"At the cross."

Where is He now?

"On the throne."

Will He ever go back to the cross to be made sin again?

"No."

He is through, eternally, with sin?

"Yes."

So are you!

God says you also in Christ are through with sin forever. Sin is no longer your master. Remember, sin pays wages and the wages of sin is death (Romans 6:23). But you died—the wages were paid. You are joined to Jesus Christ and "the life you now live in the flesh," says Paul, "you live by the faith of the Son of God, who loved you and gave himself for you. I do not frustrate the grace of God, for if righteousness come by the law [by works], then Christ is dead in vain" (Galatians 2:20-21).

I'm asking you not to look at your feelings or your experience, but to dare to believe that what God says is true. Am I going to believe God, or am I going to believe my experience? Look at what Paul says in verse 11:

6:11. *Likewise reckon ye also yourselves to be dead indeed unto sin, but alive unto God through Jesus Christ our Lord.*

Here now is the reckoning of faith. We are to know the facts—when Christ died, we died. That was the end of our history as sinners. I am no longer a child of wrath, I'm a child of God. I'm no longer in sin, I'm in Christ. Death has severed my relationship to sin as a master. Just as Christ died to sin once, we died to sin once. In that He lives, He lives to God. And we live to God. Christ, being raised from the dead, dies no more. Death has no more dominion over Him. Neither does it have dominion over you or me. Death has lost its authority. Sin has been rendered powerless by our Savior. If sin comes into a believer's life, it comes in as a test. This is God's way of holiness, God's way of sanctification. You are a new man, you are a new woman in Christ.

We Are Delivered from Sin as a Principle (6:12-15)

6:12-15. *Let not sin therefore reign in your mortal body, that ye should obey it in the lusts thereof. Neither yield ye your members as instruments of unrighteousness unto sin: but yield yourselves unto God, as those that are alive from the dead, and your members as instruments of righteousness unto God. For sin shall not have dominion over you: for ye are not under the law, but under grace. What then? shall we sin, because we are not under the law, but under grace? God forbid.*

We have a new master; we are no longer under the tyrant, sin. Our new master is Christ. In Luke 2, Simeon took the baby Jesus in his arms to bless Him, and said, "Lord, now lettest thou thy servant depart in peace, according to thy word: For mine eyes have seen thy salvation." What he really said was, "Now, Master, release your bondslave, according to your Word." He recognized God as his Master.

Christian friend, who is your master? Sin or the Lord Jesus Christ, your risen Lord? Romans 5 says we were freed from Adam's race through the death of Christ. Romans 6 says the only way to get rid of sin as a master is through death. We died with Christ. If you are "dying daily to sin," you are not satisfied with your new Master. You are still struggling with the old master and there is no victory—there is no deliverance. Take what God says as fact. We have died to sin once in the person of Christ. We no longer live in sin as a principle of operation.

Before we were Christians, sin used our bodies with all our gifts, our tongue, our minds, our hands, our eyes, our feet. It used all of us for the performance of sinful acts. Now, says Paul, you are joined to a new Man and sin has no longer any authority over you. Just as you once yielded your members to sin, now yield your members to God.

It's so easy to become a slave to sin. People are tied down under the bondage of sin even though they think they can give sin up. Often men say to me, "I can give it up or leave it alone. I can take it or leave it." Well, I know they'll take it because they're slaves to sin and sin is a tyrant. It may be alcoholism, it may be drugs, it may be immorality or any number of other things, but whatever it is, they can become slaves to it.

Often men seek deliverance in this philosophy and that psychology. They try everything and they are still not delivered. When they finally come to the place where they receive Jesus Christ as Savior, often they are freed immediately from the slavery of that sin.

"But Mr. Mitchell," you say, "I know some Christians—people who really accepted the Lord—and they are still slaves to certain sins."

That's right. They try again and again to get delivered and they can't. They pray, they fast, and still they get no deliverance. In desperation, they turn to the Lord and say, "Lord, I can't do this thing. You've got to do it." And immediately they're delivered.

Some years ago, I was invited to speak in a certain town, and after the morning meeting, a man invited me to his home for dinner. I got into his buggy, and we followed a trail down through the forest. After a bit we came to a clearing where he had built a house and was farming and ranching. Now this man had six daughters and, at that time, I wasn't married.

He said to me, "Mr. Mitchell, you go into the house and Mom and the girls will take care of you." I didn't want to go into a house with six girls, so I decided to wait for him. As he got out of the buggy, he stooped down and didn't see me still standing there. Just as he was going to take the tracers off of the buggy, he took a big plug of tobacco out of his pocket and bit off a chunk of it. Just as he did, he saw me, and he began apologizing to me for the tobacco.

"Well," I said, "it's okay with me if you want it. I don't want it. Thank God, I've been delivered from it. You go ahead. It's up to you."

So he took the tracers off and put the horses away, and on our way to the house he said, "When I was a boy, we lived in Virginia and we raised tobacco. On the way to school every day we kids used to take a leaf of the tobacco plant and chew it. I've done this all my life."

I said, "Well, do you know the Savior?"

"Oh, yes," he said. "I've been saved and I've been sanctified, but I can't get rid of it."

I said, "I think you better trust the Lord to deliver you. You've been struggling to get rid of it and you can't."

A few years after this, I met a friend of mine who used to preach up in that area, and I asked him, "By the way, do you ever see So-and-so?"

"Oh, yes," he said, "he was addicted to chewing tobacco. Do you know how he was delivered? After you left, he was so embarrassed that he decided to go out into the timber and fast and pray for two or three days. But the moment he got back home, he just made for the tobacco can.

"Then one day in desperation he got on his knees and said, 'Lord, I'm going to heaven trusting the blood of Jesus Christ, tobacco or no tobacco.' And, you know, when he got up from his knees, he became violently sick. From that day on, he wasn't able to even stand the smell of it. When his Dad came up from the south, puffing on his old pipe, he said, 'Dad, would you mind going into the barn? I can't stand the smell of it.' "

I tell you that story for a reason. This man had tried everything, including praying and fasting (and, by the way, I'm not opposed to praying and fasting), but he was trusting what he was doing for deliverance instead of trusting the Lord. Paul tells us to yield ourselves to God. Let God do the delivering. Let God have the victory. You can't win the victory; God wins the victory, and we enjoy the deliverance.

I don't know what you struggle with, Christian friend, but I'm sure I'm talking to some who have tried and prayed and agonized about being delivered from certain things in their lives that are hindering their spiritual growth and hindering their ministry. It may or may not be outbroken sin, it may or may not be some filthy habit, but it is hindering the work of God in them.

God wants you for himself. Sin is no longer your master. Just as you once yielded your body, your mind, your tongue to sin and sin reigned in you as your master, now you have a new master, Jesus Christ, and you yield your members to Him. Perhaps before you were saved your tongue was full of filthy talk, cursing, and bitterness. Now yield your tongue to the Lord. Let Him put a new song in your mouth so that, instead of cursing and bitterness, there will be blessing.

We belong to the risen Savior. We belong to the One who wrought salvation for you and me, the One who loves us with an everlasting love, even when we fail Him. He is always waiting for us to come and have fellowship with Him. This is God's way of sanctification where the Lord becomes the center of your love, the center of your life. You have a new Master, a new life with new hopes and new aspirations.

You and I criticize the world and how far it has gone in its sin. We say, "My, the world is getting terrible—lawlessness, moral corruption, legalizing sinfulness, legalizing the things that cause the wrath of God to come down upon men." We forget that the world can't help itself. That's the way it is under the tyrant of sin.

But, Christian friend, you and I are not under that tyrant any more. Paul says that God wants us to yield ourselves to Him so that our lives may be a benediction. You have a new Master, Jesus Christ. Live for Him.

We Are Delivered from Sin as a Practice (6:16-23)

We've been delivered from sin as a place in which to live, and we've been delivered from sin as a principle of operation. Now, in the last part of Romans 6, we discover that we are delivered from sin as a practice in our lives. In verse 16, we have a brand new experience. We are going to be living for God instead of sin and self:

> **6:16.** *Know ye not, that to whom ye yield yourselves servants to obey, his servants ye are to whom ye obey; whether of sin unto death, or of obedience unto righteousness?*

Some Christians take verse 16 entirely out of context and conclude they can lose their salvation. They think, "If I yield myself to sin by obeying my members, if I obey the lusts of the flesh, then I become a slave of those lusts and am no longer a child of God."

But Paul doesn't even have that in mind. He's saying, "Don't you know that, if you yield yourselves to sin, you are its bond-slave and the end is death? Don't you know that if you yield yourselves to obedience the end is righteousness?" Either your life is characterized by sin as your master or it is characterized by a great desire to please God even though you may fail.

Again, we are getting right down to motives of the heart in the life of a Christian. If you are a Christian, if you have taken Christ as your Savior, even though you may be a failure and struggle with weaknesses, you will have a great yearning in your heart to do the things that are pleasing to God. (When we get to Romans 7, we will see more of this.) The person who is not regenerated is controlled, dominated by sin. He may be a moralist and he may be self-righteous, but he is not the servant of God. He's serving himself or serving the devil instead.

In verses 17 and 18, Paul begins to encourage God's people:

6:17-18. *But God be thanked, that ye were the servants of sin, but ye have obeyed from the heart that form of doctrine which was delivered you. Being then made free from sin, ye became the servants of righteousness.*

Paul is bringing assurance to the hearts of Christians. His great desire for us is that we not yield our members to unrighteousness and sin. Sin no longer should dominate the life and the heart of a believer in Christ.

6:19. *I speak after the manner of men because of the infirmity of your flesh: for as ye have yielded your members servants to uncleanness and to iniquity unto iniquity; even so now yield your members servants to righteousness unto holiness.*

In other words, we have a new experience. We're no longer going to be dominated by sin. We're going to live for God instead of sin.

If I've accepted Jesus Christ as my Savior, then I have been delivered—translated, as Colossians 1:13 says—out of the kingdom of darkness into the kingdom of God's dear Son. Having been translated from the place where sin and death reign, I am now in a new kingdom where righteousness and love reign.

Do you see what Paul is after? He wants us to see our position in Christ so that it will affect our daily living. This is practical sanctification. All I need so that I may stand before God is what Jesus Christ did for me at the cross. Our Lord put away our sins. He defeated death and the grave. He made it possible for God to pronounce us righteous and to give us eternal life.

But I'm still in a body not yet delivered, not yet redeemed. How shall I live for God when my body has certain desires and lusts that are dishonoring to Him? What shall I do?

Before we were Christians, we just naturally yielded our members to sin. In fact, we had no righteousness. No unsaved man can produce righteousness. This is what Paul is saying in verse 20:

6:20-21. *For when ye were the servants of sin, ye were free from righteousness. What fruit had ye then in those things whereof ye are now ashamed? for the end of those things is death.*

We are now ashamed of some of the things we used to do. When a man accepts Jesus Christ as his Savior, he is forgiven every transgression, every sin. He has a new life. He has a new standing before God, a new relationship as a child of God. And some of the things he used to do, he is ashamed to do them today. There are some things I did before I was a Christian that I wouldn't think of doing today. I would be ashamed of them.

What has made the transformation? Paul is telling these Roman Christians that the very fact we are now ashamed of some of the things we did before we knew Christ, is one of the proofs that we have a new master—not sin, but the risen Lord of glory.

6:22. *But now being made free from sin, and become servants to God, ye have your fruit unto holiness, and the end everlasting life.*

Don't be afraid of that word *holiness*; it's a good word. The joy of it is the guarantee that we have everlasting life. Paul doesn't mean that everlasting life is the fruit of living a holy life. So he guards that in verse 23 when he says, "The wages of sin is death." Then why does he mention everlasting life in verse 22? To show the contrast. Before we were saved, we were free from righteousness. We had none. But now, having been made free from sin as a master and having a new Master, the Living Son of God, what is the fruit of it? A life glorifying to God. And what is the end? Enjoyment, the assurance, the certainty of everlasting life—not because of our walk, but because of our union to this Risen Son of God we now recognize as our Master.

> **6:23.** *For the wages of sin is death; but the gift of God is eternal life through Jesus Christ our Lord.*

Sin pays wages, and you can't quit the job. You can't go on strike. The wages must be paid. Either you pay the wages or somebody else does, and the wages of sin is death. Death reigns today over the human race, and the only way one can be delivered from sin's wages is to trust the One who died for us, the One who took our place, the One who died our death. "For he hath made him to be sin for us, who knew no sin, that we might be made the righteousness of God in him" (2 Corinthians 5:21).

Isn't this good news? God has made provision whereby any man or woman may be saved, wherever they are, whoever they are, whatever they have done. Jesus Christ bore our sins, took our wages, and now offers to us—as a free gift—eternal life. And eternal life can only be received from God as a gift.

Jesus could say, "He that believeth on me has everlasting life." In Him is life. To have the Son of God is to have life. Not to have the Son of God is not to have life. I don't care how good or religious you are, unless you have a relationship to the Savior, you are lost. Come to Christ, receive Him as your Savior, and yield your members to God so that Christ will be glorified in your life.

This is practical sanctification where the Lord, the Righteous One, lives out His life through you and produces righteousness in you. As Paul says, "I was crucified with Christ. I no longer live, but Christ lives in me: and the life that I now live in the flesh, I live by the faith of the Son of God who loved me and gave himself for me."

Romans 7

In Romans 7 we hear the cry of the human heart—longing to please God, longing to live a holy life. But the more this man tries to keep the law, the more he breaks it. The more he reads the Word of God and sees what the law was made for and what it demands, the more he must cry out, "O wretched man that I am, who shall deliver me?"

The law never saved anyone. It was never given to save. It was never given as a means of life for sinners, nor was it given as the rule of life for the believer in Christ.

"But can one use the law today lawfully?"

Yes, in 1 Timothy 1:9, Paul says, "The law is not made for a righteous man, but for the lawless." One can use the law to prove to men that they need a Savior. That's the purpose of the law. As Paul could say in Galatians 3:24, "The law was our schoolmaster to bring us unto Christ." Having come to Christ, we are no longer under the schoolmaster.

The danger with us is that we know we are saved by grace, saved through the precious blood of Christ. But we think that to be good we must keep the law. The more we try, the more we realize we can't be good by keeping the law. So we have in Romans 7 two wonderful things: We are delivered from the law through the death of Christ, and we were delivered so that we can bring forth fruit unto God.

DELIVERANCE FROM THE LAW (7:1-25)

The Principle of Deliverance from the Law (7:1-6)

7:1-3. *Know ye not, brethren, (for I speak to them that know the law,) how that the law hath dominion over a man as long as he liveth? For the woman which hath an husband is bound by the law to her husband so long as he liveth; but if the husband be dead, she is loosed from the law of her husband. So then if, while her husband liveth, she be married to another man, she shall be called an adulteress: but if her husband be dead, she is free from that law; so that she is no adulteress, though she be married to another man.*

Here is the principle of deliverance from law. Paul turns from the thought of being a slave in chapter 6 to being one who delights now in a new master and in a new relationship that will bring forth fruit unto God. *The principle of a holy life is not obedience to the law but union with the risen Lord.*

Paul is not discussing here the question of marriage and divorce and remarriage. He is using the illustration of marriage to show that when the husband dies, the wife also "dies." No one can be the wife of a dead man. When the husband dies, the law of marriage is broken by that death and the woman is free to marry somebody else.

Take any kind of law. The only way man knows to keep down sin is by making laws, and when you have a law, you must also have a corresponding penalty. There is no mercy in law. There may be mercy in a judge, but there is no mercy in law. The law of Moses says if you sin, you shall die. The only thing that can deliver you from law is death.

Go to any town or city and you will find a graveyard. But you will never find any policemen there, patrolling the graveyard (unless they're looking for vandals). Death has severed the relationship between those who are buried and the law under which they once lived.

My friend, the man who has accepted Jesus Christ as Savior has not only been freed from death, having been the recipient of eternal life, he has not only been freed from sin as a master and as a tyrant, but he has also been delivered from the law. The law has had nothing to say since the cross.

I repeat it, the law "was made for the lawless." The law has teeth in it—if you sin, you die. The only way you will ever get freed from it is by death. As long as you live under the law, you have to obey the law. You break the law in one point and you are guilty of all. As Galatians 3:10 says, "Cursed is everyone that continueth not in all things which are written in the book of the law to do them."

Remember, the law demands two things. The law demands that you do not break it, and the law demands righteousness. You have no capacity to measure up to either one. You neither have righteousness nor are you innocent. You have broken the law.

You say, "But, Mr. Mitchell, I'm doing the best I can."

It makes no difference. Have you broken it? Did you ever break it? "Yes." You must die. Either you die or somebody else dies for you. And the fact is that Jesus Christ took your place and died your death that you might bring forth fruit unto God. God wants fruit, and you and I can bring forth fruit, recognizing that we are no longer under the law which is a taskmaster, which has no mercy, and which insists that we die.

> **7:4.** *Wherefore, my brethren, ye also are become dead unto the law by the body of Christ; that ye should be married to another, even to him who is raised from the dead, that we should bring forth fruit unto God.*

Some of you may be saying, "But we must keep the law."

But what does the Word of God say? You have become dead to the law (not alive to the law, but dead to the law) that you might be married to another—to Jesus Christ. Paul continues:

> **7:5-6.** *For when we were in the flesh, the motions of sins, which were by the law did work in our members to*

*bring forth fruit unto death. But now we are delivered
from the law, that being dead wherein we were held;
that we should serve in newness of spirit, and not in the
oldness of the letter.*

Death severs the relationship. Some people even fight this.
Once in a meeting, Dwight L. Moody asked, "Do you know anyone who is perfect?" A man put up his hand and said, "My wife's
first husband."

But death must sever that relationship. Here we are, joined to a
risen Christ, trying to keep the memory of that old husband, the
law, alive. Paul says in Galatians 2:19, "I through the law, am
dead to the law, that I might live unto God."

You cannot live unto God, Christian friend, if you are going to
live under the law. Romans 10:3-4 talks about the Jews' going
about to establish their own righteousness. They have not submitted themselves to the righteousness of God. "For Christ is the end
of the law for righteousness to everyone that believeth."

Have you taken Jesus Christ as your Savior?

"Yes."

Have you been covered with all the righteousness of Christ?

"Yes."

Have you been justified by faith?

"Yes."

Then, my friend, the Book says Christ is the end of the law for
you. He is not the beginning of the law, but the end of the law.
Law has no more to say to a Christian. All the law can do is kill,
curse, and condemn. But Christ took my place, and now in Him,
my risen, glorified Savior, I have been set free from the law.

Someone is going to say, "Well, Mr. Mitchell, we are saved by
the grace of God. We are saved through what He accomplished for
us at the cross. But we must keep the law as a rule of life."

Friend, you are putting yourself back under the law. And, if you
put yourself back under the law as a rule of life, then you must
come back under its curse. "Cursed is everyone who continueth
not in all things which are written in the book of the law to do

them." This is strong language, isn't it?

The law doesn't die, but we die to it in Christ. Now that we are joined to the risen Christ, we are dead to the law by the body of Christ. We are joined in heart and love to the risen Savior with all His rights, with all His inheritance, with all His righteousness, with all His life, in order to bear fruit unto God in living, loving, willing obedience to Him. Our former life, the passions of our sins which were energized by the law, brought forth fruit unto death. It was not unto God.

Some of you have struggled and worked and struggled and worked to be pleasing to God by keeping the law, and you are not happy. You have no enjoyment or peace; you are struggling. You have become legalistic. You are trying to merit favor with God. You are not saying salvation is just Christ's death for me. You are saying it is Christ plus my keeping the law.

If one is saved by trusting the Savior plus keeping the law of God, then none of us will be saved because it is impossible for any one to keep the law. If you break the law in one point, you are guilty of all.

None of us can live unto God unless we realize that we have a new life in Christ, that we've been joined to the risen Savior, and that the law has no more jurisdiction over us. Did you hear me? *The law has no more jurisdiction over a Christian.* Just as sin is no longer our master, we are no longer under the jurisdiction of law. We belong to a risen, glorified Savior. Hallelujah! Rejoice in your new life in Christ.

What the Law Did (7:7-13)

> **7:7-13.** *What shall we say then? Is the law sin? God forbid. Nay, I had not known sin, but by the law: for I had not known lust, except the law had said, Thou shalt not covet. But sin, taking occasion by the commandment, wrought in me all manner of concupiscence. For without the law sin was dead. For I was alive without*

the law once: but when the commandment came, sin
revived, and I died. And the commandment, which was
ordained to life, I found to be unto death. For sin, tak-
ing occasion by the commandment, deceived me, and
by it slew me. Wherefore the law is holy, and the com-
mandment holy, and just, and good. Was then that
which is good made death unto me? God forbid. But
sin, that it might appear sin, working death in me by
that which is good; that sin by the commandment might
become exceeding sinful.

The law is not sinful, but through the law, sin wrought in Paul
all manner of lusts. The law is all right—I'm the one that's wrong.
Without the law, sin was dead; it was dormant. But the old master,
sin, woke me up when the law came.

Let me give you what the law can and cannot do. Why was the
law given?

1. The law makes sin exceedingly or utterly sinful (vv. 7-8, 13).
   The law gives a distinctive character to sin.
2. The law works wrath (Romans 4:15). It never works righteousness.
3. The law is the ministration of death (2 Corinthians 3:7-9).
   All the law can do is kill you.
4. The law is the strength of sin (1 Corinthians 15:56). It is not
   the strength of righteousness. The law demands righteousness but gives you no power to produce it. It is the strength
   of sin.
5. The law brings a curse (Galatians 3:10). The legalist (and
   most Christians) will not admit that all the law of God can
   do is to curse. When Jesus Christ took our place and bore
   our sin, all the law of God could do with Him was curse. But
   Christ has redeemed us from the curse of the law by becom-
   ing a curse for us.
6. The law was "added because of transgressions" (Galatians
   3:19). The Jews didn't know themselves, nor did they know

the law of God. So the Lord gave the law to prove what they were.

7. The law brings the knowledge of sin (Romans 3:20; 7:7).
8. The law is a schoolmaster to bring us to Christ (Galatians 3:24-25). Having come to Christ, we are no longer under the schoolmaster.

These eight things show what the law is like. The law stirs up what is in me and brings it out.

When I was growing up, sometimes my mother would put things in the living room (we called it the "front room") and shut the door. Then she made a law and would say, "Now, you children, don't go into the front room today." We weren't even thinking about going into the front room—we were in the kitchen most of the time—but when mother said, "Don't go in there today," what do you think we did? The first chance we got, we went in there. Why? She made a law that said we couldn't, and that stirred up something in me and my brothers. What in the world does she have in there? It stirred up sin and disobedience in us.

Or suppose you have some cherries in your backyard, and you don't want the children passing by to pick them. They can't see the cherries. They're not even thinking of cherries. But if you make a law and put it on a sign in your yard—"Keep away from the cherries"—the moment they see that law, they want the cherries. The desire for cherries was dormant, but seeing the law put up on the front lawn brought this lust for cherries to life.

Man says, "I'm pretty good. I'll do everything God says to do." But the law says, "You shall not do this, and you shall not do that," and it stirs up sin which was dormant.

Let me give you three more characteristics of the law:

9. The law is not of faith (Galatians 3:12); it is contrary to faith. In the Old Testament, people were never saved by keeping the law (Romans 4:6-8). You have to turn from works and accept by faith what Christ has done. You can't have both faith and works. They just don't mix.

10. The law cannot justify, it cannot save (Romans 3:20). The law doesn't give you righteousness, it demands righteousness, and you haven't any at all. Your righteousness is in God's sight as filthy rags.
11. The law cannot give life (Galatians 3:21). When Christ died, He delivered us from the law. Now God is free to give eternal life to as many as will put their trust in him.

How can you and I help but fall in love with the Savior? He is the Savior not only from sin and from death, but also from the law. We now live unto God instead of unto sin or under the law. We are new people, new creatures in Christ, living unto God. Remember, God wants you to love the Savior with all your heart.

THE LAW CANNOT DELIVER FROM SIN (7:14-25)

Paul is not concerned with pardon or with salvation. That's already settled. He is dealing with deliverance from indwelling sin. In chapter 6, he tried to do it by keeping sin down; in chapter 7, he tries to do it by keeping the law. But the more he tries, the more he fails.

In verses 12 and 13, Paul vindicates the law. It is just, it is holy, it is good, it is spiritual, it came from God—but it cannot deliver. There's nothing wrong with the law—I don't throw the law out as being no good—but I cannot meet the law's demands. Neither can you nor anyone else. It was not given to save. It was not given to help you be good, but it demands that you be good. The law prescribes a holy walk, but it gives no power to do it. And here is the frustration of the quickened soul, desiring to be holy but unable to. He wants to please God, but the more he tries, the more he fails. The old nature is unable to overcome sin in the flesh. Nothing is wrong with the law; the trouble is with me.

> **7:14-17.** *For we know that the law is spiritual: but I am carnal, sold under sin. For that which I do I allow not: for what I would, that do I not; but what I hate,*

that do I. If then I do that which I would not, I consent unto the law that it is good. Now then it is no more I that do it, but sin that dwelleth in me.

Paul says, "I am carnal, sold under sin." In 1 Corinthians 2:14, he describes the natural man, the unsaved man, the unregenerate man who does not understand the Spirit of God. Then in the following chapter, the first four verses, he describes the carnal or worldly man. This man is a Christian who should grow but is not growing. At times he lives like the unsaved. He is living in the flesh. He loves the law, he wants to be holy, he wants to please God, but he finds that the more he tries the less he can do it. He is the Christian who has not experienced deliverance from the power of sin in his life. He can say:

7:18-23. *For I know that in me (that is, in my flesh,) dwelleth no good thing: for to will is present with me; but how to perform that which is good I find not. For the good that I would I do not: but the evil which I would not, that I do. Now if I do that I would not, it is no more I that do it, but sin that dwelleth in me. I find then a law, that, when I would do good, evil is present with me. For I delight in the law of God after the inward man: But I see another law in my members, warring against the law of my mind, and bringing me into captivity to the law of sin which is in my members.*

He is saying, "My body is full of lusts and desires. Oh, how I want to please God, but the more I seek to please Him, the more I fail. Am I really saved?"

Yes, thank God, you are not saved by what you do or don't do. You are saved by trusting the Savior. The more you read the Word of God, the more you want to please God. But if you try to please God in the energy of the flesh, you will fail to realize that in your flesh dwells no good thing. God has no confidence in the flesh, neither yours nor mine. Paul found that out; he speaks here from personal experience, I believe. He wants to please God in the flesh, but he finds he can't make the flesh behave. But we can get deliverance:

> **7:24.** *O wretched man that I am! who shall deliver me from the body of this death?*

This is a cry for help, a cry for a deliverer. How can I be free of this thing? Paul says, "Here I am living in a body that is full of desire. When I want to do the right thing, I do the bad thing. When I want to leave a thing alone, I can't do it." Sometimes we begin to wonder if there is any deliverance from indwelling sin for us. Is there any way we can keep our body from doing the things it does?

Let's be realistic about it. Don't try to live like an ascetic and then tell me, "I'm holy and I don't sin." I don't believe you. If you don't sin in action, you sin in your thoughts and words. All of us do. Of course, we can see the badness in the other fellow, but he sees the badness in us. We criticize each other, and we are both bad. Oh, how quick we are to judge the weakness and failure and frailty in some other Christian. And the world is quick to judge that sin in us.

So there is a yearning in my heart, and I try to make my body behave. I try to keep the lust down by keeping the law of God. The law says, "Don't do such-and-such," but I go ahead and do it, and the law says, "You must die." I'm living in a body of death—who will deliver me? The deliverance must come from the outside.

> **7:25.** *I thank God through Jesus Christ our Lord. So then with the mind I myself serve the law of God; but with the flesh the law of sin.*

Paul learned something. He learned that sin was dwelling in his body and that he was powerless against it. Is that your experience, my friend?

Notice something else. The sinful self was not the real self. The real self wanted God. The new man panted after God; the old man panted after sin.

Romans 7 is full of "I," "me," "mine," "what I can do," "what I hope to do," and "what I am trying to do." Here is a man who is trying to be holy and good without the power of the Holy Spirit. He is trying by his own strength to conquer frailty and weakness and failure in his life. He wants to please God and finds he can't do it.

But he learns something. He learns that sin is in his members. He learns that he is powerless against it. He learns that he has a new life patterned after God even though sin is in his members. And he learns that there is only One who can deliver him and that is Jesus Christ, the risen Son of God.

My friend, are you struggling? Are you discouraged?

You're trying to live for God and your life has been full of weakness and failure? Just turn the whole business over to the Savior. Say with Paul in chapter 8, "We are more than conquerors through him that loved us." Oh, when we stop our deadly doing and just trust the Lord Jesus, what wonderful things happen.

Isn't it wonderful to have a Savior who not only saves us from the penalty and guilt of sin, but a Savior who can deliver you and me daily from the power of sin and from the curse of a broken law?

Romans 8

Now we come to the crowning chapter of the book of Romans, a chapter where the Spirit of God is so evident and so available for God's people.

We've seen that our relation to the old life has been annulled by the death of Christ. In chapter 6, our relation to sin as a master was broken. In chapter 7, the death of Christ severed our relation to the law. Christ did a perfect work at the cross. When He died, we were identified with Him so that now a risen Christ in glory, not the law, is the rule of our life.

In Romans 7, the personal "I" was prominent; the Spirit wasn't even mentioned. Romans 8 is just the opposite. The Spirit of God is prominent, and the "I" is left out. In Romans 6, we had sanctification because of our union with Christ. In chapter 8, we have sanctification because of the indwelling Spirit. Instead of experiencing the weakness and defeat of chapter 7, we now have life and power and victory by the indwelling Spirit.

It is one thing to possess the Spirit of God—to have the Spirit of God indwelling you and me as believers—but it is an entirely different thing for us to use the vast resources God has given us. A great many Christians are ignorant of what they have. Hence, they're in bondage; they're full of fear; they don't experience that peace of God that passes understanding. So it's a wonderful thing to discover in this eighth chapter of Romans the marvel of what God has for us.

Let me first give you a telescopic view of the chapter. We are in a new position—we are in Christ. We have a new life experience in the power of the Spirit. We have a new deliverance, having been emancipated forever from the law of sin and death. We have a new place in which to live—in the Spirit. We have a new relationship—we are the sons of God. We have a new hope—we are going to be transformed and made just like Him. We have a new provision—we have two advocates, one in heaven and one on earth. And then we have the blueprint of God's purpose and plan for His people. No power on earth or in hell or even in heaven can destroy this wonderful union and relationship we have with our wonderful God. The chapter starts with "no condemnation" and ends with "no separation." I tell you, there is life and liberty and assurance as we read this blessed chapter.

IN CHRIST JESUS (8:1-39)

We Are in a New Position (8:1)

8:1. *There is therefore now no condemnation to them which are in Christ Jesus.*

The King James version adds "who walk not after the flesh, but after the Spirit." It repeats these words in verse 4. In the Greek text, these words occur only in the fourth verse. Freedom is not limited to the few who "walk not after the flesh, but after the Spirit." It is for any and every believer in Christ—strong ones, weak ones, spiritual ones, carnal ones. It's for every child of God. There is no condemnation, and the ground of this is two-fold.

The first ground is that *there is no condemnation because of what Jesus Christ did at the cross*. In John 5:24, Jesus said, "He that heareth my word, and believeth on him that sent me, hath everlasting life, and shall not come into condemnation [into judgment]; but is passed from death unto life." We have that in Romans 3:21 through 4:25. The question of judgment is past. Righteousness has become our portion. We have been redeemed, forgiven, cleansed, and pardoned (Romans 3:24; 2 Corinthians 5:21; Ephesians 1:7; Colossians 1:14; Hebrews 9:12, 26). The very evidence of our sin has been destroyed, and we stand before God in all the beauty and righteousness of Christ.

Just as it is impossible for the Lord Jesus Christ ever again to come into judgment because of sin—Christ risen from the dead is through with the sin question once for all forever (Hebrews 10:12)—so it is impossible for the believer to come under the judgment of God. We have been united to Christ. The sin question is settled.

The second ground is that *our union in Christ makes us free.* In chapter 6, He has delivered us from the power of sin. In chapter 8, He declares that He has delivered us from the judgment of sin. The apostle John writes in 1 John 4:17 that we "have boldness in the day of judgment: because as he is, so are we in this world."

I had been a Christian only a few weeks the first time I saw that verse. I was living in Calgary, Alberta, and I used to spend time with the wonderful Christian man I mentioned earlier, the bald-headed barber. I was in my room reading the Bible, and when I came across that verse, I jumped up and ran the three or four blocks to his barber shop. It was past closing time, so I knocked, and when he saw who it was, he opened the door and let me in. He was stropping his razor, about to give a fellow a shave. I said, "Listen to this," and read him the verse. He just kept on stropping his razor, as if to say, "Well, what of it?"

I said, "Man, don't you see it?"

And he said, "Oh, yes, I've known that for a long time."

"Do you mean to tell me that you've known this for a long time and didn't tell me?"

He kind of laughed and said, "Son, there are so many things in the Word of God that you've never seen; but as you grow in the grace of God, you'll come to them."

He pricked my bubble, to be frank with you. I sneaked out of the shop and went back to my room. I don't think he was wise in dealing with me like that because I was a babe in Christ and didn't know much. Instead of encouraging me, he discouraged me. Please don't discourage young believers. If they come to you full of joy because of some truth you've known for years, just nod your head and say, "That's wonderful! Isn't that wonderful? My, that's wonderful."

So in this first verse of Romans 8, we have a new position in Christ where there cannot be any condemnation. There wouldn't be any peace or joy if there was condemnation.

"Do you mean to tell me, Mr. Mitchell, that you are going to go into the presence of God without any fear of condemnation?"

That's correct.

"Do you mean that you will not come into judgment for sin?"

That's correct. Jesus Christ bore all my sin. By His death, Christ paid the wages for our sin; we go free. We are no longer under the power of sin and the bondage of death, we are under a new principle of operation.

We Have a New Deliverance (8:2-4)

Notice there are two laws in these verses:

> **8:2-4.** *For the law of the Spirit of life in Christ Jesus hath made me free from the law of sin and death. For what the law could not do, in that it was weak through the flesh, God sending his own Son in the likeness of sinful flesh, and for sin, condemned sin in the flesh: that the righteousness of the law might be fulfilled in us, who walk not after the flesh, but after the Spirit.*

Oh, what a wonderful, wonderful thing—no condemnation, never to come into judgment, and to be eternally free from the law of sin and death. Don't you revel in this wonderful fact? Christ did such a perfect work for you and for me that we come into His presence with no condemnation. No one is going to be able to produce any evidence in the presence of God that we were ever sinners. No wonder we sing, "Hallelujah! What a Savior!"

What a wonderful thing to know that you are saved and that you can come into the presence of God at any time and have fellowship with Him. Why don't you do that today? Read Romans 8, come into the presence of the Lord, and discuss the chapter with Him. Pour out your heart to Him. He just loves to have you come into His presence and talk to Him face to face. This is why He made you the way you are. He gave you the power to communicate with Him. Why don't you do it? Enjoy the Lord. Don't endure some "religion." Enjoy the Lord Himself, enjoy your salvation in Christ.

The law of the Spirit of life has delivered us, has emancipated us from the law of sin and death. We are now free to serve God. We are now free to live for Him, to live a new life for Him which we didn't have under the law. The law never supplied anyone with power to perform what it demanded. It demanded holiness, but it did not produce holiness. What the law could not do, God's Son did.

I remember an elderly woman who had been delivered out of a life of bondage to alcoholism. This dear woman didn't know much about theological training, but, believe me, she knew the Lord. In her testimony, she often paraphrased 2 Corinthians 5:21, "Jesus Christ who knew no sin was made sin for me who knew no righteousness, that I who knew no righteousness might be made the righteousness of God in Him."

This is what you have in Romans 8:3-4. He made provision not only to put away our sin but to destroy the power of sin so you and I could go free—in order that the very righteous requirement of the law might be fulfilled in us who do not live according to the flesh but according to the Spirit. Our Lord released us from the bondage, penalty, and guilt of sin. Sin has no more right to the Christian; it comes as a trespasser. The Savior bought us and set us free. And what is the result? The very righteous requirement of the law is fulfilled in us. In the power of the blessed Spirit of God who indwells us, each one of us can live the life that is pleasing to God.

We Have a New Place in Which to Live (8:5-13)

> **8:5-9.** *For they that are after the flesh do mind the things of the flesh; but they that are after the Spirit the things of the Spirit. For to be carnally minded is death; but to be spiritually minded is life and peace. Because the carnal mind is enmity against God: for it is not subject to the law of God, neither indeed can be. So then they that are in the flesh cannot please God. But ye are not in the flesh, but in the Spirit, if so be that the Spirit of God dwell in you. Now if any man have not the Spirit of Christ, he is none of his.*

In these verses, we have a contrast between living according to the flesh or living according to the Spirit. I believe we have two classes of people here. In Romans 7 we had two natures, the new nature that longs for God and the old nature that lusts after the flesh. Here we have the mind of the flesh and the mind of the Spirit. The mind of the flesh speaks of death, enmity, a life dominated by the flesh, the things the unregenerate nature prefers to God's will (1 Corinthians 2:14). In contrast, you have the mind of the Spirit, a life dominated by the Spirit and full of life and peace (v. 6).

Paul goes on to say in verses 7 and 8 that the mind of the flesh is hostile to God. It does not submit to the law of God, nor indeed can it. Those who are in the flesh cannot please God; it is a moral impossibility. The first few verses of Ephesians 2 tell us that at one time we lived to gratify the cravings of our flesh, following its lusts, and were by nature children of wrath. What could we do? We were incapable of submitting ourselves to God. Hence nothing but sovereign mercy could redeem us. You can't, my friend, so fix up the flesh that it is pleasing to God.

Now look at verse 9: "You are not in the flesh"—I'm not saying that, the Book says it—"but in the Spirit, if so be the Spirit of God dwell in you. Now if any man have not the Spirit of Christ, he is none of his." There are some who tell us that a person can be saved and not have the Holy Spirit. Some who have accepted the

Savior have been told to wait, to tarry until they receive the Spirit of God. They have agonized and done all kinds of things to try to make it happen. This is false doctrine. You cannot be saved and not have the Spirit of God. This verse says, "If any man have not the Spirit of Christ, he is none of his." My friend, the moment you accept the Savior the Spirit of God dwells in you, the Spirit of Christ dwells in you, the Holy Spirit dwells in you. These are used synonymously. The whole Godhead is not only *for* His people, but *in* His people.

The Lord Jesus is at the right hand of His Father. That's where His resurrected body is, and He is in us in the power and presence of the Holy Spirit. As Paul could say, "I no longer live, but Christ lives in me." If we do not have the Spirit of God, the Spirit of Christ, the Holy Spirit, we do not belong to Him.

> **8:10-11.** *And if Christ be in you, the body is dead because of sin; but the Spirit is life because of righteousness. But if the Spirit of him that raised up Jesus from the dead dwell in you, he that raised up Christ from the dead shall also quicken [make alive] your mortal bodies by his Spirit that dwelleth in you.*

If Christ is in you, your body is under the sentence of death because of sin. That's the present experience of Christians—if our Lord tarries, our bodies will die because they are not yet redeemed. Although sin is in the body, it ought not to control the body. The Spirit of God which indwells us should control our bodies.

If you have in you some things that are displeasing to the Lord, breaking your fellowship, affecting your testimony, then, my friend, come to the Lord and confess your sins. The Spirit of God will enable you to live the kind of Christian life that will glorify God. He is not going to force Himself. The question is, will you yield yourself to the Holy Spirit who indwells you? Galatians 5:25 says, "If we live in the Spirit, let us also walk in the Spirit." This is our responsibility—to walk in the Spirit. As I yield myself to the Spirit of God, then the righteousness of God is manifested in my life.

Though the body is under the sentence of death because of sin, a time is coming when our bodies are going to be transformed and freed from death. Already we Christians have in us the Spirit that is going to quicken, to transform our bodies. The Spirit of God will never leave us until our bodies are transformed and made like Christ's. We have the hope that one of these days, in God's own time, our bodies are going to be made alive (1 Thessalonians 4:13-17; 1 Corinthians 15:35-58). In fact, we are going to be just like God's Son; we are going to be like the Lord Jesus (Romans 8:29; 1 John 3:2). Oh, what a transformation!

If we already have in us the power of resurrection, the power of transformation, cannot that same Spirit who indwells us control us now? Can He not give us daily deliverance from the lusts of the flesh, the pride of life, the weakness of the body? It is up to us to yield ourselves to the Spirit who indwells us so that He will control these very bodies which are under the sentence of death. This is life in the Spirit.

> **8:12-13.** *Therefore, brethren, we are debtors, not to the flesh, to live after the flesh. For if ye live after the flesh, ye shall die: but if ye through the Spirit do mortify the deeds of the body, ye shall live.*

We owe the flesh nothing. Remember that. It was God who saved us, justified us, pronounced us righteous, freed us from the law of sin and death, freed us from Adam's race which is under death. He has freed us from the tyrant of sin as a master. He has freed us from the law with its bondage. My, what we owe God!

We are joined to the eternal Son of God. We have the hope of a body that is going to be changed, a body that is going to be fashioned like His glorious body. Wouldn't you like that to happen now? Wouldn't you like to have your body transformed and changed? If so, consider the second half of verse 13: "Mortify the deeds of the body." Hold your body under the sentence of death; put to death the deeds of the body. The body wants to do things that do not glorify God, things that dishonor Him and that hinder the work of the gospel in others' lives. Throw yourself upon God. Let the Spirit who lives in you live out His life in and through you. This is what He wants.

We Have a New Relationship (8:14-17)

8:14-15. *For as many as are led by the Spirit of God, they are the sons of God. For ye have not received the spirit of bondage again to fear; but ye have received the Spirit of adoption, whereby we cry, Abba, Father.*

The old race had nothing to give us. It had proved to be incurably bad. So what is God going to do? He is going to bring in something entirely new, a new race of people. "But as many as received him [Jesus Christ], to them gave he power to become the children of God, even to them that believe on his name: which were born, not of blood, nor of the will of the flesh, nor of the will of man, but of God" (John 1:12).

Is there any need for a new race? Why, of course. We just learned in verses 7 and 8 that the mind set on the flesh is hostile to God. Adam's race is in rebellion against God. Man has despised God's grace, spurned His love, killed His prophets, despised His Word, crucified His Son. Sin has ruined everything. What can God do? He is bringing into being a new race of people. So I read in verse 14, "As many as are led by the Spirit of God, they are the sons of God."

Paul talks about our position and our standing before God. We not only stand before Him as His children (Ephesians 1:5), but God also determined that we should be adopted into His family as sons (Galatians 4:5). It was by the Spirit of God through the Word of God that you became a child of God. The moment you and I accepted the Savior, we were led into the family of God, forgiven our sins, and declared righteous. Not only has He put us into a new family, having a new head, but He has delivered us from the tyranny of sin (Romans 6) and from the bondage of the law (Romans 7).

As you go about your business today, think of the dignity of it all. We are children of One who is God. We are members of an entirely new race. We are partakers of the divine nature, adopted, placed in the family of God as His sons. What a wonderful thing! Hence we can say, "Ye have not received the spirit of bondage again to fear; but ye have received the Spirit of adoption, whereby we cry, Abba, Father."

This is an amazing word, "Abba." If you were to go to the Near East today, whether it be Israel or the Arab world, you would notice that the children call their father "Abba." Here is a sweet relationship. Oh, the wonder of it—He is "Abba," He is my Father. Wouldn't it be a wonderful thing if today you could just lift up your heart to the eternal God and say, "Abba, Father," and then pour out your heart to Him just like a child pours out his heart to his mother or daddy? "You have loved me with an everlasting love. You are sufficient for my need. You have a tremendous interest in me. I am the object of your love."

Is it not a wonderful thing that God can take men and women like you and me, transform us into His children, and put us into a race of people, into a family where death never comes? Everyone in the family has eternal life. Why don't you come today and spend some time in the presence of your Father? Oh, the wonderful intimacy of relationship between the Father and His people.

I find in verse 16 that the Spirit of God Himself bears witness to this relationship:

> **8:16-17.** *The Spirit itself beareth witness with our spirit, that we are the children of God: and if children, then heirs; heirs of God, and joint-heirs with Christ; if so be that we suffer with him, that we may be also glorified together.*

The Spirit of God and the believer have been joined together in mutual love, in mutual life. Furthermore, not only are we brought into the family of God, but because of this relationship we share an inheritance with Him. We are joint heirs with Jesus Christ.

I question if our minds are able to comprehend the wealth of this truth. Hebrews 1:2 says that God speaks to us "in his Son, whom he hath appointed heir of all things." Jesus Christ is the heir of all things, on earth and in heaven. The whole universe belongs to Him, and I am a joint heir with Christ!

Oh, Christian friend, how rich we are. The riches of God—the riches of glory, as well as the riches of grace—are for His people. When we say, "I'm a child of God," I wonder if we realize for a moment what that means. It means we have come into a position far beyond angelic beings. We've come into a relationship that no other created intelligence has. We are the children of God, made in His image. He has redeemed us; He has bought us back to Himself; He has given to us life eternal and then said, "You are my children. You are my sons. You are joint heirs with the Son of God." Oh, the wonder of this!

Too many of us Christians, with all the wealth we have in Christ, are living like paupers. Oh, that we might live in the goodness of this marvelous relationship. We are the sons of God. We may not be recognized by the world, but one of these days we will be recognized by all created intelligences in heaven and earth. God is going to put you and me on display and say to the myriads of angelic beings, principalities and powers, and nations of the earth, "These are my sons; these are my children."

A preacher once told me that you are not a joint heir with Christ unless you suffer with Him. I want you to mark this: Inheritance is not based on suffering. Inheritance is based on relationship. It's true in the human family, and it's true in God's family. We are joint heirs with Christ because we are His children.

It is suffering and glory that go together. Second Timothy 2:12 says, "If we suffer with him, we shall also reign with him." Relationship and inheritance go together. Suffering and glory go together.

WE HAVE A NEW HOPE (8:18-25)

There is a certain sense in which all the people of God are going to be glorified together with Christ. Colossians 3:4 says,

"When Christ who is our life shall appear, then shall we also appear with him in glory." That's true of all believers. But whenever Paul speaks of the sufferings of God's people, he always brings in the glory. He wants to encourage us even though we suffer for the Savior to remember that God takes thought of everything.

> **8:18.** *For I reckon that the sufferings of this present time are not worthy to be compared with the glory which shall be revealed in us.*

The end of verse 17 opens the door for the hope we have (vv. 18-25). We have no hope in the flesh. It's incurably bad. Therefore, we live in the Spirit and walk by the Spirit so that His character and His love and His compassion will be revealed through us. This may bring us suffering and opposition of one sort or another—in the first century it often meant martyrdom—but, in view of the glory, we can consider our present sufferings not worthy to be compared with the glory that will be revealed in us. We don't judge life in the light of the present twenty-four hours. We judge it in the light of eternity. This is our new hope.

It's a wonderful thing to be a Christian. Don't hang your head down, my friend. Lift it up. You are a child of One who is God. And the sufferings of this present time are not even worth talking about when you think of the glory that shall be revealed in you and me in that day. We have a guarantee not only of an inheritance but of the glory we will know in Christ Jesus. Who would turn down such a Savior? Who would be indifferent to such a Lord? I plead with you, live as the child of One who is God.

This hope deals not only with the believer, but it also deals with all creation. There is hope for creation.

> **8:19-22.** *For the earnest expectation of the [creation] waiteth for the manifestation of the sons of God. For the [creation] was made subject to vanity, not willingly, but by reason of him who hath subjected the same in*

> *hope, because the [creation] itself also shall be deliv-*
> *ered from the bondage of corruption into the glorious*
> *liberty of the children of God. For we know that the*
> *whole creation groaneth and travaileth in pain together*
> *until now.*

The creation is eagerly waiting for the unveiling of the sons of God. All creation is waiting for the day when you and I who believe in the Lord Jesus Christ will be manifested before it. There is nothing of that now, but just you wait! We have not yet seen what God intends creation to be. But He has a plan, He has a purpose, and He has a hope for creation.

This old earth and all creation is groaning, groaning because of man's sin. When man sinned, he not only dragged the human family into bondage, but he also dragged the creation with him. Not only are men and women experiencing the fruits of sin, but the very earth upon which we walk is suffering from it. When God said, "Cursed is the ground for man's sake," what did it give forth? Weeds, weeds, and more weeds. We use all kinds of chemicals to control bugs and plant diseases. The curse of sin is not only on the human race, it is also on the earth. My friend, you can't account for the disharmony in creation in any other way.

You fly over our forests and everywhere you see the curse of man. Everything he touches, he ruins. Thank God, a day is coming when the ground is going to be delivered from the curse. A day is coming when the animal creation is going to be freed from the curse. And not only they, but we too.

> **8:23-24a.** *And not only they, but ourselves also, which*
> *have the firstfruits of the Spirit, even we ourselves*
> *groan within ourselves, waiting for the adoption, to*
> *wit, the redemption of our body. For we are saved by*
> *hope . . .*

In verses 23-25, we believers have hope, the animal creation has hope, the ground has hope. We enjoy the liberty of grace now, but all heaven and earth is waiting for our complete redemption. Oh, how much hinges upon God's purpose in the church. Did you ever think of it? The whole universe waits for the manifestation of the children of God. It is waiting for the full redemption of the believer. We are not known now as the children of God, but I tell you, we will be when we get our glorified bodies. We are waiting for that day when the dead in Christ shall be raised and when we together with them shall be reunited and caught up to meet the Lord in the air. What a prospect! What a hope!

The creation has hope, the believer has hope, but the unbeliever has no hope. The only place in God's universe where there is no hope is among unbelievers here on earth. This just about breaks a person's heart when you think of it. The human family is the only place where there is any question mark about who Jesus is, for the angels, even the fallen angels, know who He is.

So, who has hope?

The earth has hope. The desert is going to blossom like a rose. The curse is going to be removed, and the earth is going to give forth its increase. We have never seen the earth give forth its full increase. By our scientific research, we have been able to increase the productivity of our land, but we haven't begun to see what God will do when the curse is removed from the earth.

The animal creation has hope. In Isaiah 11:6-9 and 65:25, the lion will lie down with the lamb, the bear will lie down with the kid, and a child will play with a viper. There will be nothing to hurt or to mar in all the holy mountain of God. The Book of Joel, the book of the Day of the Lord, tells us what God is going to do in the millennial kingdom. In that time the animal creation, as well as the earth, is going to be removed from the curse.

The believer in Christ has hope. This is what Paul says in verses 23-24. A day is coming when our bodies will be redeemed from the curse and bondage of sin. Romans 13:11 says, "It is high time to awake out of sleep, for your salvation is nearer than when we believed."

"Why, I thought we were already saved," you say.

Yes, we were saved when we believed in Christ. The Lord saved us and we are being saved and we are yet to be saved. The time is still coming when our bodies will be delivered from sin and death (1 Corinthians 15:51-54; Philippians 3:20-21; 1 Thessalonians 5:23-24; 1 Peter 1:5).

Our inheritance is eternal, our redemption is eternal, our life is eternal, and our family is eternal. Everything that God gives to us, my friend, is eternal. We belong to an eternal family if we have taken Jesus Christ as our Savior. We are now the children of God and we partake of what our Father has. It is a wonderful thing!

8:24-25. *For we are saved by hope: but hope that is seen is not hope: for what a man seeth, why doth he yet hope for? But if we hope for that we see not, then do we with patience wait for it.*

When we receive what we hope for, we no longer have hope; when we receive our new bodies, we no longer hope for them.

If I were to ask you, are you saved by hope, I think many of you would say, "No, I am saved by grace" or "I am saved by faith." That's true, but we are also saved by hope. The base of our salvation is His grace (Ephesians 2:8-9), and we receive our salvation by faith (Romans 5:1). But we are also saved by hope, and this is the completion of our salvation that takes in the body.

We are saved by grace! Saved by faith! Saved by hope! God starts salvation, continues it, and completes it. We've been saved from the penalty and guilt of sin, we're being daily saved from the power of sin, and we are yet to be saved from the presence of sin.

Only Christians have a hope like that. The philosophies of men give you no hope. How wonderful that God has given us a message, a gospel that brings us real, down-deep hope. As Peter could say in 1 Peter 1:3, "Blessed be the God and Father of our Lord Jesus Christ, who according to his abundant mercy hath begotten us again unto a living hope by the resurrection of Jesus Christ from the dead."

We Have a New Provision (8:26-30)

> **8:26-28.** *Likewise the Spirit also helpeth our infirmities: for we know not what we should pray for as we ought: but the Spirit itself maketh intercession for us with groanings which cannot be uttered. And he that searcheth the hearts knoweth what is the mind of the Spirit, because he maketh intercession for the saints according to the will of God. And we know that all things work together for good to them that love God, to them who are the called according to his purpose.*

We do not know how to pray, but the Spirit knows how to pray (8:26-27). That always staggers me. How many Christians today know how to pray? (And I speak to myself as well as to you.) We all know something about praying. We've all heard sermons and Bible readings and exhortations on prayer, but how many of us pray? I recommend you get that little book by E. M. Bounds, *Power Through Prayer*. It will stir your heart to pray. The Spirit of God will stir you up.

Get down and pray, and if you can't pray, let the Spirit of God pray through you. Read your Bible and let the Lord talk to you and you will soon be praying. The Spirit of God pleads; He intercedes for us. You remember Ephesians 6:18, "Praying always with all prayer and supplication in the Spirit, and watching thereunto with all perseverance and supplication for all saints." The Spirit of God is in us taking care of God's interests down here.

God has a tremendous interest in every believer, even the weakest believer. Do you think He will leave us alone and let the world take its venom out on us? Oh, no! Do you think God is going to trust us to keep ourselves? He couldn't do it. What does He do? The Spirit of God comes to indwell us and to take care of His interests. We don't know how to pray, but the Spirit of God makes intercession for you and me with groanings that can't be uttered.

But mark something else in verse 27. The Lord Jesus also is praying for us. He is making intercession for us according to the will of God. I have a great interest in heaven, and my Savior is taking care of my interests up there. God is leaving nothing to chance. He is leaving nothing, my friend, for you and me to work out. Hebrews 9:24 says, "He now appears in the presence of God for us," and 1 John 2:1 tells us that He is our advocate before the Father. The Savior never gets tired of praying for us.

What a wonderful thing! The Spirit of God in you and me is praying for us, representing God to us, taking care of God's interests in us, and sealing us for the day of redemption. He'll never leave us. And Jesus, too, is pleading our cause before the Father. Oh, the wonderful provision God has made for us. Our Savior never leaves us for a minute, and He guarantees that we shall stand in the Father's presence just like Himself.

Just look at the amazing truths in this chapter. We are in Christ Jesus. We have been delivered from the law of sin and death. We are living in a new place in the Holy Spirit. We have a new relationship as the children of God, the sons of God, the heirs of God, having an inheritance in Him. And then we have a new hope—He guarantees our bodies are going to be redeemed because the salvation we have is a complete salvation (spirit, soul, and body). God will never be satisfied with you or me until we stand in His presence, conformed to the image of His Son. Our salvation starts in God, is continued by God, and is going to be completed by God.

It's no use my reveling in the fact that I am a child of one who is God if I do not seek to please Him and if I do not seek to come into His presence to spend time with Him. I must read the Word of God and know what His purpose is for the church and for me individually.

Christian friend, you are in God's hand, you are in His family. You are His child, His heir. And don't revel in that without realizing that, as a member of God's family, you come under His discipline (Hebrews 12). Sometimes the discipline is hard, but it always produces something. We are tested and tried, not to be destroyed but to be purified so we will be to the praise of the glory of His grace.

All things work together for good (8:28). It's a good thing to know that "all things work together for good," but oftentimes I think Christians quote this verse a little too glibly. Let's remember that this is a tremendous affirmation. We've seen our sonship, our future glory, His care for us, and now we affirm that the million details that come into our life are all for our good—the heartaches, the sorrows, the joys—and work together for our good because we love God.

"Do you mean to tell me he knows all about every little detail of my life?"

Of course He does. Doesn't Job say that God numbers our steps and bottles our tears. He counts the hairs of our head. He knows all about you and me. There is not a detail of our lives He doesn't know about. And every part of our experience is working together for our good and God's glory. I want you to think about that.

I like hot biscuits and honey, don't you? But I wouldn't want to take a spoonful of flour or salt or yeast or baking soda—whatever you use to make biscuits—and put it in my mouth, and you wouldn't want to either. But you put them together and cook them a wee bit and you get hot, luscious biscuits.

Friend, don't take one little detail of your life and let that discourage you. The Lord knows how much is good for you. I may not understand everything that comes into my life, but I know that God, in His wonderful grace and love, can take the most outlandish things, the finest detail or the greatest sorrow and suffering, and make that work together for my good and for His glory. He has me on His heart, and if I murmur against circumstances, I am actually murmuring against God. In fact, I have heard Christians blame God for certain things. Don't blame God. We are His workmanship, and He never stops loving us and conforming us to the image of the Savior.

For whom is this? The verse goes on, "To them who are the called according to his purpose." And who are the ones who are called according to His purpose? Those who love God, those who are trusting the Savior. This is a fact; it is not an experience only.

Ephesians 1:11 says He works "all things after the counsel of his own will."

Our hindsight is often pretty good. When we look back over our life and recall certain experiences, we can often see how God used those for our good. We didn't enjoy what we went through at the time, but now we thank the Lord for them because it was through those things that He brought eternal glory to Himself and blessed His people.

The extent of God's purpose (8:29-31a):

> **8:29-31a.** *For whom he did foreknow, he also did predestinate to be conformed to the image of his Son, that he might be the firstborn among many brethren. Moreover whom he did predestinate, them he also called: and whom he called, them he also justified: and whom he justified, them he also glorified. What shall we then say to these things?*

When you are going to build a house, you don't just go out and build it. You call an architect, you buy plans, or you draw plans yourself. A person doesn't build a house without some idea of what he is going to build.

God has an eternal purpose that He is working out, and we who are Christians and who love the Lord are a distinct part of that purpose. We see in these verses the blueprint of just what God is going to do with us, the church of Christ. He does not reveal His purpose until He has a people redeemed and justified and united to Himself, a people who love Him, a people who are in His family and who are in the care of the Spirit of God. Now, having this people, He begins to open His heart and reveal His sovereign purpose to us. He is not doing things by happenstance. He doesn't do things on the spur of the moment. Way back, God purposed that certain things would take place.

Isaiah tells us, "The Lord of hosts hath sworn, saying, Surely as

I have thought, so shall it come to pass; and as I have purposed, so shall it stand. . . . For the Lord of hosts hath purposed, and who shall disannul it? and his hand is stretched out, and who shall turn it back?" (14:24, 27).

God is sovereign. He does what He wants to do, and none can change His purpose or hinder Him in the completion of that purpose. He never starts something He doesn't finish.

You don't have to look far to see where men start things and don't finish them. We start a project and somebody else has to finish it. God never starts a work He doesn't finish. The moment you accept the Lord Jesus Christ as your Savior, God has already started a work in you to bring you to Himself, and He will not be through with you until you are conformed to the image of His Son. You are going to stand before God holy and without blame.

Ephesians 1:4 says we were chosen in Christ before the foundation of the world to be holy and without blemish, and in chapter 2 of the same epistle, Paul writes, "That in the ages to come he might show the exceeding riches of his grace and his kindness toward us through Christ Jesus." Here you have an eternal picture of the purpose of God for you and me. He chose us in Christ to be holy and without blame. When? Before the foundation of the world. Why? That in the ages to come, He might put you and me on exhibition, if you please, to show forth the incomparable riches of His grace expressed in His kindness to us in Christ Jesus.

God doesn't say much about eternity for His people, but what He has intimated is beyond all human comprehension. If any of us were ushered into the presence of God the way we are, apart from what we are in Christ, I question if we could stand it for one second. So God begins to prepare us. He begins to loosen our feet from this old world.

Having been a pastor for a great many years, I have been privileged to be with some of God's dear saints when they have left this world. They tell me, "Dear Brother Mitchell, please don't pray for me to stay here. I just want to go home." God's purpose for them on earth is finished, and God has taken out of their hearts any desire for things down here. They have a little glimpse of the glory, and they can hardly wait to get home.

I don't know when God wants to call me home, but I know He numbers my steps and He bottles my tears and my times are in His hands.

God is on the job day and night. He never leaves us. He never forsakes us. He has made us the object of His love and affection. He is working out His divine plan and purpose, and none can say to Him, "What doest Thou?" God has a purpose in your life and my life. So we can say in verse 28, "Everything works together for good." Everything! The blessings and the trials and the tests and the sorrows and the joys, all the details that come into your life, "everything works together for good." We are in the hands of the omnipotent, sovereign God, and no power in heaven, earth, or hell can change His purpose for us.

Friend, today you have disappointments. You have failures, weakness, tests. You wish you were living someplace else. You wish you had a different job. You wish you lived in a different neighborhood. You wish this and you wish that. Ah, listen. The Lord has put you right where you are because He is working out something in your life. In His own good time—and He is always on time—He works things out after the counsel of His own will.

Sometimes God has to hedge us in to get us to do what He wants us to do. My, how stubborn we are, how we want our own way, how willful we can get. And so the Lord, in His wonderful love for us—that blessed unchanging love—puts things into our lives to hedge us in. Sometimes the things He hedges us in with are not very pleasant, but He does it because He loves us, because He is working out a purpose.

Just think of it! "He predestined us to be conformed to the image of his Son." My friend, go look in the mirror. Thank God for His grace and say, "All right, that's the way I look now; but just wait until God gets through with me." The eternal sovereign God has purposed that I'm going to be just like Jesus, His wonderful Son.

When I look at God's people, I say, "Well, that hasn't taken place yet!" That's true in our experience, but I'm just as sure as God is on the throne, just as sure as God is sovereign, the Lord of lords and King of kings, the almighty God, the One who holds the keys of death and of hell, that He is going to work it all out. And when He gets through with you and me, we are going to be just like the Savior.

Isn't that a wonderful prospect? Live in the joy of that instead of growling over your tests and trials. Say, "Praise the Lord, He is using this to make me just like the Lord Jesus."

When we stand in the presence of God, we are not going to be strangers. Did you ever go to some part of the country where you didn't know anybody and you were alone. It's an awful feeling. Or you've gone to some foreign country where you couldn't communicate with anyone. It's a terrible feeling when you are not known. But it's a wonderful thing to come into the presence of God in eternal glory and be known. He will know me and I will know Him. I shall see God, and behold, He is not a stranger. God has determined that we shall be conformed to the image of His Son.

Do you know He is already on that job, and He is doing that work now? This work of transformation has already begun. He not only took us out of the kingdom of darkness and put us in the kingdom of His Son, but 2 Corinthians 3:18 says, "We all, with open face beholding as in a glass the glory of the Lord, *are changed* into the same image from glory to glory, even as by the Spirit of the Lord."

Oh, that our hunger for God may be increased and our hearts may be opened to see, to receive, to rejoice in a God who is faithful and who will do exactly what He says. He didn't call us to go to heaven, He called us to be like His Son. He didn't predestine us to go to heaven, He predestined us to be conformed to the image of His Son. And it's going to be a permanent likeness.

We have been joined to the eternal Son of God. We are members of an eternal family where everyone is going to stand before God absolutely perfect and complete and like the Son of God.

This is God's determination. This is God's purpose and program for everyone who receives His Son. Think of it! We are cleared of every charge, declared righteous, given the blessed hope and, God says, glorified. This is His purpose for His people. As far as God is concerned, it is a finished transaction. And we demonstrate our faith in what He has done and what He is doing and what He is going to do by our obedience, by our love for Him.

My, what a privilege that you and I should become the children of God.

The Summing Up (8:31-39)

8:31-32. *What shall we then say to these things? If God be for us, who can be against us? He that spared not his own Son, but delivered him up for us all, how shall he not with him also freely give us all things?*

Before we discuss the marvelous conclusion to this chapter, let's quickly review where we've been. God takes man in chapters 1-3 and proves him absolutely unrighteous with none doing good. Then He reveals to us the wonderful provision of God who takes sinners who receive His Son and forgives their sins. He pronounces them righteous. He frees them from the bondage of death, from the mastery of sin, from the bondage of the law. He puts them in His Son, Christ Jesus. He indwells them by His Spirit, calls them to be His sons and heirs, gives them the hope of a new body transformed like the body of His Son. And then He provides two Advocates, one in heaven and one on earth—the Lord in heaven, taking care of our interests there; the Spirit in us, taking care of His interests here. God leaves nothing to chance; He does not trust the flesh to do anything. We also discovered God's blueprint, His purpose that we shall be conformed to the image of His Son. So far as God is concerned, we are already glorified.

These are the facts. Because the eternal Sovereign God declares that they are true, we can look forward with expectancy to our experiencing what He has purposed.

It's wonderful to be a Christian. It's wonderful to belong to the Savior. We are bound not only for heaven, but we are going to be conformed to the image of Jesus Christ and to be numbered among those with whom God is going to have eternal, unbroken fellowship through the countless ages of eternity. And we are going to display the grace of God and the wisdom of God to the whole universe. What are you going to say to these things? What can you say except "Amen," so let it be.

God carries out a perfect salvation, from condemnation to glorification. Who does it? God does it. The opposition doesn't even count. Who can be against us? Well, who can? God is for us and who will oppose or destroy the purpose of God? "He that spared not his own Son, but delivered him up for us all, how shall he not with him also freely give us all things?" Having given to us His Son, what else can He give us? He won't withhold anything from us.

I don't think the human mind can really get hold of this. In 2 Peter 2:4 we read that "God spared not the angels that sinned." I can understand that. And God spared not the world in Noah's day. I can understand that because the thoughts and the imaginations of the heart of man are evil continually. And God spared not Sodom and Gomorrah. I can understand that because of their gross immorality. I can understand all those things, but how do you account for God's not sparing His Son?

God didn't send an angel. He didn't send an archangel. He didn't send some good man. He sent His only begotten Son, who took my place. The judgment of God that should have fallen on you and me fell on Him. When Jesus took our place at the cross of Calvary, all the law of God could do was to curse Him.

I am not surprised that the Lord Jesus cried out, "My God, my God, why hast thou forsaken me?" Did you ever think of it? He spared not His Son. God went to the limit in giving up His Son at frightful cost. He could go no further. He gave heaven's best. What for? To redeem you and me.

Oh, listen, Christian friend, why don't we fall in love with God's Son? Why don't we love Him more? We take so much for granted. We talk so glibly about being Christians and about going to heaven. What about your daily experience in magnifying Christ among men?

Will you please, sometime today, meditate on this? God loved you so much that He spared not His only begotten Son. All the judgment, all the wrath of God that should have fallen on you and me fell upon Him; and no human mind can begin to explain or to express what the Son of God went through when He went to the cross. No wonder in the Garden of Gethsemane He cried out, "Father, if it is possible, let this cup pass from me." No wonder He cried out, "Now is my soul exceeding troubled, even unto death." No wonder He said, "Father, what shall I say? Deliver me from this hour? For this cause came I to this hour."

Did you ever think of it? Just meditate on the price God paid to redeem you and to redeem me. I just don't find the words to express this amazing truth.

When you have the Lord Jesus Christ, you have everything. Every once in a while, someone tells me I should have this experience or that experience or some other experience. As wonderful as those experiences may be, I have Jesus Christ and you can't add anything to Him. I have everything in Him, and thank God, the day is coming when through eternity I'll continually be experiencing what I have in Him. These are eternal things.

"If God be for us, who can be against us?" There is not a created intelligence in the whole universe that can thwart the purpose of God in His Son and in His people. There is not a created intelligence in the universe that is going to prevent every believer, the weakest as well as the strongest, from being glorified with all the glory of the eternal God. My, what a salvation is this! What a Savior is this!

8:33. *Who shall lay any thing to the charge of God's elect? It is God that justifieth.*

Who can charge anything to any of God's people when God says they are righteous? To charge us is to impeach the Judge who has cleared us of every charge. The evidence of all our sins has been destroyed. He has pronounced us righteous, and whoever brings a charge against us has to reckon with God. I say again, the opposition counts for nothing.

8:34a. *Who is he that condemneth?*

Who can? No angel can. No man can. No demon can. Satan can't. No one—no one in the universe can come before God and condemn us when God has pronounced us righteous. This, too, is an amazing thing.

There are two things that break my heart. First, Christians have so little knowledge of the wonderful salvation we have in Christ, of the wonderful Savior we have and of all that God has done for us. All that God is, all that God has is for His people. So many of God's people know so little of this union with the living God and what it means.

The other thing that breaks my heart is that there are so many wonderful people who have spurned the Savior or at best are indifferent to Him, coldly indifferent. It isn't that they oppose the gospel, they are just indifferent to it.

Like one man said, "Dr. Mitchell, I don't need Jesus Christ. I have all I need." But that man will have to stand before God, and He will be either His Savior or His Judge. Each one must decide what he is going to do with God's Son. He has said, "Come unto me, and I will give you rest." "He that cometh to me, I will in no wise cast out." "To as many as received him, to them he gives the right to become the children of God." Oh, why won't they receive Him as their Savior?

Christian friend, why don't you fall in love with your Savior? Oh, what that would mean to Him and what it would mean to you. God grant that our vision of Christ may be enlarged so that we will fall in love with Him.

8:34. *Who is he that condemneth? It is Christ that died, yea rather, that is risen again, who is even at the right hand of God, who also maketh intercession for us.*

We have four remarkable things in this verse. First, Christ died. That means the sin question was settled and we have been pronounced righteous before God.

Second, He is "risen again" from the dead; He is no longer in the tomb. When Christ rose from the dead, He had already defeated Satan and put away sin and death and the grave. And when you and I took the Lord Jesus as Savior, we were not only declared righteous (having our sin question settled), but we were identified with this risen, glorious Savior. Through the death and resurrection of Christ, our relation to the old Adam was severed, our relation to sin as a master was severed, our relation to the law and its bondage was severed. We were joined to the One who came forth in resurrection. We became new creatures. We received a new life. We are in only one place—in Christ Jesus. What a marvelous thing!

Third, Christ "is even at the right hand of God." Do you need any help in the court of God? Our Lord is there. The One to whom you have been joined is there. He represents us (Hebrews 9:24), and if any one were to condemn us before God, all the Father needs to say is, "Do you find any fault with my Son?" No. "These are in my Son." What a wonderful thing to be in Christ, saved, righteous, fitted, glorified in Him.

Fourth, Christ "also maketh intercession for us." He is not only representing us, but He is our High Priest, interceding for us in our frailty. We are still down here in weakness. That's why Christ "was made like unto his brethren that He might be a merciful and faithful high priest in things pertaining to God" (Hebrews 2:17). He is our Intercessor, He is our Advocate, He is our Mediator. He is the One who is praying for us (John 17; 1 John 2).

You may be one of God's weakest children, but if you mean business and you have taken Him as your Savior, my friend, you have in the presence of God One who not only prays for you, but you have One who pleads your cause, One who represents you. God has left nothing to chance, has He? We have justification, identification, representation, and intercession here. What more can God do for you and me? Well, He is not through yet.

8:35-39. *Who shall separate us from the love of Christ? shall tribulation, or distress, or persecution, or famine, or nakedness, or peril, or sword? As it is written, For thy sake we are killed all the day long; we are accounted as sheep for the slaughter. Nay, in all these things we are more than conquerors through him that loved us. For I am persuaded, that neither death, nor life, nor angels, nor principalities, nor powers, nor things present, nor things to come, nor height, nor depth, nor any other creature, shall be able to separate us from the love of God, which is in Christ Jesus our Lord.*

Nothing is left out. No circumstance on earth can separate us from God's love which is in Christ Jesus our Lord. Nothing in God's universe can separate us from Him. Nothing affects His love for us or toward us. At times circumstances may indicate that God has forgotten us, but He hasn't. There is nothing, nothing, nothing in this whole wide universe that can separate us from the One who loves us with an everlasting love.

Paul adds, "We are counted as sheep for the slaughter" and we are "more than conquerors." Sheep for slaughter and yet more than conquerors? Yes, the Son of God cannot be conquered. And where are we? In the Son of God. He has guaranteed victory.

Oh, do you see the impossibility of separation? Think of every conceivable adversary in the universe, and not one of them can separate you from the love of God which is in Christ Jesus our Lord. Death doesn't separate you from Him—death may separate you from your loved ones but not from Him—and nothing in life will separate you from Him. He loves us in death, and He loves us in life with all its successes, with all its failures, with all its tests, with all its sorrows, with all its circumstances.

Things present, things future, things known, things unknown, things above, things beneath—you name it, my friend, there is not a thing, not a created intelligence in the universe that can separate you from the love of God which is in Christ Jesus our Lord. God gave us His Son and He gave Him to us in love.

After all that's been said in these first eight chapters of Romans, the only logical thing for you and me to do is to turn our lives over to Him that He might be glorified in and through us here on earth (Romans 12:1-2). Is that asking too much? He gave heaven's best—He spared not His own Son—and with Him God has given us everything. Can't we give ourselves now over to Him so that He might be all in all in our lives?

You say that means dedication. That's exactly what it means. You dedicate yourself and He will consecrate you and set you apart that you might be to the glory of His Son.

> *Father, I pray that You will take these amazing lessons in the Book of Romans and make them a living reality in the heart and life of everyone who has been reading this. Oh, that those of us who are Christians might give ourselves wholly to You, the Living God, and our wonderful Savior.*
>
> *And Father, should there be an unsaved one who has read this far, may he or she come into this wonderful place of accepting Jesus Christ as Savior, and be numbered among those who shall stand in your presence, conformed to the image of our Lord Jesus Christ.*
>
> *Grant this . . . for His Name's sake.*

Romans 9

The first eight chapters of Romans deal with the wonderful grace of God. We've seen in chapters 1-3 how God can take men who are unrighteous and who are away from Him and bring them to Himself through the blood of Christ. They have accepted the Lord Jesus Christ as Savior. They have been redeemed. They have been forgiven every trespass. They are covered with all the righteousness of the Son of God. They have been joined to Him, identified with Him not only in His death and burial but in His resurrection. Through that death, God has severed the relationship of the believer to sin as a master and to the law with its bondage. He has put us in Christ who made us members of His family and who represents us before God. We end up in chapter 8 where no one can condemn, no one can bring any charge against God's people, and nothing in this wide universe can separate us from the love of God which is in Christ Jesus our Lord.

What a tremendous transformation! That's why, when we come to Romans 12, Paul beseeches you and me, in view of God's mercy, to present our bodies as living sacrifices, wholly acceptable to God, which is our reasonable service.

GOD IS RIGHTEOUS IN HIS DEALINGS WITH ISRAEL
9:1-11:36

Between chapters 8 and 12, however, the question is raised, "Is God righteous in His dealings with the people of Israel?"

You remember at the end of chapter 2, after Paul said that a Gentile who is uncircumcised can be justified in the sight of God yet a Jew who has been circumcised may be lost, he asks, "What is the advantage of being a Jew?" (3:1). Paul answers that God gave the Jewish people the Word of God, the revelation concerning Himself; God called the nation to witness to the Gentile nations of the oneness of God; and God called the nation to be the family through whom Messiah should come. That's the three-fold purpose for which God chose the nation Israel. So Israel has a tremendous place in the purpose and program of God for the earth.

GOD IS RIGHTEOUS IN ELECTING GRACE (9:1-33)

Was God righteous in choosing Israel to be His witness to the nations? Was God righteous in giving His truth to Israel, making it the depository of His Word? Why, of course. There is nothing wrong with that. God had a right to do that if He wanted to. He had a right to say through what people His Son should come into the human race. This is the subject of Romans 9. In chapter 10, you have God righteous in disciplining Israel. He chose the Jews to be His witnesses, and they failed the job. When you come to chapter 11, you have God righteous in restoring the nation Israel to its place of privilege in the fulfillment of prophecy.

All the promises of God for Israel will be fulfilled. Some believe that God is through with Israel and that all the blessings He promised in the Old Testament to Israel are going to be given to the church. But I say very bluntly, the church is not Israel and Israel is not the church. They are two entirely different companies of people. If you want to know God's purpose for the church, you have to go to Ephesians and Philippians and Colossians. Romans 9-11 is dealing with what God is doing with the nation Israel.

One of the tragedies through the centuries has been that the church has taken the promises of God to the nation Israel and tried to apply them to itself. God has not given the church any worldly ambition or any earthly inheritance. Our Lord said in John 16, "In the world you shall have tribulation; in me you shall have peace." The promises of God to the church are entirely different from the promises of God to Israel. Unless we see that, we are going to take the promises of God to Israel and try to work them through the church, and we will be neither fish nor fowl. We will have ruined the heavenly promises for us and destroyed the earthly promises for Israel.

When God deals with the nation Israel, He deals with the nations of the earth. Today, He is not dealing with the nations, He is dealing with individuals. He is gathering out a people for His name, made up of Jews and Gentiles. When God begins to deal with the nations, He is going to deal in righteousness and in judgment. In fact, the nations of the earth will never know righteousness except through the judgment of God (Isaiah 26:9).

For nineteen hundred years, the Jews have been a scattered people. They have been the butt of abuse and scorn and ridicule and persecution and martyrdom. In December 1947, they again became a nation, but they are still the object of persecution and trouble.

Why has God permitted this if they are His people? And why has the gospel gone out to the Gentiles? Why did God scatter the Jewish people to one side and pick up the Gentiles and form a new thing called the church? The much misunderstood answer is in these three chapters.

Paul's Great Desire (9:1-3)

> **9:1-3.** *I say the truth in Christ, I lie not, my conscience also bearing me witness in the Holy [Spirit], that I have great heaviness and continual sorrow in my heart.*

For I could wish that myself were accursed from Christ
for my brethren, my kinsmen according to the flesh.

Paul is not writing as one who hates Israel but as one who loves his people. He writes with a heavy heart.

It is easy for us to stand to one side and see what the apostle experienced and to have none of it in our own hearts. But if we glory in the truth of the first eight chapters of Romans and yet have no burden for those on the outside of the truth of God, then we have missed out entirely. The truth of Romans 8 has never gripped our heart. The more we see of the glories we have in Christ and of our position in Him, the more there should be a yearning in our souls for men and women who are outside of Christ. If the one is real in our hearts, the other will be the evidence of it. If there is no evidence of love for souls, then we have to question the reality of our faith.

The Jews were religious, they were moral, they searched the Scriptures; but they were not saved, and their unbelief greatly distressed Paul. Therefore, he stands before God with his heart laid bare and calls on God to be his witness to the sorrow and anguish he feels for Israel. (When a person calls God to be his witness, he better be speaking the truth, don't you think?) Paul has just said in chapter 8 that nothing can separate us from the love of God. Yet, he says here, "I have come to the place where I would be willing to be separated from Him if by so doing, my brethren, my kinsmen might be saved."

Isn't it strange that in the experience of one man there could be these two extremes? In chapter 8, he is full of ecstasy and wonder and glory and praise as he sees the matchless grace of God through Christ for him. Now we find him full of continual sorrow and unceasing pain. Actually, this is nothing less than the compassion of Christ revealed in a man. Here we have the heart of God manifest in Paul. The Lord Jesus, because of His love for you and me, became an accursed thing. As Galatians 3 says, "Cursed is everyone who hangeth on a tree." Paul is willing to become an accursed thing. He is willing to go to any length for the sake of his brothers, those of his own race. He is in continual sorrow, in unceasing pain, broken-hearted before God, suffering in the very depth of his soul that his brethren might be saved.

You find similar passages in the Old Testament. When Moses pleaded with God on behalf of the Jews who were worshiping the golden calf, God said, "Leave me alone and I'll blot them out and make you a great nation." And Moses said, "You can't do that. Remember your Name and remember your Word. If you blot Israel out, you can't keep your promises to Abraham and Isaac and Jacob. And what will the Egyptians say as to the kind of God Israel has—that he took them out in the wilderness to kill them?" Then Moses pleads, "Forgive them their sin," and adds, "If not, then blot me out of the book you have written." He made himself one with the people (Exodus 32).

Jeremiah, the weeping prophet, stood before God, a broken-hearted man pleading for Israel. But God said, "Jeremiah, I'm not going to listen to you." Three times God said to him, "Don't you pray for this people. I won't listen to you." Did that stop Jeremiah? No, sir.

In Jeremiah 5, God said, "If you can find one righteous man in the city, I will save the city for the one man." That shows you how far down in corruption and idolatry and rejection of God the Jews had gone. Did that deter Jeremiah? Oh, listen to him: "The harvest is past, the summer is ended, and we are not saved. . . . Is there no balm in Gilead; is there no physician there? why then is not the health of the daughter of my people recovered? Oh, that my head were waters, and mine eyes a fountain of tears, that I might weep day and night for the slain of the daughter of my people!" (8:20, 22-9:1). It was for a wicked people that Jeremiah was broken-hearted.

In Ezekiel's day the priests had become corrupt, the princes were trafficking in souls, the people were in corruption. And God said, "I looked for a man to make up the hedge and plead for my land so I would not have to destroy it, but I found none" (22:30).

If God were looking for men today who would get down before Him in intercession and travail for lost men and women, I wonder how many He would find. Would He find you? God looked for a man to intercede and found none, and God wondered that there was no intercessor.

I wonder, my Christian friend, have you ever touched the heart of God? Has the compassion of the Son of God ever gripped your soul? Did you ever come into the presence of God and plead with Him, not for yourself, not for things, not even for experiences, but for lost men and women for whom Christ died?

I have met Christians—and I'm sorry to say this—who claim that we must not pray for the unsaved, that nowhere in the New Testament are we urged by the Spirit of God to pray for the unsaved. That's not true. In 1 Timothy 2 we are exhorted to pray for all men, all in authority, for God wants all men to be saved and to come to the knowledge of the truth. When the believer in Christ prays for the lost, then we will see God move. It is impossible for a believer to come into the presence of God and plead with Him for lost men and women without having the privilege of seeing lost souls saved. Witnessing and intercession are partners; they are coupled together. The more you plead with God for men, the more you are going to plead with men for God.

That's the heart of Paul. He informs his Jewish brethren that he has no bitterness in his heart although they have persecuted him, although they have stoned him, although he has been in prison because of them. Nevertheless, he still loves them, and what he writes is because of his love for them.

Oh, that God might put upon your heart and mine a burden, a compassion, a tenderness of yearning over lost men and women that they might be saved. This doesn't come on you overnight or for a few minutes. This burden grows on your heart. I'm sure Paul spent many, many hours on his knees before God praying for Israel. Oh, friend, may the Lord give us something of the compassion and tenderness of Christ and a heart that yearns for the salvation of men and women.

Israel's Place of Blessing (9:4-5)

9:4-5. *Who are Israelites; to whom pertaineth the adoption, and the glory, and the covenants, and the giving of the law, and the service of God, and the promises; Whose are the fathers, and of whom as concerning the flesh Christ came, who is over all, God blessed for ever. Amen.*

This is an important passage because Paul is dealing with the sovereignty of God, and he is going to prove that whatever God does, He is righteous in doing it.

Being in the natural descent of Abraham, Isaac, and Jacob doesn't make you a child of promise; the promises and the purposes of God are going to be accomplished in those in Israel who are the spiritual seed of Abraham. God said to Moses that Israel would be the head of the nations, not the tail, and that through Israel the nations of the earth are going to know God. The Gentile nations are going to come into blessing through Israel.

In His sovereignty, God chose Abraham, Isaac, and Jacob and their descendants for a place of privilege. They had the covenants, they had the prophecies, they had the Word of God. Through them Christ would come, and they were privileged to be God's witnesses to the nations of the earth.

Jonah was a prophet in Israel, and he ran away from the responsibility. He was told to go to Nineveh and preach a message of judgment that would bring the people to their knees in repentance. And Jonah said, "I won't do it."

Likewise Israel should have preached a message of repentance to the Gentile nations, but it didn't do it even though it was chosen for this purpose. God gave Israel a place of privilege, a place of blessing, and it failed to live up to its calling.

The Question of Privilege (9:6-13)

9:6-9. *Not as though the word of God hath taken none effect. For they are not all Israel, which are of Israel:*

*neither, because they are the seed of Abraham, are they
all children: but, In Isaac shall thy seed be called. That
is, They which are the children of the flesh, these are
not the children of God: but the children of the promise
are counted for the seed. For this is the word of
promise, At this time will I come, and Sarah shall have
a son.*

God in sovereign grace and mercy picked Abraham. God
would have been righteous, perfectly righteous, if He had left
Abraham in his sin and idolatry. Didn't He have the right in His
sovereign grace to pick him up and say, "I am going to bless
you"? Was God unrighteous in doing that? Of course not.

Was God righteous in choosing Isaac, the son of promise,
instead of Ishmael? God was not unrighteous in letting Ishmael
go. He blessed Ishmael. But in sovereign mercy He picked up
Isaac, and it is through Isaac that the line of God's promise is to
be traced. Those who are the children of promise are those who,
like Abraham, believe the promise of God and are therefore
Abraham's true offspring.

9:10-13. *And not only this; but when Rebecca also had
conceived by one, even by our father Isaac; (for the
children being not yet born, neither having done any
good or evil, that the purpose of God according to
election might stand, not of works, but of him that
calleth;) it was said unto her, The elder shall serve the
younger. As it is written, Jacob have I loved, but Esau
have I hated.*

You find that story in Genesis 25. But please mark something:
Paul says God chose Jacob over Esau before the children were
born. It wasn't a question of whether one was good and the other
bad, one religious and the other irreligious. God in His infinite
grace and mercy said, "The elder shall serve the younger." Does
that mean God was unrighteous concerning Esau?

No. God wanted a people who would become His messengers, a people to whom He could give His Word, a people through whom Messiah would come. He wanted a people, and He had the right to choose. He didn't choose Ishmael, nor did He choose Esau. By His sovereign will and for His own sovereign purposes, God chose Jacob.

You could say, "He didn't choose Ishmael because Sarah wasn't his mother. God couldn't take him because he was a child of the flesh." But what about Jacob and Esau, who both had the same father and mother? There was nothing lacking in their parentage. God chose Jacob over Esau before they were born or had done anything good or bad to show that His election is a matter of His choice and has nothing to do with achievements, but is entirely a matter of His will. God was perfectly righteous in choosing Jacob instead of Esau to be the one through whom His Son should come.

GOD IS SOVEREIGN IN BESTOWING MERCY (9:14-33)

Is God Righteous? (9:14-18)

9:14. *What shall we say then? Is there unrighteousness with God? God forbid.*

God is never, never unrighteous. You and I may not understand all that He does or says, but He is never unrighteous.

Otherwise, He wouldn't be God.

Is God righteous in choosing Isaac instead of Ishmael? Yes. Is God righteous in choosing Jacob instead of Esau? Yes. Then isn't God righteous in putting the Jew to one side and picking up the Gentile? That's what Paul is after. God·has put Israel to one side because of her unbelief, because of her disobedience, and for the purpose of bringing in the Gentiles that they might come into relationship with Him.

9:15-16. *For he saith to Moses, I will have mercy on whom I will have mercy, and I will have compassion on*

*whom I will have compassion. So then it is not of him
that willeth nor of him that runneth, but of God that
showeth mercy.*

Now, this question, "Is there unrighteousness with God?" is
answered in verses 15 to 18. And here Paul uses the example of
Israel and the Egyptians. To the people of Israel, God manifests
His mercy; to the people of Egypt, His wrath. To know something
of His dealings with Egypt, you have to read Exodus 5-12. To
understand His dealings with Israel, you have to read Exodus 30-33
where God wants to blot out Israel because of its idolatry and corruption.

Now Paul begins moving away from the question of natural
descent as regards Abraham, Isaac, and Jacob. He wants to prove
that it is by the mercy of God in His sovereign power that Israel
has experienced through the centuries the blessing of God. He has
had infinite mercy on the people. If they had received their just
deserts, they would have been obliterated. They had forfeited
every right to God's blessing.

Israel had come out of Egypt under the power of God. They
had crossed the Red Sea and come into the wilderness. God fed
them, watered them, clothed them, and took care of them. He protected them from the terrors of the night with the pillar of fire. He
protected them from the heat of the day with the cloud. He
revealed Himself to them as Jehovah Rapha, "I am the Lord that
healeth thee." A whole race, possibly three million people, were
shut up entirely to God. He was doing a new thing—He wanted to
dwell in the midst of His people. He wanted to teach them how to
live so they could glorify Him.

Yet they corrupted themselves by making an idol in the shape
of a calf, bowing down to it and saying, "These be thy gods, O
Israel, that brought thee out of the land of Egypt."

God was angry with His people and said to Moses, "Get thee
down; for thy people . . . have corrupted themselves" (Exodus 32:7).
Then God made this amazing statement, "Let me alone, that my

wrath may wax hot against them, and that I may consume them: and I will make of thee a great nation" (32:10). And, as Psalm 106 says, "If Moses my servant had not stood in the gap, they would have been utterly destroyed."

God would have been righteous if He had just blotted out the entire race. But Moses interceded. He stood in the gap three times in the book of Exodus and pleaded for Israel. And God said to Moses, "I will be gracious to whom I will be gracious, and will show mercy on whom I will show mercy" (33:19). Therefore Paul concludes, "So then it is not of him that willeth, nor of him that runneth, but of God that showeth mercy." There was no will, there was no work in Israel except corruption; but God in sovereign grace displayed His mercy and delivered the people.

May I be a little personal? Are you saved? Is it because you willed it? Is it because you worked for it? No, it is because God showed mercy on you. Ephesians 2:4-5 says, "God, who is rich in mercy, for his great love wherewith he loved us, even when we were dead in sins . . . " When did He start to love us? When we were dead in sins. When did He manifest His mercy? When we were dead in sins.

God was righteous in manifesting mercy to Israel. The very righteousness of God demands judgment upon sin; but His mercy endures forever and is for every heart. But was God righteous in His dealings with Pharaoh?

9:17-18. *For the scripture saith unto Pharaoh, "Even for this same purpose have I raised thee up, that I might show my power in thee, and that my name might be declared throughout all the earth." Therefore hath he mercy on whom he will have mercy, and whom he will he hardeneth.*

"There you are now, Mr. Mitchell," you say. "Don't you see that God has already purposed to judge some people and to damn others?"

The Bible doesn't say that. You can't interpret these verses without reading history. You must go back to Exodus 5 through 12. Is God unrighteous if He does not show mercy to someone who is arrogant and who defies Him? That's what we have here.

Moses came to Pharaoh at the instigation of God, who had told him, "Go and stand before Pharaoh and I'm going to be with you. Tell Pharaoh, 'Let my people go that they may serve me in the wilderness.' "

Pharaoh was the head of possibly the greatest empire in the world. He was being worshiped as the representative of the gods, and his response to Moses reveals his arrogance: "I don't know this Jehovah. Why should I obey His voice? Shall I, the mighty pharaoh, the favorite of the gods, bow down and obey the god of slaves? I should say not!"

"All right, Pharaoh," God responds, "I'm going to prove to you that I am the only living God." And the judgments of God fell upon Egypt. After each plague, God hardened the heart of Pharaoh—strengthened it, if you please. He made it strong in his opposition to God. Why? Until every god in Egypt had been broken down. God proved that He was sovereign (Exodus 12:12).

Was God righteous in showing mercy to Israel? Was God righteous in revealing His power and His might and His sovereignty to Pharaoh? Perfectly righteous. God would be righteous in damning the whole human race because of our sin and rebellion. And if God has brought you into a relationship with His blessed Son, the Lord Jesus Christ, as your Savior and Lord, then you ought to get down and thank God for His mercy. We have become the sons of God because of divine grace and mercy and love. Oh, how we ought to thank God! How we ought to worship Him!

Today, I see all around me the arrogance of the human heart. It has neither time nor room nor thought for God. God is gracious and merciful, but there is a time coming when the day of grace and mercy will end and men will perish. I can't guarantee when that day may come. It may be today. It may be tomorrow. All I know is that God wants men everywhere to repent, to turn around from the way they are going, and to take His way which is the way of life and of salvation and of redemption. God is longsuffering. He has mercy for all. But if a person deliberately turns against God, opposes God, refuses to believe in God, spurns His message of salvation, then God just takes His hands off and the man is left to himself on a path that leads to destruction. You can't blame God for this.

Man's Objection to God's Sovereignty (9:19-21)

9:19-21. *Thou wilt say then unto me, Why doth he yet find fault? For who hath resisted his will? Nay but, O man, who art thou that repliest against God? Shall the thing formed say to him that formed it, Why hast thou made me thus? Hath not the potter power over the clay, of the same lump to make one vessel unto honour, and another unto dishonour?*

"Why hast thou made me thus?" is not the cry of a heart that wants the truth. This is not the cry of a heart that is yearning for God. This is an arrogant heart, a heart that puts itself in judgment upon God. This is an unbelieving heart, the heart of a man who blames God for his own sin, his own unrighteousness.

I am reminded of 1 Corinthians 2:14, "But the natural man receiveth not the things of the Spirit of God; for they are foolishness unto him: neither can he know them, because they are spiritually discerned." Man's heart is alienated from God by his wicked works. When a man sits in judgment upon God, it is the revelation of the heart that does not want God, of a heart that is not thinking of God.

Hasn't God the right to do what He pleases? Will He not always do the right thing?

It's true that some have more privileges than others, but the more privilege you have, the greater is your responsibility.

No man can say to God, "You didn't give me a chance." God offers His mercy to all. The question is: "Do you want God?"

Down through the centuries, He has been offering His mercy and His grace to men, and He still is offering it to mankind today. "God is not willing that any should perish but that all should come to repentance."

God may take one man and make him a vessel of honor. He may take another man and make him a vessel of dishonor. Each one has a different place of usefulness, but His mercy is for all. Is God unrighteous by giving one man a gift and not giving the other man the same gift? No, of course not. God is absolutely righteous in everything He does and His mercy is for all.

The Purpose of God's Sovereignty (9:22-29)

9:22-24. *What if God, willing to show his wrath, and to make his power known, endured with much longsuffering the vessels of wrath fitted to destruction: and that he might make known the riches of his glory on the vessels of mercy, which he had afore prepared unto glory, even us, whom he hath called, not of the Jews only, but also of the Gentiles?*

Today, God is calling men, whether Jew or Gentile, who will accept His mercy. If a man accepts the mercy of God, God is righteous in bestowing that mercy. And if a man rejects His mercy, then God is righteous in not giving him mercy and in casting him into utter darkness. Indeed, I would say that having spurned the mercy of God, unregenerate man will be glad to get out of the presence of God. Hell would be preferred by the unregenerate heart to heaven with its holiness.

Some people say to me, "Why, Mr. Mitchell, God won't send anyone to hell." Where can man go, once he's spurned God? He would not be comfortable in the presence of God or in the presence of the holy angels. He doesn't even like the people of God here on earth, so how is he going to stand us in heaven when we are just like God's Son? Paul says in 2 Thessalonians 1:8-9 that the Lord is going to come "in flaming fire taking vengeance on them that know not God, and that obey not the gospel of our Lord Jesus Christ: who shall be punished with everlasting destruction . . . "

The judgment of God is going to fall upon men because they did not know God (they didn't want to know Him), they did not believe the gospel (they didn't want to believe it), and they did not love the truth (they spurned the truth).

Not one of us is worthy of being saved in ourselves. There is no reason at all why God should save any of us. The reason is in Himself: "For God so loved the world that he gave his only begotten Son that whosoever believeth in him should not perish but have everlasting life."

God is gathering out those who will accept His mercy, those who appreciate His longsuffering, those who accept the Savior and come under blessing. The purpose of His sovereignty is to make His power known to those who are lost and to make His mercy known to those who will accept it.

> **9:25-26.** *As he saith also in [Hosea], I will call them my people, which were not my people; and her beloved, which was not beloved. And it shall come to pass, that in the place where it was said unto them, Ye are not my people; there shall they be called the children of the living God.*

Hosea is talking about the Gentiles coming in. Israel had forfeited every right to be the people of God, and now the Gentiles, by accepting the Savior, are called the people of God.

This was one of the hardest things for the early church to accept. There were Jewish Christians who wanted the Gentiles to be saved but wanted them to come to Christ through Judaism. No, the sinner comes immediately to the Savior and accepts His mercy. If he wants the mercy of God, it is there for him.

> **9:27-29.** *[Isaiah] also crieth concerning Israel, Though the number of the children of Israel be as the sand of the sea, a remnant shall be saved: for he will finish the*

*work, and cut it short in righteousness: because a short
work will the Lord make upon the earth. And as
[Isaiah] said before, Except the Lord of Sabaoth had
left us a seed, we had been as [Sodom], and been made
like unto Gomorrha.*

Isaiah's testimony is that Israel never did stand before God on
the ground of merit, but always on the ground of mercy. Though
the number of the Israelites be like the sand of the seashore
because of disobedience and unbelief, only a remnant will be
saved, and only then on the ground of grace.

Paul's reference to Sodom and Gomorrah makes me think of
Revelation 11 where the city of Jerusalem is figuratively called,
"Sodom." Israel as a nation in the last days will be so corrupt it's
going to be just like Sodom. Think of it! And even though the
nation is corrupt and God is going to purge out every rebel, God
still has a remnant. But if God hadn't manifested His mercy, there
wouldn't be one person left.

God Will Always Answer to Faith (9:30-33)

Paul now passes from the sovereignty of God to the responsibility of man.

*9:30-33. What shall we say then? That the Gentiles,
which followed not after righteousness, have attained
to righteousness, even the righteousness which is of
faith. But Israel, which followed after the law of
righteousness, hath not attained to the law of righteousness. Wherefore? Because they sought it not by
faith, but as it were by the works of the law. For they
stumbled at that stumblingstone; as it is written,
Behold, I lay in Sion a stumblingstone and rock of
offence: and whosoever believeth on him shall not be
ashamed.*

What the Jew rejected by his works, the Gentile received by faith. The Gentiles didn't follow after righteousness. They were afar off. They were under the curse. They went their own way. As Romans 1 says, they were given up to sin, given up to uncleanness, given up to vile affections, given up to a reprobate mind. But God followed them with the gospel of His righteousness, and they received the righteousness which is by faith.

The Jews rejected this. They tried to obtain righteousness by their own works, and they couldn't do it. They boasted about the law of righteousness but didn't follow it. Hence, having more light than the Gentiles, the Jews were in a worse plight. They stumbled at the rock of offense because they were looking for a glorified, reigning Messiah, not for a suffering, crucified Lord. They were looking for one who would free them from their enemies, not for One who would save them from their sins.

The first promise in the New Testament is, "Thou shalt call his name Jesus for he shall save his people from their sins" (Matthew 1:21). It was not "save his people from their enemies." He will deliver them from their enemies when He returns the next time. But He came as a Savior from sin, and they stumbled at that stumblingstone and rock of offense. Again, what the Jews missed by their works, the Gentiles received by faith. If righteousness comes by works, then Christ died in vain (Galatians 2:21).

But we who call ourselves Christians need to be sure that we have received the righteousness that comes by faith and not by our works. From Genesis to Revelation, no one is ever saved and fitted for the presence of God on any other ground but the ground of grace, received by faith. The poor man on the street who is a sinner, who has no righteousness of his own, accepts the Savior by simple faith, and God puts His own righteousness to his account. What the religious man misses by his works, the sinner receives by faith in Christ.

We who have accepted the Savior must realize that God has chosen us not only for salvation but also to be a testimony to our neighbors and our friends of God's grace. Oh, that they too may know about the Savior who redeems and saves with an everlasting and perfect salvation. My prayer is that our hearts will be stirred first of all with thanksgiving and worship because God has had mercy on us and then that we will bring others to the same Savior, the same Lord, that they too may experience the mercy of God, the love of God, and the grace of God in Christ Jesus.

Romans 10

God today is not dealing with nations; He is dealing with individuals—you and me. The question is, what is your relationship, what is my relationship to the living God? He has already made clear that there is a way open whereby any man or woman, whoever they are, whatever they may be, can come to know Him. This is the emphasis of Romans 10.

Although the nation of Israel is under governmental discipline, having been scattered among the nations of the earth, God is dealing with Jews and Gentiles as individuals.

GOD'S PRESENT DEALINGS WITH ISRAEL IN GOVERNMENTAL DISCIPLINE (10:1-21)

In the first eleven verses, Paul gives to us the difference between righteousness by works and righteousness by faith. The tragedy is that too many of God's people today have never seen the completeness of Christ's work on the cross nor have they seen the value and the importance of the resurrection.

**The Difference between Righteousness by Works and
Righteousness by Faith (10:1-11)**

*Israel's Ignorance of God's Righteousness and the Righteous-
ness God Provides (10:1-4)*

10:1. *Brethren, my heart's desire and prayer to God for
Israel is, that they might be saved.*

We had the same thing in the first two or three verses of
Romans 9 where Paul called God to be his witness that he had
great heaviness and continual sorrow in his heart. He could wish
himself accursed from Christ that his brethren, the Israelites,
might be saved. He was burdened before God for the salvation of
these people.

10:2-3. *For I bear them record that they have a zeal of
God, but not according to knowledge. For they being
ignorant of God's righteousness, and going about to
establish their own righteousness, have not submitted
themselves unto the righteousness of God.*

Israel is ignorant concerning God's righteousness—and the
same thing can be said today of Christendom. Even among many
professing Christians there is an appalling ignorance of the
righteousness of God. Our very lives manifest that. Our theology
manifests it. Man is so occupied with man, so occupied with self-
image, with love of self, and with the importance of self-esteem,
that he is blind to the righteousness of God.

They had a zeal for God, but zeal and sincerity are no ground
for safety. Having zeal doesn't imply that a person's heart is right
with God. Read the history of Israel, especially between the fourth
and the first century B.C., and you will find that the Jews suffered
because they refused to deny the law of God. They had a tremendous zeal for God, but they didn't know God personally.

The Jews claimed they were following God's law. Did God not
give them the law? Did they not say to God, "All that the Lord our
God has said, we will do"? Yes, they believed that the law was

given to them by God. They believed they were the only ones who had the revelation of God through the law. Gentiles have no law. The law was given to Israel. What for? To make them good? Oh, no. The law of God was given to prove they were no good so that they might turn to Him in simple faith and accept His mercy.

We have that same problem today. A great many people are depending upon their goodness, their morality. They pay their debts, they're good husbands, they're good fathers, they don't do anything really bad, they go to church every Sunday.

"Why, Mr. Mitchell, what more do you expect?" I don't expect anything. But if you are depending on your goodness, then the evidence is that you are ignorant of the righteousness of God.

From the time a Jew entered his world until he died, his whole life was interlocked with the religious life of his people.

Yet the apostle Paul could say that all those things that were gain to him—born a Jew, of the tribe of Benjamin, a Pharisee, a fundamentalist with plenty of zeal in persecuting the church, blameless concerning the righteousness which was in the law— did nothing to save him (Philippians 3). He was blameless but lost. But once he caught a glimpse of God's righteousness, the rest just faded out of the picture.

That was the Jew's trouble. His eyes were not open to the righteousness of God. He knew the character of God—he knew that God was righteous and holy—but he was ignorant of the fact that nothing short of God's righteousness would stand. Legal righteousness can never stand in God's presence.

The Jew never saw two things: He never saw his own frailty and weakness and sinfulness, and he never saw the righteousness of God. The third verse brings this out. Being ignorant of God's righteousness, this righteousness that comes by faith, he tried to establish his own righteousness and didn't submit himself to the righteousness of God. When anyone seeks to establish his own righteousness, he is manifesting ignorance of God's righteousness.

We do anything but face up to the reality that God of necessity must be righteous and I must be a sinner who has no righteousness. So how can we come together? How can I come into the presence of God and be accepted? Verse 4 is the answer.

10:4. *For Christ is the end of the law for righteousness to every one that believeth.*

This is God's method. Christ is the end of the law, not the beginning of the law. Christ is the end of the law for righteousness. The law has had nothing to say since the cross. When our Lord was raised from the dead, He started something entirely new, and the law doesn't belong to this new creation. The law was an added thing, imposed upon the people of Israel to show them how bad they were and how they needed a Savior. No Jew—and no Gentile—will ever be able to stand before God, the righteous God, unless he is covered with the righteousness of Christ.

Don't jump to the conclusion, as so many theologians have, that Jesus Christ kept the whole law for us. He didn't. You can't find that in the Scriptures. Some say that, because Christ kept every demand of the law, that is put to our account. That is not true. Christ kept the whole law that He might be a perfect, satisfactory sacrifice for you. You are not joined to Christ because He kept the law. You were joined to Him when He bore your sins and died on the cross.

Christianity starts on the resurrection side of the cross. The law is through, either as a means of life or as a rule of life. The bill is canceled. Christ is the end of the law, outside of its jurisdiction entirely. The law came to the cross, and the law was satisfied in what Christ had done for us at the cross.

I wish in some way this amazing truth of the righteousness of God by faith would get hold of your heart. If I were to ask you to give me your testimony, you would probably say, "Well, thank God, I was saved by faith in Christ." Why don't you say, "Thank God, I was declared righteous by God when I accepted Christ." It might stagger your imagination if you said that, and yet faith and righteousness are coupled together over and over again.

God has pronounced us righteous with a righteousness that

equals His own. As Paul could say in Philippians 3:8, "I count everything but loss." What for? "That I might be found in Jesus Christ, not having mine own righteousness, which is of the law, but that which is through the faith of Christ, the righteousness which is of God through faith."

Works and Faith Are Contrasted (10:5-11)

Christianity is not a life of do's and don'ts. It's a life of walking with Him. There are many things we push to one side because we love Him and want to attract people to Him. We are now under the law of love because of our union with the God of love.

> **10:5-8.** *For Moses describeth the righteousness which is of the law, That the man which doeth those things shall live by them. But the righteousness which is of faith speaketh on this wise, Say not in thine heart, Who shall ascend into heaven? (that is, to bring Christ down from above:) or, Who shall descend into the deep? (that is, to bring up Christ again from the dead.) But what saith it? The word is nigh thee, even in thy mouth, and in thy heart: that is, the word of faith, which we preach.*

The law's demand of righteousness would be satisfied if one never broke the law in one point. But the moment you break the law—just once—the judgment of God falls upon you. You see the utter frailty and hopelessness and helplessness of man. If anybody is going to be saved, God has to do it, and He has to do the whole thing (Leviticus 18:5; Galatians 3:11-12).

What we need is not more strength to keep the law. What we need is a power from the outside. God has made His salvation apart from man, and that salvation is in His Son. "Christ is the end of the law for righteousness to everyone that believeth."

Verses 6-8 point to "by faith righteousness" and quote from Deuteronomy 30:11-14: "For this commandment which I command thee this day, it is not hidden from thee, neither is it far off. It is not in heaven, that thou shouldest say, Who shall go up for us to heaven, and bring it unto us, that we may hear it, and do it? Neither is it beyond the sea, that thou shouldest say, Who shall go over the sea for us, and bring it unto us, that we may hear it, and do it? But the word is very nigh unto thee, in thy mouth, and in thy heart, that thou mayest do it."

The Spirit of God applies these words to Christ. Our Lord did come. He did die. He was raised again from the dead. The work is all done, the whole work of redemption is completed. God doesn't need to do another thing.

Righteousness by law is dependent upon doing. The righteousness of God is received by faith, and it shuts out all doing. No man can stand in the presence of God without Christ. As I have so often said, "Oh, that men would stop their deadly doing and trust the Lord Jesus."

Righteousness Is Realized (10:9-11)

10:9-11. *That if thou shalt confess with thy mouth the Lord Jesus, and shalt believe in thine heart that God hath raised him from the dead, thou shalt be saved. For with the heart man believeth unto righteousness; and with the mouth confession is made unto salvation. For the scripture saith, Whosoever believeth on him shall not be ashamed.*

The great thing here is not the nature of your faith. It is the object of your faith. People say, "As long as you believe and are sincere in what you believe, you will be all right." Well, the Muslim believes, the Shintoist believes, the Animist believes, the Buddhist believes. They believe their doctrine, they believe in their gods. They are sincere, and sometimes they may put you and me to shame with their devotion. That doesn't mean they are saved and fit for the presence of God. No, the object of one's faith is essential.

Jesus Christ must be the object of our faith. We recognize His position—He is Lord. This One, whom men put on a cross, God put on the throne. Men crucified Him as an accursed thing; God exalted Him to be Lord. Men cast Him out; heaven took Him in. The world repudiated Him, but heaven rejoiced in exalting Him as Prince and Savior.

We are to confess with our mouth that this Jesus is Lord, and we are to believe that God raised Him from the dead. It is our confession of a Person and our belief in His work. Nothing is said here about the work at the cross. There is no need to. Paul has already spent eight chapters on that. He is writing now about the confirmation, the guarantee that the work Christ did on the cross absolutely satisfied the righteous character of God. When you confess with your mouth that Jesus is Lord and you believe in your heart—the very depths of your being—that God raised Him from the dead, you are saved.

I'm not saved by confessing, but because I am saved, I confess. If you were to give someone a gift, you would expect the recipient at least to say "thank you." There would be a response to it. If we receive eternal salvation from God as a gift, the least we can do is thank Him for it. By so doing, we confess that Jesus Christ is our Savior, our Lord.

When the risen, glorified Savior is the object of our faith, then we receive His salvation and His life. We are covered with His righteousness, His beauty, and His merit. As Paul says in Romans 8:1, "Therefore there is now no condemnation to those who are in Christ Jesus." My, what a place to be! Just to be in Christ. You can't work your way into that. There is only one way—God's way—and that's the way of faith.

Righteousness by Faith Is for All (10:12-18)

Righteousness by faith is open for all, regardless of whether you are a Gentile or a Jew. In the first eleven verses, Paul dealt with personal salvation. Now He is going to deal with a salvation for anyone. It's for all. It's not limited to any group, it's not limited to any nation or country. This righteousness through faith is open to everyone.

> **10:12.** *For there is no difference between the Jew and the Greek: for the same Lord over all is rich unto all that call upon him.*

God's character declares this. If God is righteous, He is not going to show any favoritism. God is righteous and He offers this righteousness to anyone and everyone who will receive it. In Romans 3:23, Paul said there was no difference in sin—"All have sinned [Jew and Gentile] and come short of the glory of God." Now he is saying that there is likewise no difference in salvation. All are lost and need a Savior, and the same Lord is rich to all who call upon Him.

Not only His character declares this, His promises also declare it:

> **10:13.** *For whosoever shall call upon the name of the Lord shall be saved.*

Paul quotes God's promise recorded in Joel 2:32. (It is cited also in Acts 2:21, and there's a "whosoever" in John 3:16 that includes you, too.) The Jews wanted to keep salvation for themselves. Because they did that, they became occupied with themselves and missed God's salvation. Now Paul is saying it is for all. God's character declares it in verse 12, His promises declare it in verse 13, and His servants declare it in verses 14-18.

> **10:14-18.** *How, then, shall they call on him in whom they have not believed? and how shall they believe in him of whom they have not heard? and how shall they hear without a preacher? and how shall they preach, except they be sent? As it is written, How beautiful are the feet of them that preach the gospel of peace, and bring glad tidings of good things! But they have not all obeyed the gospel. For [Isaiah] saith, Lord, who hath believed our report? So then faith cometh by hearing,*

*and hearing by the word of God. But I say, Have they
not heard? Yea verily, their sound went into all the
earth, and their words unto the ends of the world.*

The servants of God, the called of God, are sent with good
news. The law is not good news. The law says if you sin, you die.
There is no recourse. But God has raised up men and women to go
and tell their friends, their family, their neighbors, everyone
around some good news. God wants to communicate to men the
good news concerning His Son. How is He going to do it?
Through those who know the Word of God.

The last words of our Savior were, "Go into all the world and
preach the gospel to every creature." Our Lord said in Acts 1 that
the Spirit of God will come upon you "and ye shall be witnesses
unto me both in Jerusalem, and in all Judea, and in Samaria, and
unto the uttermost part of the earth."

What a change from the Old Testament. When the Jews were
called, their nation was set apart from others so they could reveal
to the world the wonders of our God. They failed and so what is
God doing now? He has turned to saved men and women, including the Gentiles, and said, "You take my good news. Tell your
friends. Go into all the world. Wherever there is a man or a
woman that doesn't know the Savior, you go and bring the Word
of God to that person."

I say with a great deal of sadness that we still have not touched
the whole world, though we've had the gospel of the grace of God
for over nineteen hundred years. Is God's purpose going to be
defeated? No. Even now, God's good news is being beamed to vir-
tually every part of the globe. God has seen fit to use mass com-
munications such as radio, television, and shortwave so that the
whole world may hear the gospel of God revealed in Christ.

The coming of the Lord is near, and I plead with you, my
Christian friend, as I plead with my own heart—may the Lord
deliver us from our indifference to the salvation of men and
women. "Faith cometh by hearing and hearing by the Word of

God." If you have the Word of God, then by your life, by your testimony, bring the good news to those around you that they may know Him whom to know is life eternal. Be much in prayer that God will send forth laborers into His harvest field.

The "sound" Paul refers to in verse 18 is the voice of creation (cf. Psalm 19). Everyone has, through creation, heard of the living God. There is no excuse for unbelief. No one will be able to stand before God and say, "I never heard of you." They may not have heard about the Savior, but they have heard about the living God.

Oh, how we Christians have failed to get behind God's messengers who will go to the ends of the earth, sacrificing themselves and family and friends, to reach those who have never heard of the Savior. It often takes missionary candidates two years to gather their support. This is to our shame. And how often do we pray for them when they are on the field? I plead with you to spend some time remembering these servants of God.

What a wonderful thing that God should call you and me to pass on the good news to our generation. It is a universal salvation—it is for everybody—and this is right. If God is righteous, it has to be that way. His very character demands it, His promises declare it, and His servants declare it.

There Is No Excuse for Israel (10:19-21)

The people of Israel should have known that God is not only the God of the Jews, He is also the God of the Gentiles. They believed there was only one God, but they didn't want the Gentiles to come under His blessing. Human nature is a strange thing. We want things for ourselves but not for anybody else. This was Israel's attitude.

So Israel was cast away under the discipline of God. For more than nineteen hundred years, the Jews have been in bondage, scattered over the earth.

10:19-21. *But I say, Did not Israel know? First Moses*

saith, I will provoke you to jealousy by them that are no
people, and by a foolish nation I will anger you. But
Isaiah is very bold, and saith, I was found of them that
sought me not; I was made manifest unto them that
asked not after me. But to Israel he saith, All day long I
have stretched forth my hands unto a disobedient and
gainsaying [contrary] people.

If the Gentiles in their heathendom discovered the wonderful
truth of righteousness by faith, then Israel, which had the Word of
God, has no excuse for unbelief. And if there are people coming
to know the Savior in Africa, in Southeast Asia, in South
America, then there is no excuse for us in America who have
heard the name of Jesus all of our lifetime. Whether we were
raised in a Christian family or not, we knew about the Savior. We
knew about the Bible. We knew something. That these men and
women in so-called pagan countries have come to know the
Savior is a rebuke to those of us who in our arrogance have turned
away from the Savior. We are in the same position as Israel.

"Did not Israel know?" Of course they knew. The fact that
Gentiles were coming under the blessing of God should have
stirred Israel to jealousy to seek their God and to obey Him. God
had already declared through the prophet Isaiah that He would
save Gentiles. Hence, there is no excuse for Israel because they
knew it. Why should they get mad at Paul for going out among the
Gentiles and preaching the unsearchable riches of Christ? Why
seek to persecute him when their own Scriptures declared that
God would speak to them through other nations?

The Gentiles, who did not seek God, accepted Him. Israel,
which had the Word of God, was indifferent to Him and full of
unbelief. Oh, the blessings, the mercy, the love He poured upon
them; but they never turned to Him. They became colder and
colder in spite of God's outstretched hand toward them. They
didn't care anything about God.

My, how God loved Israel, how He yearned for them. What

broke His heart? They rejected His offer of salvation which was both free (vv. 1-11) and universal (vv. 12-21). Because they have rejected His salvation, has God cast away His people? Paul answers this question in chapter 11.

Romans 11

God's future dealing with Israel in the fulfillment of prophecy is the subject of this eleventh chapter. Israel's rejection is neither total nor final. The bringing in of the Gentiles, which God has been doing for nineteen hundred years, will not alter the promises of God to Israel. The Lord has manifested His grace and His love and His patience to Israel, and He is going to fulfill every word, every promise, every covenant He made with this people.

GOD'S FUTURE DEALINGS WITH ISRAEL
(11:1-36)

God Has Not Cast Away His People (11:1-10)

11:1-2a. *I say then, Hath God cast away his people? God forbid. For I also am an Israelite, of the seed of Abraham, of the tribe of Benjamin. God hath not cast away his people which he foreknew.*

The Jew is liable to say, "What's the use? God has cast us off, and we are done for." Paul says, "Wait a minute. I'm a Jew. I'm an Israelite. I'm of the tribe of Benjamin. I'm of the seed of Abraham. God hasn't cast me off. I know the Lord. God has not cast away His people whom He foreknew."

Thousands and thousands of other Jews who have accepted the Savior can say the same thing. Paul was living proof that God had not cast his people off. Remember, He did not choose them because they were many. He chose them because He loved them.

> **11:2b-5.** *Wot ye not what the scripture saith of Elias? how he maketh intercession to God against Israel, saying, Lord, they have killed thy prophets, and digged down thine altars; and I am left alone, and they seek my life. But what saith the answer of God unto him? I have reserved to myself seven thousand men, who have not bowed the knee to the image of Baal. Even so then at this present time also there is a remnant according to the election of grace.*

God has always had those who were faithful to Him, even when the nation was away from Him in apostasy, idolatry, and corruption. He always had a remnant of the nation, who trusted Him.

Take this man Elijah. The nation had followed Ahab, the wicked king, and was worshiping Baal. Ahab said, "If you find any prophet of Jehovah, kill him. Get rid of him." He tried to stamp out the worship of Jehovah. Elijah saw the overwhelming flood of unbelief, and he said, "Lord, you might as well get rid of me since I'm the last one." But God said, "Listen, I have seven thousand who have never bowed to Baal."

Elijah didn't know who they were. Obadiah, who was the governor of Ahab's household, "feared the LORD greatly," but nobody knew about it. That's just like today. We have a great many Christians (and I'm not going to question whether or not they are Christians, that's between them and the Lord) who give no public indication that they are the Lord's. My heart doesn't run after Obadiah. My heart runs after Elijah.

I have talked to many Christians who have become so discouraged they think they are the only ones who love the Savior. I have met preachers who felt they were the only ones who proclaimed the truth. But God will always have a remnant of those who love Him, even in America. When one sees the way things are going, I tell you, it makes the heart grieve. It ought to drive us to our knees in intercession in behalf of our country as we see, even in so-called Christendom, cold indifference to the person of Christ. It's bad enough to be indifferent, but it's terrible when one is satisfied in his indifference.

Are you one of God's remnant? Are you, as one who loves the Savior, standing for Him in the midst of a world of corruption and compromise with the truth? God always has His people. He always has a remnant that loves Him.

> **11:6.** *And if by grace, then is it no more of works: otherwise grace is no more grace. But if it be of works, then is it no more grace: otherwise work is no more work.*

No one has ever been saved by his works—no one. No one, from Adam to the present, has ever been fitted for the presence of God on the ground of works of any kind. One is saved only on the ground of the matchless grace of God. Not grace plus something. Grace by faith *alone*.

> **11:7-10.** *What then? Israel hath not obtained that which he seeketh for; but the election hath obtained it, and the rest were blinded (according as it is written, God hath given them the spirit of slumber, eyes that they should not see, and ears that they should not hear;) unto this day. And David saith, Let their table be made a snare, and a trap, and a stumblingblock, and a recompence unto them: Let their eyes be darkened, that they may not see, and bow down their back alway.*

Israel did not obtain what it sought for because it was seeking it by works. As a result, eyes were darkened and all its national hopes came to nothing. It became so much the enemy of its own good that David's curse on the enemies of Jehovah's servant (Psalm 69:22-23) fell on Israel.

What is God's purpose for Israel in the future? Is God through with Israel? We see her people scattered all over the face of the earth. Only a small remnant has gone back to Israel. Is God through with the Jews?

God's Purpose for Israel in the Future (11:11-32)

11:11-15. *I say then, Have they stumbled that they should fall? God forbid: but rather through their fall salvation is come unto the Gentiles, for to provoke them to jealousy. Now if the fall of them be the riches of the world, and the diminishing of them the riches of the Gentiles; how much more their fulness? For I speak to you Gentiles, inasmuch as I am the apostle of the Gentiles, I magnify mine office: if by any means I may provoke to emulation them which are my flesh, and might save some of them. For if the casting away of them be the reconciling of the world, what shall the receiving of them be, but life from the dead?*

You can see what the Lord is doing. If He can stir the Jews up to jealousy, then they might turn to Him. In the Book of Acts, Paul went from city to city, preaching the gospel in the synagogues, and certain Jews were saved. But the Gentiles also heard the Word of God and a great multitude of them believed. Then the Jews became envious. But instead of being stirred up to jealousy to turn to the Lord, they turned against Him.

For nineteen hundred years the Gentiles have had the gospel and have preached it to the world. Yet today, hundreds of millions of people know nothing of the Savior. If Israel failed in its job of making known to the nations the wonders of God, the church of Jesus Christ hasn't done its job either. There will not be a reaching of the nations of the earth until Israel is gathered in, purged, and its people sent out as God's messengers. This will mean the salvation of the world, and then we will enter the millennium.

11:16-18. *For if the firstfruit be holy, the lump is also holy: and if the root be holy, so are the branches. And if some of the branches be broken off, and thou, being a wild olive tree, wert grafted in among them, and with them partakest of the root and fatness of the olive tree; boast not against the branches. But if thou boast, thou bearest not the root, but the root thee.*

The olive tree represents Israel in its place of privilege and testimony, and the wild olive shoot represents the Gentile nations. The breaking off of some of the branches of the olive tree and the grafting in of the wild olive shoot represent Israel's present rejection and the Gentiles' acceptance. But Gentile believers must not look down upon the Jews. They are indebted to the Jews. But for the grace of God, they would still be in unbelief.

11:19-24. *Thou wilt say then, The branches were broken off, that I might be graffed [grafted] in. Well; because of unbelief they were broken off, and thou standest by faith. Be not highminded, but fear: for if God spared not the natural branches, take heed lest he also spare not thee. Behold therefore the goodness and severity of God: on them which fell, severity; but toward thee, goodness, if thou continue in his goodness: otherwise thou also shalt be cut off. And they also, if they abide not still in unbelief, shall be graffed in: for God is able to graff them in again. For if thou wert cut out of the olive tree which is wild by nature, and wert graffed contrary to nature into a good olive tree: how much more shall these, which be the natural branches, be graffed into their own olive tree?*

The Jews were cut off through unbelief, and we Gentiles were grafted in, contrary to nature. Galatians 3:7 says, "They which are of faith, the same are the children of Abraham." In other words, we were grafted into salvation by faith.

You don't graft a wild branch onto a good tree. You generally do the opposite. And if God cut Israel off because of its failure and disobedience, then a time is coming when God is going to cut the Gentile off—and I believe that time is near.

When the church is gone from the scene and our testimony is through, God is going to turn around, pick up the people of Israel, and restore them to the place of privilege. Isaiah 43 says the Jews will be witnesses for God to the nations of the earth. Every Jew in that day is going to be a witness for God.

The Gentiles will call the Jews "priests unto God." Nations will recognize that the Israelites are God's people, God's witnesses. And what we have not been able to do in nineteen hundred years, the nation Israel is going to do when this godly remnant is restored to a wonderful relationship with Him.

God Is Not Through with Israel (11:25-32)

11:25. *For I would not, brethren, that ye should be ignorant of this mystery, lest ye should be wise in your own conceits; that blindness in part is happened to Israel, until the fulness of the Gentiles be come in.*

What is the mystery? It is that Israel has in part experienced a blindness, a hardening. For nineteen hundred years, the Jewish people have been scattered among the nations of the earth under the discipline of God. They are blind. They will be blind as a people until the full number of the Gentiles has come in. We Gentiles are to recognize this mystery so that we may not be conceited. We are not to be ignorant of the fact that this blindness has occurred.

There is a difference between "the times of the Gentiles" and "the fulness of the Gentiles." Jesus says in Luke 21 that Jerusalem will be trampled on by the Gentiles until "the times of the Gentiles" is filled full. The "times of the Gentiles" started with the reign of Nebuchadnezzar in Babylon (when he took the people of Israel into captivity), and it runs right through until the Lord begins to deal with Israel in the tribulation period and then sets up His kingdom.

Then what is the "fulness of the Gentiles"? This I believe has to do with the church of Jesus Christ. We are living in a time when God is gathering out a people for His name, called the church. This is the period of "the fulness of the Gentiles." It starts with the resurrection of Christ and lasts until the translation of the church. And when you see what is happening in Israel today, you can lift up your head, my friend, if you are a Christian, because your redemption draweth nigh.

> **11:26-27.** *And so all Israel shall be saved: as it is written, There shall come out of Sion the Deliverer, and shall turn away ungodliness from Jacob: for this is my covenant unto them, when I shall take away their sins.*

Even though Israel has been unfaithful to God, God will still be faithful to His covenant, to His promise. Does that mean every Jew in the world is going to be saved? No. When this occurs not every living Israelite will be saved, but Israel *as a nation* will be saved.

In the time of tribulation, after the church has been taken away, God will begin to deal with Israel. Then the nation of Israel is going to be saved in a single day by the personal appearance of Jesus Christ. The people shall see Him whom they pierced and shall say, "Where did You receive these wounds?" And He shall say, "I received them in the house of My friends" (Zechariah 13:6). And there will be national repentance. When they see the Lord Jesus Christ come, they are going to say, "This is our Lord. We have waited for Him."

He came the first time to the earth to Israel to fulfill the promises made to the fathers. "I am sent but to the lost sheep of the house of Israel." He is going to come the second time to the earth for the salvation of Israel, to deliver it from its enemies and to judge the nations of the earth.

For the believer, we wait for the translation of the church. We are not going to meet our Lord on earth; we are going to meet Him in the heavens. We are going to be caught up to meet the Lord in the air and be with Him forever. But Israel, when the Lord comes the second time, will be surrounded by its enemies. All the nations of the earth will be against it, and the only way of deliverance will be up. That's when God begins to pour out His wrath upon the nations. He is going to judge them, and He is going to reign on the earth. He is going to turn ungodliness away from Jacob and make a new covenant with the people of Israel.

"But, Mr. Mitchell," you say, "the new covenant is what God made with the church." I'm well aware that there is a certain sense in which the new covenant takes us in. But God promised to make a new covenant with the people of Israel when He takes away their sins. God is going to take away their heart of stone and give them a heart of flesh.

This is the essence of the new covenant, recorded in Jeremiah 31 and quoted in Hebrews 8. It is written to Israel, not to us as members of the church. It's true that when you and I accepted the Savior, we were forgiven every sin, cleansed from every transgression. We passed from death to life. We will never again come into judgment as sinners. We are covered with the righteousness of Christ. We have become the children of God, the recipients of eternal life, fitted for eternal glory.

But don't be jealous of what God is going to do with Israel. Two-thirds of Israel will be cut off, and one-third will be brought through the fire. This will occur in the tribulation period, according to Jeremiah 30. This is "the time of Jacob's trouble," the time when God is going to purge Israel. And then, when He comes, He is going to make a new covenant with the house of Israel. He is going to make them a wonderful people, and they are going to know the Lord.

11:28. *As concerning the gospel, they are enemies for your sakes: but as touching the election, they are beloved for the fathers' sakes.*

When God made His covenant with Abraham, Isaac, and Jacob, He made an everlasting covenant. When He made His covenant with David, it was an everlasting covenant. When God made those covenants, He knew all about Israel. Don't forget that. He knew exactly what the people would do. If you read the section in Deuteronomy where Moses declared the blessings and the curses (chapters 28-30), you will notice he is positive that the people are going to come under the judgment of God. Nevertheless, they are still beloved for the fathers' sakes. But because of their enmity, God opened the door to the Gentiles. That doesn't mean He doesn't love the Jew. That doesn't mean He's not going to complete His promises to the Jew. Every covenant He made He is going to fulfill.

You talk about the grace of God and the mercy of God. They don't deserve mercy any more than you and I do, but God has manifested His grace to us. He forgave us our sins and blotted them out, never to see them again. Cannot God do the same for Israel?

11:29. *For the gifts and calling of God are without repentance.*

When God starts a thing, He finishes it. He may not do it in a split second, but He will do it in His own good time. When God called Israel to be His people, He knew exactly what they would do—yet He still chose them. His word to them is as eternal as the new heavens and the new earth He is going to make. God never repents in manifesting His grace to man. He still saves and He still keeps. Even Israel's rebellion and idolatry will not turn God from fulfilling His purpose and His plan.

11:30-32. *For as ye in times past have not believed God, yet have now obtained mercy through their unbelief: even so have these also now not believed, that through your mercy they also may obtain mercy. For God hath concluded them all in unbelief, that he might have mercy upon all.*

If the mercy of God was free to the Gentiles, the mercy of God is going to be free for Israel. And, my, what will God not do for the Jews when they come in?

If you and I were to write verse 32, we would write, "God has concluded Jew and Gentile in unbelief that He might judge them all." No, thank God, it doesn't say that. God has included all, Jew and Gentile, in unbelief that He might have mercy on them all.

God doesn't make distinctions between sinners. You and I make distinctions. We say, "That fellow over there is a vile sinner; only the grace of God can reach him. Me? I'm a good man. I'm a moral person. I'm a religious person."

But, my friend, you need the mercy of God just as much as that fellow in outbroken sin. His outbroken sin reveals the condition of his heart, and if we could examine your heart and see its thoughts and desires . . .

"Oh, brother," you say, "don't do that!"

If we could see those things you would like to have done . . .

"Oh, no. Don't look at those!"

You see, when God looks on the heart of every man or woman, He finds we are all under sin, all in unbelief. He could have left every one of us in our sins. He could have left Abraham in idolatry. He could have left Israel in its unbelief, and He could have left you in your sin. God didn't have to save anybody. But He did.

The Great Doxology (11:33-36)

No wonder Paul overflows with his great doxology. I don't know of any Scripture so marvelous as this.

> **11:33.** *O the depth of the riches both of the wisdom and knowledge of God! how unsearchable are his judgments, and his ways past finding out!*

Paul's heart was bursting with rapturous praise as he thought of the grace of God—grace that has taken Gentiles given over to sin and fitted them for eternal glory; grace that will regather the Jews, cleanse them, forgive all their iniquities, and fulfill in them the promises of God in the millennial reign of our Savior.

Oh, to be so overmastered by that wonderful, divine love of the Savior so that you and I become channels displaying that same love to our generation.

"O the depth of the riches." Did you ever think of the divine wealth, the inexhaustible riches of Christ? I am reminded of that verse in Ephesians 3 when Paul speaks of the "unsearchable riches of Christ." You can't exhaust them, and you can't get to the end of searching them out. I tell you, we have a God who is rich in mercy, rich in love, rich in grace toward any open heart that will come to him (Ephesians 1-3). My friend, He excludes nobody.

Then think of the depth of His wisdom. He has no confidant, no counselor. The depth of his wisdom is beyond, way beyond, the faculty of man to plumb. First Corinthians 1 tells us the foolishness of God is wiser than the wisdom of men. In Colossians 2:3, we read that God has hidden in Christ all His treasures of wisdom and of knowledge. Hence, all we know of God is just what He has revealed to us.

My friend, you can study all the philosophies of the world, but none of them can bring you into a relationship with God. What do we know about God? Only what He has revealed. What do we know about His working? What do we know about His ways? What do we know about His wisdom and His love? Only what He has revealed.

The astounding thing is that men today question the working of God. They question His wisdom; they question His love. They sit in judgment of God. Oh, the arrogance of the human heart. Man can't begin to plumb the depths of the wisdom of God, of the riches of God. Yet, we sit back and we tell God just what we think of Him. We judge Him. We claim to have more love than He has, more grace than He has.

No, my friend, there is only one way you will ever know the grace of God, the love of God, the wisdom of God. You find it in the Word of God. Oh, the depth of His riches, the depth of His wisdom.

But it goes on. Paul celebrates not only the depth of the riches of His wisdom, but also of His knowledge—for God is omniscient. He knows everything. Our Savior manifested this. In John 2, the last two verses, many claimed to be His disciples when they saw the miracles He performed; but He did not entrust Himself to them because He knew what was in man. He knew even their thoughts.

And His ways are past finding out. Isaiah 55:9 says, "As the heavens are higher than the earth, so are my ways higher than your ways, and my thoughts than your thoughts." He does not show us His ways until we yield ourselves entirely to Him. In fact, His ways are beyond the reach of human intellect and philosophy.

He is the eternal, omniscient God. He is the One who is rich in wisdom and knowledge, whose judgments are unsearchable and whose ways are past finding out.

11:34. *For who hath known the mind of the Lord? or who hath been his counsellor?*

When God created the universe, made this world, made man, made the animals, He didn't call anybody in and consult with him—not the angels, not the archangel Michael, not His messenger Gabriel. He did not consult anyone.

Paul is actually quoting here from Isaiah 40, which gives us a tremendous picture of the incomparable character of God: "Who hath directed the Spirit of the LORD, or being his counsellor hath taught him? With whom took he counsel, and who instructed him, and taught him in the path of judgment, and taught him knowledge, and showed to him the way of understanding?" (vv. 13-14).

What do we know about our redemption? What do we know about the resurrection? What do we know about the rapture, about the new heavens and new earth, about the resurrected and glorified body? We just don't, my friend.

What do we know about what is going to happen after death? You don't know unless you come to the Word of God where He has revealed it to us. As 1 Corinthians 2:9-10 says, "Eye hath not seen, nor ear heard, neither have entered into the heart of man, the things which God hath prepared for them that love him. But God hath revealed them unto us by his Spirit: for the Spirit searcheth all things, yea, the deep things of God."

> **11:35-36.** *Or who hath first given to him, and it shall be recompensed unto him again? For of him, and through him, and to him, are all things: to whom be glory for ever. Amen.*

What can you give such a God? Have you ever given Him anything? He has given you everything in His Son. What He wants in return is our worship, our trust, our obedience—for everything we have is from Him. All we do is to use what God has given to us.

My friend, He is going to have all the glory, too. Throughout Romans and Corinthians and Ephesians the apostle Paul writes over and over again, "To him be all the glory." No flesh will glory in His presence. Not a bit.

"Oh, the depth of the riches both of the wisdom and knowledge of God! how unsearchable are his judgments and his ways past finding out."

But you and I can know them by coming into right relationship with Him through faith in the Son of God. We can walk in His fellowship and enjoy *Him*. That's what spiritual life is—the enjoyment of divine life.

Romans 12

From Romans 1 through 11, we have had (for the most part) what God has done for us. Starting in chapter 12, we have what we are to do to glorify God here on earth.

Paul begins by appealing to our wills. By the Spirit of God, God has given to us the capacity to glorify the Savior among men. Think of it. He wants you and me to be channels to express to the world something of His love, of His grace, of His compassion to men. God still loves men and women—remember that. And how is He going to display Himself except through you and me?

PRACTICAL RIGHTEOUSNESS MANIFESTED IN HIS PEOPLE
(12:1—16:27)

Relationship to God (12:1-2)

12:1. *I beseech you therefore, brethren, by the mercies of God, that ye present your bodies a living sacrifice, holy, acceptable unto God, which is your reasonable service.*

Here you have the beseeching of grace. It's not the law, demanding you do something, but rather the entreaty of grace, pleading for personal dedication to God. I think sometimes that we who have been on the way for many, many years have lost that fervency, that freshness, that sweetness of love for the Savior.

How about you, my friend? I'm not questioning your standing before God. All I ask is, how much do you love Him? When we consider how good God has been to us, there is only one thing we can do—obey this verse. Let it get hold of you. "I beseech you by the mercies of God"—not by anything else, just by the mercies and compassion of God—"that you present your body a living sacrifice." That's all He asks.

Before we were saved, we yielded our bodies to sin. We yielded to the lusts of the flesh and the mind. Now Paul says, yield those things to God. Why? To be saved? No. To get something? No. Just because we love Him.

Notice Paul calls it "a living sacrifice." God didn't ask you to die for Him. The challenge is to live for Him in the midst of a world that has no place for Him and in the midst of friends, neighbors, and relatives who scorn you because you love the Savior.

Paul said at the beginning of this epistle that he was a bondslave of Jesus Christ. A bondslave had no possessions of his own, no will of his own, no time of his own. He was given over entirely to his master.

You say, "Well, Mr. Mitchell, it's going to cost me something." Yes, it costs to be a living, holy sacrifice.

Whenever I think of this verse, I think of John Alexander Clark, a missionary who spent his lifetime in the Congo. He told of an incident when he treated a woman who had fallen into a fire and had severely burned her arm. He put some medicine on her arm and bandaged it and took care of her. Then, for a number of weeks, he went daily to her hut and massaged her arm until it became usable.

Months later, he was sitting in front of his hut when a woman came down from the village with a large basket full of corn on her head. She came up to him and put the basket down and said, "This is your corn."

He said, "No, it isn't my corn. I didn't buy it—but I will buy it from you."

"Oh, no," she said. "I can't sell this corn. It's your corn."

"No," he said. "It's not my corn."

"You don't understand," she said. "This corn is your corn. This arm is your arm. You're the one who saved this arm. It's your arm. This arm prepared the ground. This arm planted the seed and cultivated the soil. It gathered in the harvest. This arm is your arm. This corn is your corn."

The Lord Jesus gave himself for us. Can we not give ourselves to Him so we become His arm? He redeemed us from the fire, He bought us with His own precious blood, He sacrificed to save you and me. The least we can do is to offer ourselves as living sacrifices, holy, acceptable to God.

Have you done that, my friend? If not, why not? Is the Lord asking too much of us? On the contrary, it's the only logical thing we can do.

> **12:2.** *And be not conformed to this world: but be ye transformed by the renewing of your mind, that ye may prove what is that good, and acceptable, and perfect, will of God.*

Paul first makes a negative statement: "Do not conform any longer to the pattern of this world." Don't run your life according to the world that is in opposition to Christ. This age is a selfish age. It pleases self instead of God. It is dominated by Satan, not by Christ. To conform to this world is to manifest unfaithfulness to the One who redeemed us from this present evil age.

Then he makes a positive statement. We are to be "transformed by the renewing of our minds." Have your mind renewed by continual occupation with Christ so you may prove what is the good, acceptable, and perfect will of God. It is a positive setting of your mind on Christ.

Knowing the perfect will of God is the outcome of the dedication in verse 1. When I give myself as a present to Him and turn my body and all I am over to Him, then I begin to prove what His good, perfect, and acceptable will is. Put yourself, put all you are and have, in the hands of your wonderful Savior, and then, through you, the Spirit of God will reveal something of the loveliness and beauty of your Lord.

RELATIONSHIP TO THE BODY (12:3-18)

Membership in the Body (12:3-5)

12:3-5. *For I say, through the grace given unto me, to every man that is among you, not to think of himself more highly than he ought to think; but to think soberly, according as God hath dealt to every man the measure of faith. For as we have many members in one body, and all members have not the same office: so we, being many, are one body in Christ, and every one members one of another.*

First, Paul takes up the responsibility you and I have, as members of the body of Christ, to the church. Remember, your gifts have been given to you under the sovereignty of God. The Spirit of God is sovereign not only in the bestowal of gifts (1 Corinthians 12), but He is also sovereign in the place you have in the body of Christ. He is sovereign in putting you in the place where you can exercise your gifts as you serve the church, which is Christ's body.

We are put in the body for two reasons. The first reason is *for the edification of the body* (Romans 1:11-12; Ephesians 4:16; Colossians 2:19). We ought to share with each other what we know about the Savior. As we do, we encourage each other. We may impart to someone else truth he has never seen, and in like manner, he may impart to us something we have never seen. I don't care how much you know of your Bible, there is much in the Word of God that you don't know.

Some of the most wonderful truths I ever learned as a young Christian, I learned not in seminary, not in school, but in some old sod shacks way up in northern Canada, sitting on an earthen floor with a homesteader telling me what he or she knew of the Savior. It's true, I didn't know much in those days, and these homesteaders were not men of the schools—they were not scholars. But don't tell me they didn't know the things of God. There was a sweetness, an aroma about them in the things of Christ that stirred in me a tremendous yearning: "This is what I want. This is real. Not something to tickle my intellect, but something to reach the need of my heart." I saw the reality of life in Christ.

God has given to each one of us gifts, according to the measure of faith. God in His sovereignty has put us in the body of Christ and gifted us by the Spirit as it has pleased Him. It's not what we want. It's what God wants. He knows the best place for you and for me to serve Him. He has put us in the body to function so that He will be glorified.

My friend, you can't get along without me and I can't get along without you. Each of us has a different function, and God wants us to walk in fellowship with Christ, our Head. As we do, we will be able to use our gift and edify the other members of the body.

The second reason we are put in the body is *to increase the body*, and that's soul winning. It is communicating the Word to our generation. Even if you are the weakest member of the body of Christ, you have a place to function. You might be only a joint, but even so you must function. No one can take your place.

You say, "Well, Mr. Mitchell, I don't know what He wants me to do." That may be true. All I'm asking you to do is to walk in fellowship with Christ in the light of His Word. He will soon show you what to do. It will be put upon your heart what to do. God will open doors for you. Or it may be that God's ministry for you is in your room with the door shut, where you have a ministry of intercessory prayer. That is one of the most needed ministries today.

Oh, for God's people to take some time to wait upon Him, to intercede for His servants all over the world. Sometimes they feel forgotten. Nobody prayed. It would be terrible if a man or woman were to go to the mission field and have nobody behind him in prayer. Take someone upon your heart and pray for him or her. Take your place in the body of Christ as one who intercedes.

Everyone of us must minister in the body of Christ. Everyone of us. When you don't minister, the body suffers. We must buy up every opportunity of reaching our generation for Christ because the coming of the Lord is near. Will you pray that every testimony for Christ to our generation will be given in the power of the Spirit of God? How glad I am we are workers together in this blessed ministry.

Our Ministry in the Body (12:6-8)

Each of us has a ministry. Our service truly is measured by how much of a heart we have for Christ.

> **12:6-8.** *Having then gifts differing according to the grace that is given to us, whether prophecy, let us prophesy according to the proportion of faith; or ministry, let us wait on our ministering: or he that teacheth, on teaching; or he that exhorteth, on exhortation: he that giveth, let him do it with simplicity; he that ruleth, with diligence; he that showeth mercy, with cheerfulness.*

There are seven gifts mentioned here. Some are public gifts; many others are personal.

The first gift, the gift of *prophecy*, is for edification and comfort. It is giving forth the Word of Life. Prophecy doesn't necessarily mean foretelling future events. A prophet is one who speaks for God to others. When I speak from the Word of God, I am prophesying. Not everyone has this gift, but those who have it are to use it to give forth the Word.

The second gift Paul mentions is *ministry*, pouring out our lives for others (cf. Ephesians 4:12). Certain men in the gospel ministry are not evangelists or teachers, but they are good pastors. They minister to the needs of God's people. As long as you are a member of the body of Christ, you can minister. You can reveal to others things that will encourage them in the Lord. Anyone can have a ministry.

God has also given to certain men gifts of *teaching* so that they can make the Word of God clear. I have friends who have a tremendous capacity for knowledge, but when it comes to imparting that knowledge, they have a difficult time. You can ask them a question and they can answer you, but you put them before a group of people and they aren't very effective communicators. They don't have the gift of teaching.

If you have the gift of teaching, use it. You may not be a G. Campbell Morgan, but you can use your gift to impart the truth of God to others in Sunday school, young people's meetings, in home Bible studies, or wherever.

Another of God's gifts to the church is *exhortation*. A man who exhorts God's people encourages them to be obedient to the Word of God. He has the gift of encouraging God's people to do something for God. He exhorts them to perform the ministry to which God has called them. A person may not be a teacher of doctrine, but he can stand up and give a devotional to exhort the people of God, to encourage them to walk with God in the midst of a world that is lawless and sinful. That's the work of an exhorter.

If you love to exhort, don't try to be a teacher or an evangelist or pastor. Stick to your job of exhortation. We need the teacher. We need the pastor. We need the evangelist. We need the exhorter.

Some also have the gift of *giving*. One day, our Lord was standing by the treasury in the temple when the Pharisees came along and blew their trumpets and made a lot of noise so everybody could see what they put into the treasury box. And along came a little widow who slipped in her two mites and kept on going. Nobody saw it except the Lord. But he spoke wonderfully about her joy of giving and her sacrifice. He never said a word about the Pharisees and the amount of money they put in. When you give, give quietly and with simplicity.

Lest someone should say, "Well, Mr. Mitchell, I don't have the gift of giving"—don't try to rationalize your stinginess. Don't hold back. Give with a heart that is wholehearted for God. Give because you love him. And, remember, God will never be in your debt.

Others have the gift of *leadership*. If you hold a leadership position in your church, serve with diligence. Do it with a heart before God. Remember, this is a God-given responsibility. Lead with diligence, as if it were your own business.

I've seen men who were diligent in the business world, but when it came to the Lord's business, they were sloppy, they were indifferent. Be just as diligent in the work of the Lord as you are in your own business. It is God's business, and we should do it with diligence. Don't miss meetings, don't be slack in your responsibilities, lead with diligence.

The final gift Paul lists is *showing mercy*. This ministry may be to the sick; it may be to failing, stumbling believers; it may be to discouraged, disheartened Christians. They don't need a club—they need some mercy. God has been wonderful in His mercy to you and to me. Should we not show the same to God's people?

"Brother Mitchell, if you only knew what they've done!" I don't care what they have done, they need some mercy. Oh, that God would put into your heart and mine a spirit of mercy for God's people. Don't go into a hospital room as if your last day has come. When people are sick, they need to be cheered up, they need encouragement. Some Christians are downhearted because of the roughness of the path. They are having a hard time. Everything is going wrong. They're discouraged and down in the dumps. They need someone who will come along and understand them, care for them, love them, show them mercy.

And if you find Christians who have been taken over by some sin, please don't judge them. Don't come down on them. Don't go and tell everyone about them. Instead, manifest mercy and encourage them in the Lord. Put your arm around them and encourage them in the Savior. Remind them that the Lord is full of mercy and grace. Remind them that they have a throne of grace to which they can come and there obtain all the mercy and all the grace they need. Oh, for that understanding spirit that can take dear people of God in all their frailty and love them so much that they turn to the Savior in repentance or are encouraged to go on for the Lord.

Oh, how we need these seven blessed ministries today. These are God's gifts to the church, and every Christian has a gift. You and I have a tremendous place of ministry in the body of Christ. Why not begin today to exercise the gift God has given you?

Our Relationship to Each Member (12:9-18)

12:9. *Let love be without dissimulation. Abhor that which is evil; cleave to that which is good.*

Paul is saying, let love be real, let love be without hypocrisy. Love must not be something you put on like a coat. Let's be genuine in our love. First Corinthians 13 tells us that genuine love is patient and kind. It doesn't envy, it doesn't boast, it is not proud. It is not rude nor self-seeking nor easily provoked, nor does it keep record of wrongs. It doesn't rejoice in iniquity, but it rejoices in the truth. Love bears all things, believes all things, hopes all things, endures all things. This is the kind of love we are to manifest.

Paul also tells us to hate what is evil and to cling to what is good. This is to be our attitude toward evil men and evil things. Abhor what is evil. Run away. Don't put yourself in the way of temptation.

We sometimes think, "Why, I'll never do that." But we do—and we do it again and again. Why? Because we put ourself in the way of temptation. Are we not all guilty here? You say God delivered you from some of your weaknesses, habits, and corrupt sinful things you did before you were saved. And after you were saved, the Lord put in your heart a desire to please him. You think that desire is so strong now that these things won't tempt you. Listen and don't you forget it: Don't put yourself in the way of temptation or, just as sure as you were born, you will fall.

My friend, don't forget that you are weak. Just as you trusted the Lord when you were saved, you must trust Him now for everything every day. The Lord is the deliverer—your strong will is not.

12:10. *Be kindly affectioned one to another with brotherly love; in honour preferring one another.*

Sometimes I think kindness is a forgotten art. It doesn't cost you anything to be kind. A kind word, a kind act—oh, friend, how this world needs it. There are so many dear Christian people who would welcome kindness from someone. There are so many lonely people in the world. Maybe a dear woman has lost her husband, and her children are living in another part of the country. She is alone. How she needs some little kindnesses—a kind word, a kind act. If you know someone like that, show her some kindness, won't you?

And honoring someone above ourselves is not common either, is it? There is no self-exaltation here. "In honor preferring one another." Don't be envious. Don't be jealous. Oh, how it must rejoice the heart of God when self is put to one side and the other brother is given the place of honor. May God grant to you and me a generous spirit when we meet with God's people—not to be always looking for a place of honor, but to let the other fellow have it.

12:11. *Not slothful in business; fervent in spirit; serving the Lord.*

Be diligent. Don't lie down on the job. You say, "I don't like my job." All the more reason to be diligent, to do your job for the Lord, and to be the best worker on that job. A lazy man or woman is no credit to the Lord. Whatever the task is, do it as to the Lord. Remember, you are serving the Lord Christ.

You say, "I don't get what's coming to me." Can't you trust the Lord who loves you? If you are serving and doing the job as to the Lord, you can trust God to take care of you. And not only that, but your work becomes no longer a chore, no longer a burden. It becomes a real joy when you are doing it for God.

Is your heart full of fervent love and zeal for the things of God? Are you fervent in your spirit? One young man wrote on the flyleaf of his Bible, "Wanted: Wicks to burn out. Oil supplied." This is what John means in Revelation 2 when he writes about "first love"—that fervency, that freshness, that hotness of love for the Savior.

12:12. *Rejoicing in hope; patient in tribulation; continuing instant in prayer.*

Why rejoice in hope? Because the Lord is going to come soon. We must live in daily expectation of seeing the Savior. Are you living in the expectation of His coming? Are you rejoicing in hope of the glory of God? Isn't it wonderful that you and I can live today in expectation of seeing Him whom, having not seen, we love? So we are filled with joy.

But you say, "I'm in sorrow right now. I'm having a tough time right now." Even so, lift up your head, for your redemption draws nigh. The Lord is at hand. Think of the early martyrs who went into the amphitheater singing the glories of Jesus even though they were going to be torn to pieces by wild beasts. They went singing because they were rejoicing in hope of the glory of God. They were going to say, "Good night, earth! Good morning, glory!" Oh, to rejoice in hope of the glory of God. Won't you do that today?

"Patient in tribulation." It's hard to be patient in tribulation. Some people become so self-sympathetic: "Nobody goes through what I go through. No one has the tests I have." Don't get occupied with yourself or you'll get discouraged. Glory in your tribulation, says Paul, because tribulation works. It's doing something for you. "These light afflictions . . . are working for us a far more exceeding and eternal weight of glory." Our suffering is but for a short while. It will end, and God will have used it for our perfection and for His glory.

Paul also tells us to be "instant in prayer." What does he mean by that? I believe he means we are to be ready at any time to pray.

On the job, driving the car, preparing a meal, be always ready to pray. Our Lord said in Luke 18:1, "Men ought always to pray and not to faint." That doesn't mean you have to be on your knees all the time, but your heart should be so in touch with the Lord that whatever comes into your life you can talk to Him about it. If you meet some child of God going through some problems or testing, you can pray with him. You can pray while you do your job. Be always ready at any time to lift up your heart to the Lord in prayer for whatever may come.

We are workers together with God. The least thing in your life is of great interest to Him, and it's wonderful to just sit down and talk to the Lord about it or to go on about your business and commune with Him about it.

12:13. *Distributing to the necessity of saints; given to hospitality.*

If Christians can't meet other Christians in their need, who will? Be generous. God will never let you down. Do it for His glory, and for His name's sake to bring relief to someone else's burdens. Let's be generous.

And then be given to hospitality. I like what Hebrews 13:2 says about entertaining angels unaware. Be given to hospitality but don't do it with a grudging spirit (1 Peter 4:9). Don't say, "I wish they would go home. I wish they would go some place else. Don't they know I'm busy?" No, be given to hospitality.

Oh, how often, whether you know it or not, you will uplift someone by that little act of kindness of yours, that hospitable spirit of yours, that stopping the thing you are doing just to encourage some dear soul who has come to you in need. And, my, the joy it gives you when you make the effort to meet their need. Be given to hospitality. It is a responsibility, not a gift. These are very practical matters.

12:14. *Bless them which persecute you: bless, and curse not.*

Follow the example of our Lord "who, when he was reviled,

reviled not again; when he suffered, he threatened not; but committed himself to him that judgeth righteously." It is a wonderful thing not to retaliate. Somebody speaks harshly or accusingly to you, and you know they are not being just. What they are saying is wrong. The most natural thing is to want to retaliate. Instead of retaliating, just say, "The Lord bless you." Just take it quietly. Anyone can retaliate; it takes a strong man not to retaliate. "Bless them that persecute you," and, of course, do the rest of the verse, "bless and curse not." You can disarm people by manifesting a sweet spirit.

12:15. *Rejoice with them that do rejoice, and weep with them that weep.*

We are to enter into the joys and the sorrows of fellow Christians. If you are at a wedding, no matter how you feel, rejoice with the bride and groom. May their joy be filled full because you are part of their celebration. And if you are with those going through testing, sorrow, and heartache, enter sympathetically into their pain. Manifest mercy and kindness and understanding and love. This is not being a hypocrite, my friend, this is thinking about the other fellow.

12:16. *Be of the same mind one toward another. Mind not high things, but condescend to men of low estate. Be not wise in your own conceits.*

Live in harmony with all men, and be willing to associate with people of low estate. It's natural to want to be around those who are famous or popular. Forget about that. Seek out people who are lowly, humble in mind, and who live a genuine life. That's what Paul is after. Fellowship with lowly men and don't be conceited.

12:17. *Recompense to no man evil for evil. Provide things honest in the sight of all men.*

Don't return evil for evil—return good. In 1 Peter 3:9, the apostle tells us not to repay "evil for evil, or railing for railing: but contrariwise blessing; knowing that ye are thereunto called, that ye should inherit a blessing." Peter has been writing about the relationship between husbands and wives. Don't rail upon each other because that builds up a wall between you, he says. If one starts to rail on the other, let the other just turn around and bless.

I have preached on this subject several times, and I've always thought I was in control of these things. But the Lord showed me otherwise one night when I came home storming about something or someone and I took it out on Mary Mitchell. I crabbed about something she'd spent a lot of time on—something new she'd made for dinner—and she just smiled and said, "The Lord bless you, honey." Talk about putting a man in his place! We still laugh about it.

Then Paul says we should be careful to do what is right in the sight of all men. Be honest in all your dealings with the outside world and with Christians, too. Don't take advantage of another believer. Let us be honest in what we do, honest in what we say. We are children of One who is God, and he wants us to be honest in the sight of all men.

> **12:18.** *If it be possible, as much as lieth in you, live peaceably with all men.*

Be at peace with all men as far as it is possible (cf. Hebrews 12:14; Mark 9:50). I needn't go any further in this. These are practical exhortations about our relationship, our responsibility, our service, our ministry to one another. Read them over and over again. Remember, it's as we walk in fellowship with God that our lives show forth His praise. May that be true today.

Relationship to Our Enemies (12:19-21)

Paul concludes this twelfth chapter by giving us our responsibility toward those who don't love us or like us, who are opposed to our ministry and to our Christian faith. If you try to live as a Christian and please God, you are bound to receive opposition of some kind. Let's face up to it. The closer you walk to the Lord and the more you seek to please Him, the greater will be the opposition you can expect. We live in a world that has no place for the Savior. So what is my relationship to be?

> **12:19-21.** *Dearly beloved, avenge not yourselves, but rather give place unto wrath: for it is written, Vengeance is mine; I will repay, saith the Lord. Therefore if thine enemy hunger, feed him; if he thirst, give him drink: for in so doing thou shalt heap coals of fire on his head. Be not overcome of evil, but overcome evil with good.*

It is hard not to seek revenge. It is difficult to leave everything to the Lord. You feel like saying, "Lord, hurry up." But we need to look to the example of our Lord who patiently endured ridicule and suffering, entrusting Himself to Him who judges justly (1 Peter 2:21-23).

You and I cannot judge justly. We do not know all the facts involved, all the circumstances. But we can leave everything to the Lord, for vengeance belongs to Him and He will repay. God is the only one who can pay back personally and accurately. And believe me, my friend, you can trust God to repay.

And if you have any enemies, be kind to them. Your very kindness may open their eyes to their need of a Savior, or it may increase their doom. Paul says in 2 Corinthians 2:15-16, "We are unto God a sweet savor of Christ, in them that are saved, and in them that perish: To the one we are the savor of death unto death; and to the other the savor of life unto life. And who is sufficient for these things?"

Paul says the preaching of the cross is foolishness—to whom?—to those who are perishing (1 Corinthians 1:18). And when you and I give forth our testimony, often we are hindered; we are opposed and sometimes cursed. So what! Bless them. Be cheerful. In some way manifest something of the grace and the mercy and the patience of the Lord.

I want to tell you, my friend, it really works. I have seen fellows ashamed of the things they've said. They wouldn't have been ashamed if I had cursed them or reviled them back. That would have added fuel to the fire. Just bless them; overcome evil with good. It really works.

Romans 13

We've looked at our relationship as believers to God, to each other in the body of Christ, and to our enemies. Now we come to our relationship to the governing authorities.

RELATIONSHIP TO CIVIL AUTHORITIES (13:1-7)

13:1-2. *Let every soul be subject unto the higher powers. For there is no power but of God: the powers that be are ordained of God. Whosoever therefore resisteth the power, resisteth the ordinance of God: and they that resist shall receive to themselves damnation.*

When Paul wrote this passage, Nero was the emperor of Rome. He was a terrible man who came to power only because his mother Agrippina got rid of every man who stood in Nero's way. There was no question she was a wicked woman. But after Nero came to the throne, he had his mother banished from the royal palace and later condemned her to death. When the executioners came to kill her, she said, "Strike. Level your raids against the womb which gave birth to such a monster."

Here you have extremely wicked, corrupt, vicious people in authority. And yet Paul writes to the Christians living under that authority to "be subject unto the powers that be, for there is no power but of God. The powers that be are ordained of God."

We are to be subject to civil authority because rulers are ordained of God. They receive authority from Him. Neither their character nor how they rule is the question before us. Paul doesn't bring up Nero's wickedness and his temper and his murdering and his corruption. He brings up one fact—the powers, the civil leaders, are ordained of God, and they receive their authority from him.

God raised up a man named Cyrus to be head of the Median empire and called him "my shepherd" (Isaiah 44-45). Cyrus was an idolater. He was corrupt. Yet he was God's instrument to allow the captive Jewish remnant to return to Israel. Zerubbabel and Ezra went back and rebuilt the temple, and afterward Nehemiah came and rebuilt the walls of the city. Cyrus was a minister of God in that he was given the authority to liberate the remnant of Israel from Babylon. His authority came from God.

When you and I manifest contempt for the government, that's lawlessness. We are resisting the authority God has given to men. We're living in a day when people thumb their noses at the government because they don't like what's going on. But my place is to be one of subjection to the government. The power, the authority is ordained of God.

> **13:3-4.** *For rulers are not a terror to good works, but to the evil. Wilt thou then not be afraid of the power? do that which is good, and thou shalt have praise of the same: for he is the minister of God to thee for good. But if thou do that which is evil, be afraid; for he beareth not the sword in vain: for he is the minister of God, a revenger to execute wrath upon him that doeth evil.*

It's a terrible thing today that we have such strong public sympathy for criminals. We have more sympathy for the criminal awaiting judgment than we have for his victims. Men excuse the criminal because "he has a disease." So sin is no longer sin. Corruption is no longer corruption. Murder is no longer murder. Stealing is no longer stealing. It's just a disease.

My friend, God has authorized government to keep down evil-doers, and when you sympathize with those who are guilty of crime, you rebel against God. It is a sad picture when sin is no longer sin. And if Satan can get us to minimize sin, then he can minimize the work of Christ on the cross. When sin is no longer sin, no longer lawlessness, when it's just a disease, we have come to the place where nothing short of the wrath of God is going to fall on our generation. Anything that is against the righteous character of God is sin and will come under the judgment of God.

13:5. *Wherefore ye must needs be subject, not only for wrath, but also for conscience sake.*

We must be subject to the government not only because of what it can do to us when we break laws, but also for the sake of our conscience. We are to be subject to constituted authority. Whatever the law says, there is no question as to our duty.

"But, Mr. Mitchell, what about my conscience? What if the government demands something that is contrary to my conscience?" Remember this: Governments are for the earth, to keep evildoers in check. But governments don't control the spiritual realm.

In the Book of Daniel, Azariah, Mishael, and Hananiah refused to bow the knee to Nebuchadnezzar's golden image. Theirs was a question of conscience before God. They refused to bow the knee to an image the king had made. He was trying to control and direct their worship. That's a different proposition.

If I am told I may no longer preach the gospel of Christ, if I am told I may no longer worship the Lord Jesus Christ or stand for the Word of God, I would rather go to jail. If the issue is contrary to my conscience before God and concerns my relationship to God, there is no question where I will stand. I will stand for God whatever the cost may be to me.

But as long as the government doesn't interfere with my walk before God and my obedience to His Word, I will obey the government because it is ordained of God. I may not agree with some of the methods of government, but because its authority comes from God, I must be in subjection to my government.

> **13:6-7.** *For this cause pay ye tribute also: for they are God's ministers, attending continually upon this very thing. Render therefore to all their dues: tribute to whom tribute is due; custom to whom custom; fear to whom fear; honour to whom honour.*

In other words, pay your taxes. I don't like my tax bill, but I pay my taxes. I'm a Christian, and therefore I'm subject to the authority that's over me. I pay my taxes for conscience sake. I pay my taxes to support the government. The leaders are ministers of God to keep down evildoers, and they must be supported.

Even the Lord Jesus, the Creator of all things, didn't dodge his taxes (Matthew 17:24-27). Remember that. He recognized the Romans' place of authority even though the Jews squirmed a great deal because of the way Rome treated them. Nevertheless, the Son of God said to Peter, "Go and catch a fish. In its mouth you'll find some money. Pay the taxes for me and pay your taxes, too, from that same money." Why? "Lest we should offend them. Lest we should cause any trouble."

But if the time ever comes where we have to choose between our relationship to God and our relationship to our government, if the choice is between Christ or Caesar, then only one decision can be made and that is for the Savior. Whatever it costs, whether it means jail or even execution, we must stand by the Savior.

Relationship to Society (13:8-14)

> **13:8.** *Owe no man any thing, but to love one another: for he that loveth another hath fulfilled the law.*

I am not talking about the word *love* as it is used so commonly today with no depth to it. What people sometimes call love today is nothing but lust.

Paul writes this in view of the return of the Lord, who manifested

His love for His Father by obedience. He manifested His love for you and me by sacrifice, by dying for us. Likewise, we also as Christians manifest our love for our heavenly Father by obedience, by being obedient to His Word. We manifest our love for each other by sacrifice—by "dying," as it were—for the saints and for our neighbors. Love is a perpetual debt, and we are to owe no man anything but love.

Why did Paul bring the law in here? He is dealing with our relationship to man. In our relationship with God, it is a question of faith, of putting our trust in Him. God sees our faith; man experiences our love. Paul uses the law to show us our relationship to each other in practical living.

> **13:9-10.** *For this, Thou shalt not commit adultery, Thou shalt not kill, Thou shalt not steal, Thou shalt not bear false witness, Thou shalt not covet; and if there be any other commandment, it is briefly comprehended in this saying, namely, Thou shalt love thy neighbor as thyself. Love worketh no ill to his neighbor: therefore love is the fulfilling of the law.*

In the Ten Commandments, the first four laws govern our responsibility to God. Paul doesn't use them here since he is talking about our relationship to one another. The law is righteous, and the law demands righteousness. Love alone can keep the law. Love is the active principle of Christianity. When we love God and man, we fulfill the purpose of the law. The one who loves has wrought righteousness.

You see, friend, if I'm going to use the law as a means of life, then I'll never have life. The law was never given as a means of life to the unsaved, and the law was never given as a rule of life to the saved. The law has had nothing to say since the cross. But as Christians, indwelt by the Spirit of God, we will keep that part of the law that governs our relationship to society. That's why I say here, no man is ever saved by keeping the law. We are saved by grace through faith in the Savior.

But I have a responsibility to society, to my neighbors, and to other people on earth, and love is the only way I can express that. When you love people, my friend, you will do things you never dreamed of doing. Love alone can keep the law.

But don't expect the government to manifest love. God doesn't expect the government to manifest love or to rule by love. The government is to rule by righteousness. "Righteousness exalteth a nation: but sin is a reproach to any people" (Proverbs 14:34). Righteousness is the principle for reigning, but love is the principle for living with one another.

13:11. *And that, knowing the time, that now it is high time to awake out of sleep: for now is our salvation nearer than when we believed.*

Our incentive for loving our neighbor is that each day brings our salvation nearer. And if Paul could say that to the early church, how much closer the coming of the Lord is for us. This is the incentive—the Lord Jesus may come today. Philippians 4 says the Lord Jesus is at hand. Therefore, what manner of men ought we to be?

You might say to me, "Well, Mr. Mitchell, the church through the centuries believed that and He hasn't come." That's true—and that's the genius of it. *He may come today*, and I'm to live today just as Paul lived in his day, in expectation of seeing Him whom having not seen we love. Here Paul says, "Because our salvation is nearer than when we believed," we ought to love our neighbor as ourselves. We ought to manifest that love which would be for the benefit of our neighbor and to the glory of God.

Oh, our generation is so full of indifference and coldness to this appeal of the Savior that I wonder what will break us down. We are not fighting so much outbroken opposition to the gospel—we don't meet much vileness against the gospel today—we just meet cold indifference. It's bad enough to be indifferent, but it's terrible when we are satisfied with our indifference. Regrettably, this is also true of many Christians. I'm not questioning their salvation, but I wonder how much love they have for the Savior.

Oh, to be delivered from our cold indifference to the warmth of our Savior's love. You and I can be right in our doctrine and be cold in our heart and indifferent to our Savior's appeal that we should live before men as the children of God. As Philippians says, we are "the sons of God . . . in the midst of a crooked and perverse nation, among whom ye shine as lights in the world" (Philippians 2:15). We ought to buy up every opportunity to love our neighbors and live a life that will glorify God in the world.

Oh, listen, my friend, it's high time to awake out of sleep. Are you a sleepy Christian? An indifferent Christian? A lukewarm Christian? Are you so satisfied with the things of this world that in some way, somehow, you have missed Christ's appeal that you manifest the character, the heart, the compassion and tenderness of the Savior to men and women for whom He died? How are we going to reach our generation if we don't manifest that precious love of the Savior?

And please don't tell me, "I just can't stand my neighbors." The Lord loved you and died for you when you were His enemy, and that same divine love is indwelling your heart by the Spirit of God. "The love of God is shed abroad in our hearts by the Holy [Spirit] given unto us," Paul wrote in Romans 5:5. As you and I walk before God in the light of His Word and in the Spirit of God, we begin to manifest the character and the heart and the love and the compassion and the tenderness of our Savior.

Someone once asked John Wesley, "Sir, what would you do if you knew the Lord was coming today?" He said, "I would do just what I am doing. I am living today, every day, in the anticipation of the coming of our Savior." Or as G. Campbell Morgan used to say, "I am living and serving as if the Lord were coming today, and I am working as if the Lord were going to tarry a hundred years."

13:12-13a. *The night is far spent, the day is at hand: let us therefore cast off the works of darkness, and let*

*us put on the armor of light. Let us walk honestly, as in
the day . . .*

The hour for the coming of the Lord Jesus is at hand, just as He
spoke of in John 14:3, "And if I go . . . I will come again, and
receive you unto myself." In view of this, my hope being stimu-
lated, my watchfulness being aroused, what shall I do? Notice,
three times Paul says "Let us." "Let us cast off . . . Let us put on . . .
Let us walk. . . ."

What are the works of darkness we are to cast off? The next
verse tells us:

13:13b. *Not in rioting and drunkenness, not in chambering and wantonness, not in strife and envying.*

As someone has said, "Let's get rid of our night clothes, the
clothes of darkness." Cast off the works of darkness. Throw off
your night clothes, the deeds of the old man—rioting and drunkenness—which are the outbroken sins of society. I needn't go into
them. Rioting and drunkenness don't belong to the children of
God. Rioting and drunkenness are manifestation of the sins of the
night. This is the world outside of Christ.

The second couple—chambering and wantonness—are the
secret sins of society, the sexual immorality and corruption so
prevalent today. You and I are living in a day of situation ethics.
"If two people agree that they want to do certain things, what's
wrong with that? They both love each other. Let them do what
they want to do."

It's moral corruption, and with that moral corruption comes disease. I question if even medical science could give us an accurate
count of how many people suffer from sexually transmitted diseases in America. One reads that a tremendous percentage of high
school young people are already diseased. This is immorality and
corruption. Let it not once be named among us as becomes the
children of God.

Oh, listen, Christian friend, you and I haven't much more time
to magnify the Savior. We are surrounded with this wave of situation

ethics, of moral corruption, this so-called freedom of expression (which is really bondage) that is lapping over, not only into our schools but also into our society and even into our churches. The cup of iniquity is filling full in America and throughout the world. We cannot afford to live one day out of fellowship with God. As Christians, as children of God, let us walk honestly before God, not in rioting and drunkenness, not in chambering and wantonness.

You say, "Why, Mr. Mitchell, I am not guilty of rioting. I am not guilty of drunkenness. I am not guilty of immorality." All right, but what about the last couple? These are sins of our heart, sins of our emotions. Notice the company that "strife and envying" keep.

My heart was heavy the day I heard of a split in a church in a certain city, a church with a wonderful testimony for God and out of which have sprung three or four new congregations. The breakup came out of fighting and strife among the members. It was a case of envy, of jealousy, of dissension. Someone has said that envy and jealousy are the sins of Christian workers. God forbid!

How easy it is to become jealous and envious of someone, even of some other Christian that God is using. I may not agree with all he does, but God is using him, and to his own master he stands or falls. But because our own heart is out of fellowship with God, we say things we shouldn't say about him or her. There is envy and jealousy, and the first thing we know, we divide God's people. Shame on us Christians! God deliver us from envy and jealousy of those God is using. May we keep our hands off and glorify what God is doing.

Oh, no, we wouldn't be found guilty of rioting and drunkenness, of chambering and wantonness, of impurity and moral corruption. But what about strife and envy and jealousy? Proverbs says, "Envy is the rottenness of the bones." O, God, deliver us from such a thing. Cause us to be knitted together around the Person of Christ so we see each other in Christ Jesus, not in our weakness, not in our frailty, not in our failures.

The time is at hand. The day is far spent. The Lord is even at the door—He may come today! What an incentive to live for God. What an incentive to throw off rioting and drunkenness. What an incentive to throw off the sins of the flesh, immorality and uncleanness. What an incentive to throw off all strife and bickering and fighting and jealousy.

And then what are we to do?

13:14. *But put ye on the Lord Jesus Christ, and make not provision for the flesh, to fulfill the lusts thereof.*

This is the place of victory. This is the place of deliverance. "Put on the Lord Jesus Christ." Recognize your identification with the risen Lord and appropriate Him for your daily needs. We look forward to His return, but now we experience Him in a delivered life.

Paul says in Philippians, "that Christ may be magnified in my body whether it be by life or by death. For to me to live is Christ." We are to live like citizens of another world. "That I may know him and the power of his resurrection and the fellowship of his suffering. . . . I count everything but loss that I might win Christ—that I might know Christ."

Make no provision for the flesh, for its desires and lusts. All you need is found in Christ. Take your weaknesses, take your circumstances, take your frailties, take the whole business to him. He is all you need. Arm yourself with His power for your life day by day.

Oh, listen, my Christian friend, why don't you appropriate Christ today? Let Him live His life out through you and manifest His love toward society. Oh, how we need this.

God grant that you and I may walk before Him and live in the light of His presence, radiating something of the sweet aroma of Christ. Oh, that people may see Christ living in you and in me. Let us manifest a loving spirit toward others by our works, by our speech, by what we do, by where we go that Christ may be glorified.

Romans 14

Romans 14 and 15 ought to be in big letters on every church bulletin board. Oh, the confusion among Christians, the lack of love and compassion and understanding we show. How we need this passage!

Few of us know how to deal with Christians who may not be doing the things they ought to do or who are doing the things they shouldn't do. What is our attitude to be toward them? Likewise, how should we act toward weak brethren, to those who are babes in Christ?

Some of us have been saved for twenty years or more. We are well taught in the Word of God, and we know our doctrine. But others have been Christians for just as long and haven't grown at all in the knowledge of God. Are we to judge the immature in the light of our own conscience and by how much more we know? Or is there another way?

In chapter 12 we examined our relationship and responsibility to God, to the body of Christ, and to our enemies. In chapter 13 we dealt with our responsibility to the state, to our neighbors, and to society. In chapter 14 we're dealing with our responsibility to other Christians. Paul deals with the matter of receiving weak believers, some of whom have certain scruples. And in the first few verses of chapter 15, Paul will talk about those who claim to be strong and who ought to bear the infirmities of the weak. If I'm a child of God, then I ought to walk as a child of God—not only in my love for the Savior and my obedience to His Word, but also in my relationship to my friends whether they are strong or weak.

RELATIONSHIP TO WEAKER BRETHREN (14:1—15:7)

Receiving Weaker Brethren (14:1-4)

14:1-3. *Him that is weak in the faith receive ye, but not to doubtful disputations. For one believeth that he may eat all things: another, who is weak, eateth herbs. Let not him that eateth despise him that eateth not; and let not him which eateth not judge him that eateth: for God hath received him.*

I am sorry to say there are certain groups who will not accept anyone into their fellowship unless he believes just a certain way. I recognize the possibility of heresy and the need to guard believers against it, but if someone stands for the person and work of Christ and loves the Savior, there is no reason we cannot have fellowship with Him.

Sometimes it is hard for us not to judge, not to criticize when we see things we believe are dishonoring to the Lord, especially when the person we're criticizing doesn't see why he should do this or shouldn't do that.

We're to walk in love toward each other, and it's going to cost us something. Let's be realistic about this. It's not easy to stop doing something that you like to do and you feel free to do. You stop it, not because it's bad but because it's a stumbling block or it hinders another Christian who believes he can't do the same thing.

What in the world does Paul mean when he says, "Him that is weak in the faith receive ye, but not to doubtful disputations." Don't dispute with your weaker brother over things that are only doubtful.

How often we've heard, "If that fellow were a Christian, he wouldn't do that." How do you know he is not a Christian? He may be thinking the same thing about you. You see him not doing certain things, so you say, "Oh, he is a legalist. That fellow never was saved, he's just bound up in religion." And he looks at you exercising your freedom and he says, "I don't believe that fellow is a Christian. If he were a Christian, he wouldn't do that sort of a thing."

We judge each other in the light of our own knowledge, conscience, and experience. The result is we don't manifest patience toward one another. We try to decide the other man's doubts for him and so require him to walk in the light of our conscience.

My friend, he must not be forced to do so. Why don't you let him grow normally by the Word of God? He has faith. I know he's weak, but you should receive him into your fellowship. The trouble is, we cross our t's and dot our i's and split hairs, and if a person doesn't believe exactly what we believe, we won't have fellowship with him. This causes pride and divisions among God's people.

I led a men's Bible class in Portland some years ago, and seventy to eighty men attended each week. During one class, a man who was visiting for the first time began asking some questions, and it was obvious from his questions that he disagreed with what had been said. When I tried to lead the man along to see the truth as it is in Christ, I didn't get a chance to do so. Two or three of the men in the class spoke out and jumped all over this fellow. He quickly clammed up . . . and never came back.

I told those men the next Lord's Day, "It has taken the Lord ten to twenty years to get you where you are today. All you know now about the Savior and about your position in Christ was not learned in twenty-four hours. Some of you folk, when you first came to our Sunday school, believed just like this visitor did. But quietly the Word of God had its affect on your heart and your life, and you have grown in the grace and knowledge of God. Yet now you want this fellow to get there in ten minutes. It doesn't work that way."

When I became a Christian, I had no doctrine to undo. The Lord just saved me and dropped me right into the grace of God—into the wonderful position that I have in Christ as given to us in the Book of Romans. In fact, somebody asked me one time if that was the only book I had in my Bible because I reveled so much in the marvelous truth in it. But I had nothing to undo. I had no doctrines to get rid of. But other people have been raised from the time they were children in certain doctrines, and, my friend, you can't expect them to get rid of that in ten minutes. So if you meet a man who loves the Savior, who claims to believe in the Lord, but he is weak in the faith or he doesn't agree with you (and that's to be expected), then what shall you do? Bring him into your fellowship to encourage and edify and build him up.

14:4. *Who are thou that judgest another man's servant? to his own master he standeth or falleth. Yea, he shall be holden up: for God is able to make him stand.*

I am appealing to you Christians who have been taught all your life. I am appealing to you preachers and Sunday school teachers to manifest grace, tenderness, and compassion for God's people. Remember that a great many of them have never been instructed in the Word of God. They have longed and longed for scriptural food from the Word of God. They have gone from church to church and haven't received it. Friend, if you are in a church where they preach the Word of God, thank the Lord for it; but do not sit in judgment on those who have never had the opportunity.

Young believers and weak believers and possibly fallen believers do not need a clubbing. They need encouragement in the Lord, they need edification, they need someone who can pray with them and weep with them if necessary.

The Ground for Receiving Weaker Brethren (14:5-12)

14:5-6. *One man esteemeth one day above another: another esteemeth every day alike. Let every man be fully persuaded in his own mind. He that regardeth the day, regardeth it unto the Lord; and he that regardeth not the day, to the Lord he doth not regard it. He that eateth, eateth to the Lord, for he giveth God thanks; and he that eateth not, to the Lord he eateth not, and giveth God thanks.*

The first ground for receiving weaker brethren is that we have the same Lord, the same standing. We are going to glory together. We'll spend eternity together. This puts our receiving others on the unchanging absolute of our relationship to the Savior. We have no grounds for judging other Christians.

> **14:7-9.** *For none of us liveth to himself, and no man dieth to himself. For whether we live, we live unto the Lord; and whether we die, we die unto the Lord: whether we live therefore, or die, we are the Lord's. For to this end Christ both died, and rose, and revived, that he might be Lord both of the dead and living.*

There is no other law to be considered. Jesus Christ is the Lord for all believers, whether strong or weak, whether mature or babes. When you begin to judge another Christian, it's not, as a rule, an act of love as much as an act of pride. Is that not true? And, especially, if you know quite a bit of truth, the danger is to criticize and to judge the weaker brethren or those who don't agree with you.

But Paul says, "Let each one be fully persuaded in his own mind." Why? Because you walk before God in the Word of God as you see it, and others walk in the Word of God as they see it. You want to please God and to live for the Lord even though your doctrines may be different. In your heart, you all have the same yearning. There is no room for judgment because you have the same Lord and you can't live to yourself.

> **14:10-12.** *But why dost thou judge thy brother? or why dost thou set at nought thy brother? for we shall all stand before the judgment seat of Christ. For it is written, As I live, saith the Lord, every knee shall bow to me, and every tongue shall confess to God. So then every one of us shall give account of himself to God.*

The second ground for receiving weaker brethren is because the Lord is the judge. He is not only the Lord over all believers, but

He is the judge of all believers. And, remember, He is going to judge righteously. In the final analysis, friend, we have to stand before God.

As Christians, our sins have already been judged at the cross. We are being judged today on the character of our daily walk, and the result is chastisement or blessing. We are going to be judged with respect to rewards at the Judgment Seat of Christ (1 Corinthians 3:11-15; 2 Corinthians 5:10-11). The things we think are so wonderful may be nothing but wood, hay, and stubble. Did you minister, did you work and sacrifice because of your love for the Savior and for God's people? Or did you do it to earn a reputation or for financial gain? May the Lord deliver us from that. What stands the test of the fire—the gold, the silver, the precious stones—brings glory to God.

The unsaved are going to be judged at the Great White Throne judgment. These are the unsaved pictured in Revelation 20. And then will be the judgment of fallen angels and the judgment of the nations at the coming of the Savior to reign on the earth. As I have often said, the resurrection of Jesus Christ from the dead is a guarantee of salvation to everyone who will put his trust in Him. Yet the resurrection of Christ from the dead is a guarantee of judgment to everyone who rejects Him.

When we all appear before the judgment seat of Christ, then everything will be out in the open—not only our works and our actions, but our very attitudes. So wouldn't it be a good thing for you and me just to walk with God and let Him judge the brother? We do not know all the circumstances. We do not know all that is involved in the other person's life. So let's be slow to judge other Christians. Let's encourage them, edify them, and build them up in the Lord.

The Edification of All Believers (14:13-23)

The apostle now says that we are to seek the edification of all Christians, and here he takes up the use of liberty. He takes up our walk before God and our love for each other. First, we are to avoid being stumblingblocks to other Christians:

> **14:13-16.** *Let us not therefore judge one another any more: but judge this rather, that no man put a stumbling-block or an occasion to fall in his brother's way. I know, and am persuaded by the Lord Jesus, that there is nothing unclean of itself: but to him that esteemeth any thing to be unclean, to him it is unclean. But if thy brother be grieved with thy meat, now walkest thou not charitably. Destroy not him with thy meat, for whom Christ died. Let not then your good be evil spoken of.*

We either nurture young Christians in their growth or we judge them and cause them to stumble. You can do something and say, "I'm free to do it. I'm not bound. I have a free conscience about it." Yes, but your brother's conscience may not be so free.

I gave up certain habits after I became a Christian, not because I felt they were wrong nor because someone told me they were wrong. I gave them up because I found they were hindering young Christians from going on with the Lord, and they were hindering sinners from coming to the Savior. If you claim to be strong in the faith, then, my friend, you will be charitable, compassionate, tender, and understanding toward weak believers. And you will encourage them to get into the Word of God.

But we must manifest love toward one another, especially to weak believers. The more you love your Savior, the more you will love your brother in Christ. We serve the Lord Christ. If your brother is grieved by what you eat, remember him in his frailty and stop doing the thing you are doing for his sake. You want to guard his spiritual walk before God.

"Let not your good be evil spoken of"—don't let the very name of God be blasphemed among unbelievers because of your actions. Today men and women are turning away from the gospel because they know some Christians who are not walking before God. When I speak with men and women about the Savior, so often this is thrown up. "Let me tell you about Mr. So-and-so or Rev. So-and-so," they say. They run down the Savior because of the lives of Christians. And I have to say, "Pardon me, sir, but I'm not talking about them. I'm talking about the Savior. Do you find any flaw in the Savior? Do you have any fault to find with Christ?"

Please, do not criticize another Christian, whatever he has done, in the presence of the unsaved. This is a family matter. Don't give the unsaved ammunition to reject the Lord Jesus Christ because you told him about the failures and weaknesses and frailty of other Christians. If you know of some Christian who has failed God, don't tell somebody else about it. Get on your knees and pray for him or search him out and encourage him in the Lord. Don't meet him with a judgmental spirit; but rather in the spirit of love have understanding and tenderness and compassion.

God grant that you and I will so live before men and each other that we manifest something of the fragrance and love of the Savior. May we always have respect for other Christians. May we never shout about our liberty in Christ if we are not manifesting love to our weaker brother who needs our encouragement, who needs building up.

Paul goes on to tell us what the Kingdom of God is:

> **14:17-18.** *For the kingdom of God is not meat and drink; but righteousness, and peace, and joy in the Holy Ghost. For he that in these things serveth Christ is acceptable to God, and approved of men.*

Paul is dealing with the practical side of things. We have righteousness, peace, and joy in the Holy Spirit. As righteousness is evident in our lives, we experience peace and joy. This kind of life is "acceptable to God" and free from the judgment of men.

Does your walk, does my walk please God? Do our actions, our words, our attitudes, our motives glorify Him? When your life pleases God, you also have the approval of men. Even the world respects the reality of life in the Christian. You can talk to people about the Savior—you can talk doctrine to them and even give them the gospel—and they may rise up in opposition or they may be coldly indifferent. But the moment they see something of the reality of life in Christ, they take notice.

How often people say to me, "I wish I had what those Christians have. In all the problems of life they go through—their sorrows, their afflictions, their disappointments—they have a spirit about them. They have a peace I don't understand. I wish I had it." There's only one place to find it and that's in Christ.

> **14:19.** *Let us therefore follow after the things which make for peace, and things wherewith one may edify another.*

I get letters from people who don't agree with things I've said on my radio broadcast. I can understand that. No man knows all the truth. We have all the truth in the Word of God, and after studying it for seventy years, I have barely scratched the surface of what's in the Bible. You don't know all the truth either, my friend. This being the case, would it not be well for us to see each brother as in Christ and, because of our love for the Savior and our love for our brother, not destroy the work of God. Let us "follow after the things which make for peace" and build one another up.

God gave the church apostles, prophets, evangelists, pastors, and teachers. What for? For the perfecting of God's people till we all come to the unity of the faith. May we grow in our understanding, in our knowledge, in our patience, and in our love for one another.

> **14:20-21.** *For meat destroy not the work of God. All things indeed are pure; but it is evil for that man who eateth with offence. It is good neither to eat flesh, nor to drink wine, nor any thing whereby thy brother stumbleth, or is offended, or is made weak.*

Liberty misused is a sin against Christ. Christ must be the center of your walk. I'm not going to take up the question, "Is it good to drink wine." The issue is: Don't let eating and drinking cause your brother to stumble. So live, so act, so move that your life will be for the glory of God and for the blessing and edification and building up of your brother in Christ, especially the brother who is weak.

> **14:22-23.** *Hast thou faith? have it to thyself before God. Happy is he that condemneth not himself in that thing which he alloweth. And he that doubteth is damned if he eat, because he eateth not of faith: for whatsoever is not of faith is sin.*

Don't air your freedom before others. Don't say, "I'm free, I can eat, I can drink, I have perfect liberty." If the other fellow is afraid to do it, then don't say, "He is a legalist, he has no sense, he's a babe." That's not the attitude of one who loves the Savior. If you have faith to eat or drink, keep it to yourself. Don't make a show of your faith. Don't glory in front of weaker Christians about what you can or can't do. You are sinning against Christ when you do that.

Happy is the man who does not condemn himself by what he approves. But if a fellow believes that to do certain things is sin, to him it is sin. "He that doubts is judged if he eats because he eateth not of faith." So you have one who can eat and drink in faith and it's not sin. The other man eats and drinks in doubt and he sins. Whatever is not of faith is sin.

The one thing God delights in is faith. He just loves to have men and women trust Him—not only for their eternal salvation, but also for their next twenty-four hours. It's an amazing thing about us Christians. We trust God with our souls and rejoice in an eternal, perfect, complete salvation, but we are full of doubts and worry about today.

The writer of Hebrews admonishes us, "Without faith it is impossible to please him: for he that cometh to God must believe that he is [that he is God] and that he is a rewarder of them that diligently seek him" (11:6).

Romans 15

Liberty and license are two different things. With license, you do what you want to do without regard for what happens to anybody else. Liberty is the freedom not to do something that will be a stumblingblock to others. Real liberty has tremendous respect for the rights of others. No man lives to himself. No man dies to himself. As long as you are on this earth, my friend, you must live with other people and, especially, with other Christians. If you claim to be strong, you have a tremendous responsibility to those who are weak.

THE PRINCIPLE OF LIBERTY (15:1-7)

15:1-2. *We then that are strong ought to bear the infirmities of the weak, and not to please ourselves. Let every one of us please his neighbour for his good to edification.*

If we are strong, we should bear with the failings of the weak, not judge or criticize him. We should sacrifice for his sake that he may be built up in the faith, that he may be strong, that he may be able to walk on his own two feet.

A great many Christians need a lot of help. So many are on spiritual crutches, so many are in spiritual hospitals. Some churches are nothing but convalescent wards.

261

Oh, what an atmosphere of fellowship and joy and blessing there would be among God's people if we were all trying to please the other fellow. I don't mean to "tacky" up to the other fellow and pat him on the back with an enthusiasm that's not real. But let's edify him, attract him to Christ, especially if he has failed God. Let's encourage him in the Lord.

> **15:3.** *For even Christ pleased not himself; but, as it is written, The reproaches of them that reproached thee fell on me.*

This hits us pretty hard, doesn't it? What is the example? "Christ pleased not himself." Do you know of any place in our Lord's life when He pleased himself? There is only one verse where He said, "Father, I want something for myself." That's John 17:24, where He said, "Father, I will that they also, whom thou hast given me, be with me where I am; that they may behold my glory."

Oh, friend, Christ pleased not Himself. The reproaches that should have fallen on other people fell on Him, and the reproaches that men had against God fell upon Him. He is the example of one who pleased not Himself. His desire was to do the will of His Father (Psalm 40:6-8 cf. Hebrews 10:5-10; Matthew 26:42; John 4:34; 5:30; 8:29).

His whole life was one of ministering to others. He came "not to be ministered unto, but to minister" (Matthew 20:27-28). He "took upon him the form of a servant" (Philippians 2:7). In John 13 He took a towel and girded Himself and washed the disciples' feet. What a sight for angels who had worshiped Him. What a sight for them to see the Son of God on His knees, girded with a towel, washing the dirty feet of His disciples.

Oh, friend, the Lord Jesus left us an example that we should follow in his steps. To think that He should leave the glory just because He loved you. And where were you? Dead in trespasses and sins. Where was your brother? In the same position. If God the Son loved him and loved you and died for both of you, don't you think you ought to love each other? Sacrifice for each other? There is only one answer to that, isn't there?

Now for the encouragement:

> **15:4.** *For whatsoever things were written aforetime were written for our learning, that we through patience and comfort of the scriptures might have hope.*

Paul is inferring that the whole Old Testament gives to us a revelation and an example of patience and comfort.

"But, Mr. Mitchell," you say, "I can't stand that other brother. I can't stand the things he does. He is weak. He is stumbling. He's a disgrace to the Lord."

Yes, that's because you need patience. You need the love of Christ to be welling up in your heart for him. Remember, Christ pleased not himself. The whole Old Testament is a revelation of the fact, written for our learning, that we through patience and comfort of the Scriptures might have hope—not only personal hope, but also hope for the other believer that he might become strong in Christ.

> **15:5-7.** *Now the God of patience and consolation grant you to be likeminded one toward another according to Christ Jesus: that ye may with one mind and one mouth glorify God, even the Father of our Lord Jesus Christ. Wherefore receive ye one another, as Christ also received us to the glory of God.*

Why didn't Paul say "the God of glory"? Why didn't he say "the God of all grace"? Why didn't he say "the God of peace"? Because, what strong believers need is patience with the weak believer.

Tell me, how did Christ receive you? He received you in grace, in tenderness, in compassion, in love. Isn't that right? Then how should I receive my brother who doesn't agree with me? Or my brother who is weak, possibly a little worldly and frail, who doesn't know very much of the truth of God? How shall I receive him? In Christ. Have fellowship with him, so that together with one mouth you may glorify God, and receive one another as Christ received you. Remember, he is the object of the grace of God just as much as you are. He is the object of the affection of Christ just as much as you are. Then, my friend, fellowship with him and together glorify God.

Having dealt with the need for unity and fellowship between strong and weak, between mature and immature Christians, Paul begins to plead for more unity between the Jew and the Gentile. For, as Christ has received both Jew and Gentile, so we should receive each other—not on sectarian grounds or the grounds of culture or background—but because we are in Christ. In his epistle, the apostle John speaks of fathers, young men, and babies, but they are all in the same family. Paul is thinking of the family as he writes to the Christian church of his day.

EXHORTATIONS (15:8-33)

Starting at verse 8, Paul gives exhortations to the people of God. The first one occurs in verses 8 to 13 where he says the Gentiles are to be blessed through Christ and his ministry is to bring everybody, Jews and Gentiles, into one body called the church.

The Gentiles Are Blessed through Christ (15:8-13)

15:8-9. *Now I say that Jesus Christ was a minister of the circumcision for the truth of God, to confirm the promises made unto the fathers: and that the Gentiles might glorify God for his mercy; as it is written, For this cause I will confess to thee among the Gentiles, and sing unto thy name.*

Christ came to be a servant of the circumcision, a servant of the Jews, to show God's faithfulness. It's obvious, when our Lord walked among men, that He came to "confirm the promises made

264

to the fathers" and to enable the Gentiles to "glorify God for his mercy."

I'm reminded of Matthew 15:22-28 where the Canaanite woman said to the Lord Jesus, "Thou Son of David have mercy on me and heal my daughter." A Gentile, she came on the wrong ground. She came to him as if she were a Jew, claiming the mercies of David. But Gentiles have nothing in the mercies of David. Jesus rightly said, "I am sent only unto the lost sheep of the House of Israel." It was only when she began to plead, "Help me, Lord. I'll take my place as a dog for the dogs have to be fed," that she got on the right ground and her daughter was healed. You see, the Lord came to confirm the promises made to Israel.

In Matthew 10, when Jesus sent out his disciples two by two, He said to them, "Do not go to the Gentiles. Do not go to the Samaritans, but go to the lost sheep of the House of Israel." This was their limited ministry. In Acts 3 Peter said to the men of Israel, "To you first was the gospel given."

In John 12, when certain Gentiles came and said, "We would see Jesus," do you know what He said? "Now is mine hour come." What hour? The hour for crucifixion. There was no place for the Gentile until Christ died on the cross.

"He came to confirm the promises made to the fathers." He came to confirm the truth of God who had made certain promises to Israel about the coming of the Messiah and what they could expect.

But why do we have in verse 9 "that the Gentiles might glorify God for his mercy?" Both Jew and Gentile are included in the purpose of God. Paul is writing this to urge the fellowship of Jew and Gentile in the Savior. This is what God expects.

> **15:10-12.** *And again he saith, Rejoice, ye Gentiles, with his people [that is, with the Jews]. And again, Praise the Lord, all ye Gentiles; and laud him, all ye people. And again, [Isaiah] saith, There shall be a root of Jesse, and he that shall rise to reign over the Gentiles; in him shall the Gentiles trust.*

Paul is urging these Jewish Christians to accept the Gentile Christians as being one with themselves. It is hard for us to realize the tremendous difference between the Jew and the Gentile, especially in the first century. In Galatians 2, Paul rebuked Peter because Peter separated himself from the Gentiles in Antioch when certain Jewish believers from Jerusalem arrived. Paul withstood Peter on this because there was a possibility that two kinds of churches, a Jewish church and a Gentile church, would result.

And here in Romans 15, Paul informs us that our Lord came to confirm the promises made to the Fathers, not only for the Jew to be saved, but that the Gentiles also would come to know God. Then both Jew and Gentile together could be joined in their praise and in their worship of God.

Paul's Great Desire for Them (15:13)

15:13. *Now the God of hope fill you with all joy and peace in believing, that ye may abound in hope, through the power of the Holy Ghost.*

This amazing verse reflects Paul's great desire for believing Jews and Gentiles. Our hope is based, first of all, on the resurrection of the Son of God; then it is based on the faithfulness of God. The resurrection of Christ and the faithfulness of God guarantee our hope. If our Savior is not raised from the dead, then we have no hope (1 Peter 1:3).

Our Savior is a risen, glorified, exalted Savior, exalted to the right hand of authority. That, my friend, gives me hope. Furthermore, the faithfulness of God guarantees that hope. What God has said, He will surely perform.

God has declared that every Christian is going to be conformed to the image of Jesus Christ. The Lord Jesus said, "Where I am, there you may be also." So wherever Jesus is, the faithfulness of God guarantees that we will be there. God will surely keep His Word to every one of His people.

He is the God of hope not only for the Jew, but also for the Gentile. Since we have the same Savior, the same salvation, the same destination, the same hope in Christ Jesus, then every believer ought to rejoice in our fellowship together in Christ that we might glorify God for His mercy. This cancels all credibility for separate churches for saved Jews and saved Gentiles.

When a person loves and trusts the Savior, my friend, there is a bond that is eternal and complete. We ought to rejoice, whether we are Jew or Gentile, in the God of our salvation. He is the God of hope and the God of patience for all of us together.

Furthermore, hope brings joy. A hopeless person has no joy, nothing to look forward to, living only in the present. Our Lord once told us to be full of joy. He said to His disciples in the upper room, "These things have I spoken unto you, that my joy might remain in you, and that your joy might be *full*" (John 15:11). Is your joy full? When a Christian's joy is not full, you can count on one thing—his fellowship with the Lord Jesus is broken. He has lost that deep joy that is not affected by circumstances.

The Lord said, "My joy I give unto you," even though in a few hours He was going to be scourged and then crucified. As Hebrews 12:2 tells us, "Who for the joy that was set before him endured the cross, despising the shame, and is set down at the right hand of the throne of God." This is the joy you have in the midst of affliction or sorrow or disappointment or pain. You can have a real and a settled joy. The hope of the believer—even in the midst of all circumstances—that Christ may come today, fills us with joy.

What is the purpose of it all? "That ye may abound in hope through the power of the Holy Spirit." Friend, I do not need to know your circumstances. I know One who is with you in your circumstances, One who knows all about your circumstances, One who never leaves you in your circumstances. He is the God of hope who can fill you with all joy, with all peace in believing. He is the One who has caused you to abound in hope through the power of the Holy Spirit.

The foundation of the fellowship of God's people and of our joy and peace is anchored in the person of God Himself. This is what we have here in chapter 15. He is the God of patience because we need endurance (v. 5). He is the God of all comfort because we need encouragement (v. 5). He is the God of hope when all around seems to be failing because he fills me with joy and peace and he will perfect what he has started (v. 13). He's the God of peace (v. 33), guaranteeing the perfecting of God's purpose in his people, guaranteeing the completion of our salvation, and guaranteeing that he will defeat Satan under our feet shortly (16:20).

God must be the center of our fellowship. If anything else is the center of fellowship, then we are going to have confusion, not fellowship. But when hearts are gathered around the person of Christ who is the God of all patience, the God of all hope, the God of all comfort, and the God of all peace, oh friend, this knits us together in the person of Christ. He is for us every day, every hour of the day, every minute of the day. My, what a God! What a Savior we have!

Christian friend, why don't you get occupied with Him? If you look to men, they are failures. If you look to leaders, they disappoint you. You look to the Savior and He will never disappoint you. Take courage. He will work all things out after the counsel of His own will and perfect in you and me that which pleases Him.

EXHORTATION AND TESTIMONY (15:14-33)

15:14. *And I myself also am persuaded of you, my brethren, that ye also are full of goodness, filled with all knowledge, able also to admonish one another.*

What an assembly of Christians you have when you have these three marvelous things: goodness, spiritual perception, and openness to admonish one another. They had all joy, they had all peace, and they were abounding in hope, but now Paul is persuaded that they are also full of goodness. This is the proof of their faith. It's folly for you and me to talk about our faith in the Lord Jesus if it is not transforming our lives.

Remember, Paul had not met these Roman Christians, but the reports he had heard persuaded him that they were also full of goodness. It's a wonderful thing when the love of Christ is evidenced in a Christian by his being good. Barnabas was called a good man, full of the Holy Spirit and full of wisdom. He was able to bring joy and edification to God's people.

Furthermore, they were filled with knowledge. This doesn't mean they were filled with worldly knowledge, rather they were able to understand and perceive spiritual realities. It's wonderful to find Christians who are full of spiritual perception. They are able to discern what is right, what is in accord with the Word of God, what is in accord with the character and love and grace of God.

And then they were able to admonish one another. That is, they were able to guide each other and build each other up. They were able in love to correct fellow believers and to exhort one another for edification.

Admonishing one another doesn't mean that you know more than the other fellow and you crow about things or you sit in judgment on God's people in their frailty. No, the one who admonishes is able not only to perceive things spiritually, but also to have the grace and the tenderness and the understanding to encourage God's people to go on with God. Sometimes you have to say things that are difficult, and yet it is for the glory of God and for the benefit of His people. As David could say, "Faithful are the wounds of a friend." A true friend will love you enough to even wound you when you need it.

Now Paul begins to speak of his experience:

> **15:15-17.** *Nevertheless, brethren, I have written the more boldly unto you in some sort, as putting you in mind, because of the grace that is given to me of God,*

*that I should be the minister of Jesus Christ to the
Gentiles, ministering the gospel of God, that the offering up of the Gentiles might be acceptable, being sanctified by the Holy Ghost. I have therefore whereof I may
glory through Jesus Christ in those things which per-
tain to God.*

The apostle was preaching everywhere in the power of God
that he might bring the Gentiles, who at one time were in idolatry,
afar off, dead in sins, without Christ, without hope and without
God, into new life in Christ. Paul's desire was that through his
ministry of the gospel these Gentiles might be so transformed and
so set apart by the Spirit of God that they would be an offering
offered up to God with thanksgiving.

When God wanted a man who could reach the Gentile world,
He picked a man well acquainted with both the Jewish and
Gentile cultures. Paul came from the city of Tarsus where the
academies of the Stoics and the Epicurean philosophers were
located. Paul was well versed in the philosophies of the Greeks
and the Romans, as well as the Jewish people. He was a fit instrument for God to use to bring the Gentiles to Christ.

15:18-21. *For I will not dare to speak of any of those
things which Christ hath not wrought by me, to make
the Gentiles obedient, by word and deed, through
mighty signs and wonders, by the power of the Spirit of
God; so that from Jerusalem, and round about unto
Illyricum, I have fully preached the gospel of Christ.
Yea, so have I strived to preach the gospel, not where
Christ was named, lest I should build upon another
man's foundation: But as it is written, To whom he was
not spoken of, they shall see: and they that have not
heard shall understand.*

My, what an evangelist this man was! He was full of the compassion and the tenderness of Christ. When Paul spoke to the

Ephesian elders at Myletus on his way to Jerusalem, he said, "I have not kept anything back. I have given everything that I knew of the Word of God to you folk. I didn't come with a partial message, I came with the full message of the gospel in Christ. In fact, I have strived to preach the gospel not where Christ was named, lest I should build upon another man's foundation."

This gets hold of my heart. How often, do we hear only a part of the gospel. We don't hear the full truth that God has given to us. What a need we have for men and women throughout the world who saturate their lives with the Word of God, who center their affections and devotion in the person of Christ, and who derive their power from the Spirit of God, not from the things of man.

This is Paul. No wonder he could say, "I don't care whether I live or die. It makes no difference to me as long as Christ is magnified in my body. I consider everything a loss—including the good things of life—compared to the surpassing greatness of knowing Christ Jesus my Lord, for whom I have suffered the loss of all things."

Oh, that God would raise up in these last days men and women whose very passion will be the Person of Christ and whose heart will be full of tenderness and compassion for lost souls. We need men and women who will not be satisfied until they reach people everywhere with the gospel of Christ.

What a wonderful experience it is to talk to someone who has never really heard the gospel of Christ. It's wonderful to see the Spirit of God take the Word and make it live in that person's heart. And then you have the joy of building that person up in Christ Jesus. There is nothing comparable.

In my early ministry I had the joy of preaching the Word of God on the prairies where no one else had been with the gospel. They hadn't had a gospel message for some twenty or thirty years. Believe me, my friends, I love to stand in a schoolhouse and bring to people the precious Word of God. And, after preaching for an hour, to have them say, "What are you stopping for? Give us the rest of it." And I preached until eleven or twelve o'clock at night, three or four hours, to hungry people who for the first time were hearing the wonderful grace of God. What a joy to see them accept the Savior and to see the transformation of their lives and to build them up in the holy faith.

I can sense the yearning of Paul's heart. What an evangelist this man was. What a missionary. What a heart he had for God and for God's people! Oh, that God would give us big hearts that will take God's people and establish them in the truth.

Oh, to get ahold of some of these dear people for whom Christ died. God loves them, and He wants that love to be manifested through you and me so that we can reach these people with the Word of Life that they too might be saved.

> **15:22-24.** *For which cause also I have been much hindered from coming to you. But now having no more place in these parts, and having a great desire these many years to come unto you; whensoever I take my journey into Spain, I will come to you: for I trust to see you in my journey, and to be brought on my way thitherward by you, if first I be somewhat filled with your company.*

Paul's great desire, of course, was that he might go to Rome and encourage these dear Christians in the Savior. He is saying here, "I am planning to go west to Spain; and on my way I want to stop by Rome and see you folk, so that you and I both may be encouraged and edified by our mutual faith."

> **15:25-29.** *But now I go unto Jerusalem to minister unto the saints. For it hath pleased them of Macedonia and Achaia to make a certain contribution for the poor saints which are at Jerusalem. It hath pleased them verily; and their debtors they are. For if the Gentiles have been made partakers of their spiritual things, their duty is also to minister unto them in carnal things.*

When therefore I have performed this, and have sealed to them this fruit, I will come by you into Spain. And I am sure that, when I come unto you, I shall come in the fulness of the blessing of the gospel of Christ.

He came to the believers at Rome all right, but he didn't get a prosperous journey because, when he went to Jerusalem with the offering to the Jewish Christians, he was taken prisoner in the temple courtyard. The Jews would have pulled Paul to pieces—they would have killed him—if the Roman soldiers hadn't stepped in and delivered him. He was taken prisoner and was sent to Caesarea where he stayed for more than two years. From there, he sailed for Rome and was shipwrecked en route. I don't know whether he ever made it to Spain. Tradition says he did, but the Word of God doesn't tell us.

I like the confidence of this man Paul. He said, "I am sure that when I come to you, I will come with a full measure of the blessing of the gospel of Christ." That has been one of my great desires when I go to a Bible conference or some other place to have meetings. I want to go in all the fullness and blessing of the gospel of Christ. If only every evangelist, Bible teacher, and pastor every time he opens the Word of God, would be filled with all the fullness of the blessing of Christ so that, as his own heart is full, he will relate that blessing to God's people. A person who gets blessed in his own ministry of the Word of God can be sure that others are going to be blessed too.

15:30-32. *Now I beseech you, brethren, for the Lord Jesus Christ's sake, and for the love of the Spirit, that ye strive together with me in your prayers to God for me; that I may be delivered from them that do not believe in Judaea; and that my service which I have for Jerusalem may be accepted of the saints; that I may come unto you with joy by the will of God, and may with you be refreshed.*

Paul had just said in verses 18 to 20 that he had gone out
preaching to the Gentiles and the mighty power of God was manifested by signs and wonders by the Spirit of God. He said that
from Jerusalem to Illyricum the gospel had been proclaimed to
everybody. A great many people had come to know the Savior.
And yet, by the end of the chapter, an amazing thing takes place.
Paul turns to these Christians he has never seen and asks them to
pray for him. Oh, the humility of this man!

Paul urges these Christians at Rome to strive together with him
in prayer. That word *strive* means to agonize in prayer. Do you
remember Epaphras in Colossians 4:12? He was "always labour-
ing fervently for you in prayers." He was always agonizing in
prayer that God's people might stand complete in the Word of
God. The believer can come into the presence of God and plead
with Him for others. I'm not talking about saying prayers. I'm
talking about praying in earnest.

Friend, how long has it been since you got down before God
and meant business—I mean really meant business? I've had the
privilege and honor—and it's a sacred thing—to be in the presence of people who have meant business before God when they
were on their knees. They forgot about me and everybody else as
they laid hold of the Throne of Grace in behalf of somebody else.
There is something about it. It's beyond the ken of men, that
redeemed men and women can besiege the Throne of Grace and
come right into the presence of God. They come right into the
holiest place of all and plead with God for the requests on their
heart.

This is what Paul is asking—"that you agonize, that you strive,
that you mean business together with me in your prayers to God
for me."

What does he want? First, that he may be delivered from the
unbelievers in Judea, from those that hate the gospel. He knows
what he is getting into, and he asks to be delivered from the
unsaved Jews in Jerusalem.

Someone is bound to ask, "Why didn't God answer that

prayer?" Just a minute. If Paul had not been made a prisoner, the chances are we would not have such books as Ephesians, Philippians, and Colossians, those letters Paul wrote from prison. There's a purpose behind all this. How would the people in Caesar's household have known about the Savior if Paul hadn't been a prisoner there? God answers prayer in His own way. He wasn't blind. He wasn't deaf to the cry of Paul for deliverance from the unbelievers in Judea.

The second thing Paul asked them to pray for was that his service in Jerusalem would be acceptable to the saints there. Though he was taking an offering back to Jerusalem, he did not know how the Jews would receive it. He didn't want them to take offense or to reject this sacrificial offering from the Gentile churches. So he asked the believers at Rome to pray that the Jewish believers in Jerusalem would accept his offering in the same spirit in which it was given, for those dear people in Macedonia and Achaia gave out of their abundant poverty. It was a real sacrifice for them to give, but they gave because there were others in need. How perceptive and how far-reaching were Paul's concerns for the churches.

The third thing he requested prayer for was that, by God's will, he might come to them with joy so that they would be refreshed together by their mutual faith.

Paul is not so far above God's people that he doesn't need their prayers. Here are Gentiles who have come to know the Savior, and he is pleading with them to strive together in prayer for him.

I ask of you the same thing. "Do you mean to tell me, Mr. Mitchell, that you need my prayers?" I sure do. More than anything else, I'd rather have your prayers that the Word of God would go forth in clarity and power, in tenderness and compassion so that people will be saved and established and built up in Christ.

Paul prayed that he might be delivered from his enemies, that his gift to the Jewish Christians might be acceptable, and that he might come to Rome with joy by the will of God. I believe he was full of joy when he walked up the Appian highway into Rome. In

Ephesians 3 and 4, he calls himself "a prisoner of Jesus Christ for you Gentiles." I like the dignity of that. He didn't say, "Paul, a prisoner of the Romans." Joy filled his heart even though he was in chains.

15:33. *Now the God of peace be with you all. Amen.*

Paul comes right back to the "God of peace." This man had such a passion for the Savior and such a love for God's people. He would sacrifice anything, anything and everything, that they might be established in the Word of God and that their joy might be filled full.

That's my desire for you. I don't know who you are, but I tell you, my friend, God can absolutely and perfectly satisfy your heart. Remember, He's the God of comfort. He's the God of all peace. He's the God of all grace. And He's sufficient for your every need.

Romans 16

The apostle Paul is through exhorting the Christians at Rome, and now in this concluding chapter he has a few words of salutation.

SALUTATIONS (16:1-27)

God's Notables (16:1-16)

16:1-4. *I commend unto you Phebe [Phoebe] our sister, which is a servant of the church which is at Cenchrea: that ye receive her in the Lord, as becometh saints, and that ye assist her in whatsoever business she hath need of you: for she hath been a succorer of many, and of myself also. Greet Priscilla and Aquila my helpers in Christ Jesus: who have for my life laid down their own necks: unto whom not only I give thanks, but also all the churches of the Gentiles.*

Paul names a number of people in this chapter. I call them "the notables of God." This is God's hall of fame. Wherever the Word of God has gone for the last nineteen hundred years, people have read about these unknown men and women. How gracious of Paul to remember them!

May I say just a word to you who think you are unknown. It is true, you may not be known by very many on earth. You have been serving the Lord faithfully, some of you for thirty years or more, and you think, "No one knows about me. I'm one of the least significant saints the Lord has on earth."

But, my friend, you are well known to God. How glad I am that the frailest, the weakest, the simplest child of God is well known by the Savior. If Paul manifests such a heart of love for those he greets here, how much more the Lord Jesus must love every one He has received, every one He has bought for Himself. Isn't it wonderful to know you belong to Him? So what if the world does not know you? That's neither here nor there, just as long as you are known by the Lord and He knows you.

A number of women are included in this list of notables, such as Phoebe, Priscilla, Mary, Julia. You have the mother of Rufus and Paul; you have the sister of Nereus. There are some ten women in this Hall of Fame. Let's look at one or two of them for just a moment.

Phoebe is called "a servant of the church." She was possibly a deaconess of the church at Cenchrea. And Paul says, "Receive her in the Lord in a way worthy of the saints and give her any help she may need because she has been a great help to many." She has been a helper not only to the church in Cenchrea, but she has been a real helper to Paul also. In fact, there are those who believe that Paul gave her this epistle to take to Rome. He had had fellowship with her and he wanted the believers at Rome to have fellowship with her.

And then you have Priscilla, the wife of Aquila. You met them in the Book of Acts where they were making tents with the apostle Paul (Acts 18). Wherever they went, they radiated the presence of Christ and communicated the wonderful gospel of the grace of God. They even risked their lives for Paul. They were willing to die that he might be free to preach the gospel of Christ to the people in Europe.

> **16:5-16.** *Likewise greet the church that is in their house. Salute my well beloved Epaenetus, who is the firstfruits of Achaia unto Christ. Greet Mary, who bestowed much labor on us. Salute Andronicus and*

Junia, my kinsmen, and my fellow-prisoners, who are
of note among the apostles, who also were in Christ
before me. Greet Amplias my beloved in the Lord.
Salute Urbane, our helper in Christ, and Stachys my
beloved. Salute Apelles approved in Christ. Salute them
which are of Aristobulus' household. Salute Herodion
my kinsman. Greet them that be of the household of
Narcissus, which are in the Lord. Salute Tryphena and
Tryphosa, who labour in the Lord. Salute the beloved
Persis, which laboured much in the Lord. Salute Rufus
chosen in the Lord, and his mother and mine. Salute
Asyncritus, Phlegon, Hermas, Patrobas, Hermes, and
the brethren which are with them. Salute Philologus,
and Julia, Nereus, and his sister, and Olympas, and all
the saints which are with them. Salute one another with
an holy kiss. The churches of Christ salute you.

Paul knew who all these people were, where they were, what
they had done, and what a tremendous interest they had in the
people of God. I wonder if we today couldn't reflect the great
yearning Paul had for the people of God—these people who had
helped him, who were humble ones, who were not great leaders
but who had labored much in the gospel. They were approved in
Christ, and possibly some of them had gone through great testings
and afflictions for the gospel's sake.

Wouldn't you like to be approved in Christ?

Paul talks about Rufus, chosen in the Lord. He stood out in
Paul's mind as one who had proved his position. You have those
who suffered for the gospel's sake—Andronicus and Junia, his
fellow prisoners. These two men are Paul's relatives, and they
became Christians before he did. They may have been among the
group in Acts 9 when Paul went about trying to put all the
Christians in prison. Perhaps he turned on these relatives of his,
and now they are fellow prisoners. My, what a transformation in
Paul, transformed from a persecutor to a humble servant of the Lord.

The phrases "in the Lord" and "in Christ" occur eleven times in this passage. This shows the oneness of the believers. Being in Christ, they were knitted together. They were in union with Him, and they were in union with each other. Here are masters and slaves, here are rich and poor, here are Jews and Gentiles, and yet they are all one in Christ.

One of these days, you and I who love the Savior are going to meet all these men and women. It is so wonderful when you think of the marvelous grace of God in picking up these different people and approving them and calling them His beloved. They were called the "offscouring of the world." They were unknown and unwanted by the world; yet they are well known in glory, well known in Christ. God never rewards greatness. He rewards faithfulness in the task He has given us to do.

You say, "But I don't know what God wants me to do." It may be just to live for Christ and magnify Him right where you are under the circumstances into which God has put you. The best place for us to serve and please the Lord is right where we are.

I've heard Christians say, "If only I were in some other city or in some other church or in some other country—what a person I would be for the Lord." Oh, no. God knows every detail of your life. He knows your strength and your frailty, and He has put you in the best place where you can serve Him. You may not be known by men, but who cares as long as you are known by God!

Exhortations (16:17-21)

> **16:17-18.** *Now I beseech you, brethren, mark them which cause divisions and offences contrary to the doctrine which ye have learned; and avoid them. For they that are such serve not our Lord Jesus Christ, but their own belly; and by good words and fair speeches deceive the hearts of the simple.*

Someone has said, "False teaching and vile living go together." Paul here calls for separation from those who bring in false teaching and cause divisions among God's people. We see so much division today, most often on insignificant matters. It's amazing how quickly someone can come along and break up the unanimity of Spirit and the purpose and the fellowship the saints have in Christ. We are not asked to separate from those who love the Savior, but we are called to separate from those who bring in false doctrine.

Paul goes on to say that the lives of false teachers usually measure up to their doctrine. They do not serve the Lord, they serve themselves. By smooth talk and flattery they deceive the hearts of the naive. They come to deceive, to break up the unity of the Spirit among God's people. Mark them; watch them. These false teachers will come under the sure judgment of God.

> **16:19.** *For your obedience is come abroad unto all men. I am glad therefore on your behalf: but yet I would have you wise unto that which is good, and simple concerning evil.*

Our safeguard is our simplicity in Christ. I do not need to know all the ramifications of all the false doctrines. One thing I ask is what place do they give to the person of Christ? Our safeguard against false teachers who divide God's people is our simplicity in Christ. As someone has well said, "We shoot mad dogs. We quarantine infectious diseases. But we tolerate false teachers in the body of Christ."

Make Christ and His redemptive work—His crucifixion, His burial, His resurrection, and His exaltation—the center of your life and your fellowship. Oh, that we might "not know anything among you, save Jesus Christ, and him crucified . . . that your faith should not stand in the wisdom of men, but in the power of God" (1 Corinthians 2:2, 5). Oh, that we might enjoy the fellowship and the communion of God's people. And you will when Jesus Christ is your center of attraction.

> **16:20.** *And the God of peace shall bruise Satan under your feet shortly. The grace of our Lord Jesus Christ be with you. Amen.*

Way back in Genesis 3:15, when Adam and Eve sinned, God promised that the seed of the woman would crush the serpent's head and that the serpent would bruise his heel. Now Paul encourages these Roman Christians, who were suffering for their testimony's sake, by giving them this promise that the God of peace would soon crush Satan under their feet.

The one who hates God's people and stirs up persecution against them is going to come under the judgment of God and under the feet of God's people. The enemy of their souls was going to be defeated and would soon be bruised under their feet. This was to encourage them during the difficult days in which they were living.

Paul's Fellow Workers (16:21-24)

16:21-24. *Timotheus my workfellow, and Lucius, and Jason, and Sosipater, my kinsmen, salute you. I Tertius, who wrote this epistle, salute you in the Lord. Gaius mine host, and of the whole church, saluteth you. Erastus the chamberlain of the city saluteth you, and Quartus a brother. The grace of our Lord Jesus Christ be with you all. Amen.*

Paul usually had friends and fellow workers around him, and these now take the opportunity to send their greetings to the believers in Rome. Timothy, of course, was Paul's close companion and helper during many of his missionary journeys. Paul usually dictated his letters, and Tertius served as secretary for this letter to Rome.

God's Ability to Establish Us (16:25-27)

16:25-27. *Now to him that is of power to stablish you according to my gospel, and the preaching of Jesus Christ, according to the revelation of the mystery, which was kept secret since the world began, but now*

is made manifest, and by the scriptures of the prophets,
according to the commandment of the everlasting God,
made known to all nations for the obedience of faith:
To God only wise, be glory through Jesus Christ for
ever. Amen.

Only God can establish us. No religious system can ever establish any of God's people. God must do this. Though Paul said in the first chapter, "I want to come to edify you, to build you up in the faith," he recognized this must be done by God himself.

Notice also, it's going to be done, says Paul, according to "my gospel." Paul uses similar terminology in 2:16 when he says God is going to judge the secrets of men by Jesus Christ "according to my gospel."

"Do you mean to tell me, Mr. Mitchell, that Paul has a message all his own?"

No, God's message has so taken hold of Paul that it has, in that sense, become Paul's gospel. I am reminded of Elijah, who said to King Ahab in 1 Kings 17, "There shall not be dew or rain these years, but according to my word." Was Elijah's word going to close the heavens? No. He believed what God had said to Moses: If the people of Israel ever left God and became idolaters, He would withhold the rain from them and they would have no crops. Elijah had taken the Word of God, the promise of God, and made it his own.

This is what Paul is doing. The gospel of Christ, the good news from God concerning His Son, has become so much a part and parcel of Paul's life that he could speak of it as his gospel.

Are you so in love with the Savior, is He so much the center of your affections that His Word becomes your word? Has His gospel become your gospel so that as you minister the Word to others, as you bear testimony for the Lord, it becomes a living reality in your heart.

Unless truth lives in you, it is not yours. Unless you are able to impart it to somebody else, it is not yours. But when the truth gets a hold on your heart and you speak with that authority, that certainty, that assurance that this is the truth of God, it has become your word. This is what Paul is saying.

What is this "mystery" that Paul refers to which was kept secret since the world began? God gave Paul two revelations—the revelation of His grace, which you find in Romans, and the revelation of the church, the body of Christ, which you find in Ephesians.

It was no mystery in the Old Testament that the Gentiles would be blessed. The prophets spoke of a coming time when God would bless and eventually save the Gentiles. It was no mystery in the Old Testament that Jesus Christ would be born of a virgin, that he would be born in Bethlehem, that he was going to suffer and die and be raised again from the dead. That was no secret.

So what is the mystery? The mystery spoken of by Paul in Romans and established in Ephesians is that Gentile Christians will be fellow heirs with the Jews. They will be members of the same body, with the same life and the same standing. They will be one in Christ, a company of people seated in the heavenlies in Christ, citizens of heaven. It's God's desire to take all His children and bring them into His glory so that He may reveal Himself to them in all His love and grace.

This mystery was not made known to angelic beings. This has been made known to simple believers, both Jews and Gentiles. The moment you accept the Lord Jesus Christ as your Savior you become a member of the church, the body of Christ. It's to this church that God has revealed the wonders of His love and grace. He has revealed that the church is going to share with Him in His glory (John 17:22; Colossians 3:4).

Think of it, my friend! There is a company of people called the church to whom Christ is going to reveal His purposes. He is going to share with them in His glory. This is not for angelic beings, this is not for the nations, this is not even for Israel. This is for you and me who love the Savior.

The purpose of it all is found in verse 26—so that all nations might believe and obey him. The book of Romans starts with Paul wanting fruit among the Gentiles (1:5), and God has chosen to give us this tremendous opportunity and responsibility of making known to the nations, the millions who have never heard, the precious Word of God.

The time left to us to reach people with the Word of God is brief. When I read my Bible in connection with the condition of the professing church, when I read my Bible with respect to Israel and to the nations of the earth, I tell you, my friend, we have little time left to proclaim the wonderful story of Christ's redemption.

God has taken you and me out of sin and has placed us in Christ. He has taken us out of the kingdom of darkness, put us into His own kingdom, and left us here on earth with this tremendous responsibility of bearing testimony to others that they might know Him whom to know is life eternal.

I plead with you, my Christian friend, give everything over to Him. Let Him, the only wise God, the One who has all ability and all authority and all power, use you in these final days for the praise of the glory of His grace and for the salvation of precious souls.

"To God only wise, be glory through Jesus Christ for ever. Amen."